# Music and Politics

# Hans Werner Henze

# MUSIC
# AND POLITICS
## Collected Writings
## 1953–81

*Translated by Peter Labanyi*

Cornell University Press
ITHACA, NEW YORK

First published 1982 by Cornell University Press

International Standard Book Number 0–8014–1545–4
Library of Congress Catalog Card Number 82–71806

Filmset in Monophoto Ehrhardt by
Latimer Trend & Company Ltd, Plymouth
Printed in Great Britain by
Redwood Burn Ltd., Trowbridge, Wiltshire

198303

# Contents

# Contents

# Illustrations

## Illustrations

# Publisher's Note

This book is basically a translation of a collection of the composer's writings which was originally published as *Musik und Politik: Schriften und Gespräche 1955–1975*, edited by Jens Brockmeier, Deutscher Taschenbuch Verlag (dtv), Munich 1976. This English edition omits a few of the more occasional pieces in that book. It also includes a number of new pieces, several of which have been specially written for this book, such as the chapter about Montepulciano, or, like the important autobiographical essay, 'German Music in the 1940s and 1950s', have been adapted from interviews.

The dates and sources of the various writings are given in footnotes on the first page of each. Fuller details of the sources are to be found in *Musik und Politik*.

We should like to express our warm thanks to the translator, Peter Labanyi, to John Cruft for preparing the text for publication, to Helen Grob, Sally Groves, and Fausto Moroni for their help and advice, and above all to Hans Werner Henze for his active collaboration at every stage.

# Introduction

The present collection of essays and other *pièces d'occasion* has never been published in English until now (some of these writings were written nearly thirty years ago). I am very glad that they are now available to British and American readers because I think (and hope) it will help to make my music and ideas more widely known.

Unlike most of those composers of my generation who have dedicated a great deal of their working time to theoretical writings, I have never been able to contribute anything to this genre. Perhaps the reason for this is, or was, that I have had no theory. Even in those recent years when I have done a fair amount of writing—and have taken part in various public activities, such as the Montepulciano Cantiere—I have not had time to write a book or any other extensive publication (except to edit two volumes of articles on new musical aesthetics;* three further volumes are planned), so the only material I can offer to the reader is the present collection. I am at the moment working on a substantial book that might turn out to be, in spite of all the autobiographical and political sketches it will contain, something like a study in musical theory, a harmony book, a counterpoint treatise. The essays in *Music and Politics* should be considered, I think, as exploratory attempts at an understanding of myself and the world in which we are all living.

HANS WERNER HENZE

September 1981

* *Neue Aspekte der musikalischen Ästhetik*, ed. Hans Werner Henze. Vol. 1: *Zwischen den Kulturen*. Vol. 2: *Die Zeichen*. Frankfurt: S. Fischer, 1979 and 1981.

# Chronology

| | |
|---|---|
| 1926 | born 1 July in Gütersloh, Westphalia, to Margarete (née Geldmacher), wife of Franz Henze, primary school-teacher |
| 1931–42 | primary and grammar schools in Bielefeld, Westphalia |
| 1938 | first attempts at composition |
| 1942 | begins studies at the Brunswick State School of Music |
| 1944–5 | labour and military service; prisoner of war |
| 1945 | transport worker; then repetiteur at the Bielefeld Stadttheater |
| 1946 | study at the Heidelberg Church Music Institute and with Wolfgang Fortner |
| | Chamber Concerto for solo piano, solo flute and strings |
| | Sonata for violin and piano |
| | First Symphony (revised 1963) |
| 1947 | studies dodecaphony |
| | Five madrigals (Villon) for small mixed choir and eleven solo instruments |
| | First String Quartet |
| | Concertino for piano, wind and percussion |
| | Sonatina for flute and piano |
| 1948 | First Violin Concerto |
| | Musical Adviser at the Constance Deutsches Theater |
| | *The Miracle Theatre* (Cervantes): opera in one act for actors (new version for singers 1964) |
| | *Lullaby of the Blessed Virgin* (Lope de Vega) for unison boys' choir and nine solo instruments |

*Chorus of the Captured Trojans* (from Goethe's *Faust*) for mixed choir and large orchestra (revised 1964)
*Whispers from Heavenly Death* (Whitman):
    (a) for high voice and eight solo instruments
    (b) for voice and piano
*The Reproach* (Franz Werfel): concert aria for baritone, trumpet, trombone and string orchestra
Chamber sonata for piano, violin and cello (revised 1963)

1949    lessons from René Leibowitz in Darmstadt and Paris
Ballet Variations for large orchestra
*Jack Pudding*: chamber ballet in three scenes
Second Symphony
*Apollo et Hyazinthus* (Georg Trakl): improvisations for harpsichord, alto voice and eight solo instruments
Serenade for solo cello
Variations for piano

1949–50    Third Symphony
1950    Artistic director and conductor of the ballet at the Wiesbaden Hessische Staatstheater
*Rosa Silber*: ballet for small orchestra
Symphonic Variations for chamber orchestra
First Piano Concerto

1950–1    *Labyrinth*: choreographic fantasy for small orchestra
1951    Robert Schumann Prize of the City of Düsseldorf
*Boulevard Solitude* (Grete Weil): lyric drama in seven scenes (premiere 1952, Hanover Opera House)
*A Country Doctor* (Kafka): radio opera (stage version 1964):
    (a) opera in one act
    (b) version for baritone and orchestra
*The Sleeping Princess*, arranged for small orchestra from Tchaikovsky's ballet

1952    *The Idiot* (devised by Tatiana Gsovsky, with words by Ingeborg Bachmann): chamber ballet after Dostoevsky (premiere 1952, Berlin Festival)
Wind Quintet

Second String Quartet

*Pas d' Action*: ballet in two acts (new version with libretto by Peter Csobàdi 1964 as *Tancredi*)

1952–5   *König Hirsch* (Heinz von Cramer): opera in three acts (premiere 1956, Berlin Festival; abbreviated version 1962 as *Il Re Cervo oder Die Irrfahrten der Wahrheit*) Music for the radio play *Die Zikaden* (Ingeborg Bachmann)

1953   moved to Forio d'Ischia

*Ode to the West Wind* for cello and orchestra

*The End of a World* (Wolfgang Hildesheimer): radio opera (stage version 1964 as opera buffa in one act)

Symphonic interludes from *Boulevard Solitude*

Premio d'Italia of the RAI for *A Country Doctor*

1955   moved to Naples

*Quattro Poemi* for orchestra

*Drei sinfonische Etüden* (new version 1964)

Fourth Symphony (apotheosis of the second act of *König Hirsch*)

1956   *Maratona di Danza*: ballet (premiere 1957, Berlin Festival, directed by Luchino Visconti)

Five Neapolitan Songs (anonymous seventeenth-century texts) for medium voice and chamber orchestra

*Concerto per il Marigny* for piano and seven instruments

Suite from the ballet *Maratona* for two jazz bands and orchestra

1956–7   Major Music Prize of North Rhine-Westphalia

*Ondine*: ballet in three acts (freely adapted from De la Motte Fouqué, choreography by Frederick Ashton, decor and costumes by Lila de Nobili, title role Margot Fonteyn; premiere 1958, Royal Opera House, Covent Garden)

1957   Wedding music from *Ondine* for symphonic wind orchestra

*Nachtstücke und Arien* (Ingeborg Bachmann) for soprano and large orchestra

1957–8    *Sonata per Archi*

1958    *The Prince of Homburg*: opera in three acts (libretto from Kleist by Ingeborg Bachmann; premiere 1960, Hamburg State Opera, conductor Leopold Ludwig, producer Helmut Käutner)

*Three Dithyrambs* for chamber orchestra

*Kammermusik 1958* on Hölderlin's 'In lieblicher Bläue', for tenor, guitar and eight solo instruments

1959    *Sonata per pianoforte*

*Des Kaisers Nachtigall*: chamber ballet by Giulio di Majo (adapted from Hans Christian Andersen)

1959–61    *Elegy for Young Lovers*: opera in three acts (libretto by W. H. Auden and Chester Kallman; premiere 1961, Schwetzingen Festival)

1960    *Antifone* for orchestra (premiere 1962, Berlin Philharmonic Orchestra, conductor Herbert von Karajan)

*Aufstand: a Jewish Chronicle* (with Blacher, Dessau, Hartmann and Wagner-Régeny, to words by Jens Gerlach)

1960–8    Member of the West Berlin Academy of the Arts

1961    moved to Castelgandolfo, near Rome

Arts Prize of the City of Hanover

*Six Absences pour le Clavecin*

1962    Fifth Symphony (premiere 1963, New York Philharmonic Orchestra, conductor Leonard Bernstein)

*Novae de Infinito Laudes* (Giordano Bruno): cantata for four soloists, mixed chorus and orchestra (premiere 1963 Venice Biennale with Elisabeth Söderström, Kerstin Meyer, Peter Pears, and Dietrich Fischer-Dieskau, Cologne Radio Choir and Symphony Orchestra, conducted by the composer)

Incidental music to de Musset's *Les Caprices de Marianne* (adapted by Jean-Pierre Ponnelle)

1962–6    in charge of composition masterclass at the Salzburg Mozarteum

1963    film music for Alain Resnais's *Muriel*

*Los Caprichos*: fantasia for orchestra
*Being Beauteous* (Rimbaud): cantata for coloratura soprano, harp and four cellos
*Cantata della fiaba estrema* (Elsa Morante) for soprano, small chorus and thirteen instruments
*Ariosi* (Tasso) for soprano, violin and
    (a) orchestra
    (b) piano (four hands)
Adagio for eight instruments (clarinet, horn, bassoon and string quintet)
*Lucy Escott Variations* for piano or harpsichord

1964    *Divertimenti* for two pianos
*Chorfantasie* on Ingeborg Bachmann's *Songs from an Island* for chamber choir, trombone, two cellos, double-bass, portative organ, timpani and percussion
incidental music to Aristophanes' *Peace*

1964–5    *Der junge Lord*: comic opera in two acts (libretto by Ingeborg Bachmann, after a parable by Wilhelm Hauff; premiere 1965, Berlin Deutsche Oper, conductor Christoph von Dohnányi, producer Gustav Rudolf Sellner)
Intermezzi for orchestra from *Der junge Lord*

1965    took part in SPD election campaign for Willy Brandt
*The Bassarids* (libretto by W. H. Auden and Chester Kallman): opera seria with intermezzo, in one act (premiere 1966, Salzburg Festival, conductor Christoph von Dohnányi, producer Gustav Rudolf Sellner)
*In memoriam 'Die weisse Rose'* for chamber orchestra

1966    to Japan with the Berlin Deutsche Oper, for Tokyo premiere of *Elegy for Young Lovers* (conducted by the composer)
East German premieres of *Der junge Lord* (State Opera, Dresden; Komische Oper, Berlin)
moved to Marino, near Rome
film music for Volker Schlöndorff's *Der junge Törless*
*Muses of Sicily*: concerto for chorus, two pianos, wind and timpani on fragments from Virgil's *Eclogues*

*Doppio Concerto* for oboe, harp and strings
Concerto for double-bass

1967    Visiting Professor at Dartmouth College, New Hampshire, USA
*Moralities*: three scenic cantatas (W. H. Auden, after fables by Aesop) for soloists, narrator, choir and orchestra
*Telemanniana* for orchestra
Second Piano Concerto

1967–8    start of political commitment in West Berlin, in the student movement, for the SDS (Sozialistischer Deutscher Studentenbund), and the Vietnam Congress

1968    resigned (with Paul Dessau) from West Berlin Academy of the Arts; became corresponding member of the East German Academy of Arts, Berlin
May: Italian premiere of *The Bassarids* at La Scala, Milan; August: American premiere of *The Bassarids* in Santa Fé, New Mexico, conducted by the composer
October: Mexican premiere of *Elegy for Young Lovers* (by Berlin Deutsche Oper, conducted by the composer)
*The Raft of the Medusa* (Ernst Schnabel): oratorio for narrator, soprano, baritone, mixed choir and orchestra (premiere interrupted, Hamburg 1968)

1969    *Essay on Pigs* (Gastón Salvatore) for narrator (baritone), brass quintet and chamber orchestra (premiere February 1969, London, English Chamber Orchestra conducted by the composer)
April: first visit to Cuba, as guest of the National Council for Culture; October 1969 to April 1970: second visit to Cuba, teaching, studying and preparing *El Cimarrón*
Sinfonia No. 6 for two chamber orchestras (premiere by Orquesta Sinfónica Nacional La Habana, conducted by the composer)

1969–70    *Compases para preguntas ensimismadas* for viola and twenty-two players

1970    *El Cimarrón* (Hans Magnus Enzensberger) for four

performers (baritone, flute, guitar and percussion)

1971    Honorary Doctorate of Music, University of Edinburgh

*The Tedious Way to Natascha Ungeheuer's Flat* (Gastón Salvatore): show with baritone and seventeen players (premiere Rome, May 1971, RAI, conducted by the composer)

Second Violin Concerto, for violin, tape, bass-baritone and 33 instrumentalists, with the poem 'Hommage à Gödel' by Hans Magnus Enzensberger

*Prison Song* (Ho Chi Minh) for percussionist and tape

1971–2    *Heliogabalus Imperator: allegoria per musica* for orchestra (premiere November 1972, Chicago Symphony Orchestra, conductor Georg Solti)

1972    election appeal for the Deutsche Kommunistische Partei

*La Cubana* (Hans Magnus Enzensberger): a vaudeville (premiere 28 May 1975, Munich Staatstheater am Gärtnerplatz)

1973    artistic director of a composers' collective for the stage cantata, *Streik bei Mannesmann* (premiere August 1973 by the Berliner Ensemble during the East Berlin World Youth Festival)

*Voices* for two singers and instrumental groups (premiere 1974 with Paul Sperry, Rose Taylor, and the London Sinfonietta, conducted by the composer)

*Tristan*: preludes for piano, orchestra and electronic sounds (Third Piano Concerto) (premiere 1974, London Symphony Orchestra, conductor Colin Davis)

1974    British premiere of *The Bassarids* (English National Opera, produced and conducted by the composer)

1974–5    performance of the stage cantata *Streik bei Mannesmann* in factories and universities in the Federal Republic of Germany, by the instrumental ensemble Hinz & Kunst

*We Come to the River* (Edward Bond): actions for music (premiere 12 July 1976 at the Royal Opera House, Covent Garden)

1975    West German premiere of *The Bassarids* (Frankfurt

Opera House, produced by the composer)
film music for Volker Schlöndorff's *Die verlorene Ehre der Katharina Blum*
began collective composition of an opera with the working title *Der Ofen* (with Peter Maxwell Davies, Thomas Jahn, Richard Blackford, Niels Fréderic Hoffmann, Geoffrey King, Fabio Vacchi, and Wilhelm Zobl)
*Royal Winter Music*: first sonata for guitar on characters from Shakespeare
Honorary Member of the Royal Academy of Music, London

1976    Third String Quartet
Fourth String Quartet
arrangement of Carissimi's *Jephta*
First Montepulciano Cantiere Internazionale d'Arte
Spohr Prize of the City of Brunswick

1977    Fifth String Quartet
Sonata *Tirsi, Mopso, Aristeo* for solo violin
*Il Vitalino raddoppiato* for violin and orchestra
arrangement of Wagner's *Fünf Wesendonk-Lieder* for mezzo-soprano and small orchestra
*Aria de la folia española* for chamber orchestra
film music for Eichendorff's *Der Taugenichts*
*Madrigal for Herbert Marcuse* for flute, clarinet, and bassoon
Wind Quintet '*l'Autunno*'

1978    incidental music for Edward Bond's play *The Woman*
*Five Scenes from the Snow Country* for marimba
*Orpheus* (Edward Bond): ballet in two acts (premiere 17 March 1979, Stuttgart State Opera, choreography by William Forsythe, conductor Woldemar Nelsson)
*Don Chisciotte*, recomposition after Paisiello's opera

1979    Sonata for viola and piano
*Royal Winter Music*: second sonata for guitar
*El Rey de Harlem*: imaginary theatre on a poem by F. Garcia Lorca for mezzo-soprano and eight instruments

(premiere 20 April 1980 in Witten)

*Barcarola* for orchestra (premiere 22 April 1980, Ton-halle, Zurich)

*S. Biagio 9 Agosto ore 1207* for double-bass

*Etude philharmonique* for solo violin

*Pollicino*: an opera for children (written for the 5th Montepulciano Cantiere) (premiere 2 August 1980 in Montepulciano)

*Capriccio* for cello solo

1980    begins to compose *The English Cat*: comic opera with libretto by Edward Bond

starts teaching at Cologne Musikhochschule

appointed artistic director of the Accademia Filarmonica Romana

1981    *Cherubino*: three miniatures for piano

*Le Miracle de la Rose*: imaginary theatre II for clarinet player and thirteen instruments

*I sentimenti di C. P. E. Bach*, music for flute, harp and strings

1981–2    Reconstruction of Monteverdi's *Il Ritorno d'Ulisse in Patria*

# First Works[*]

Apart from private piano lessons from my sixth year and brief piano and harmony classes at the Brunswick State Music School in 1943 and 1944, my studies in composition began with Wolfgang Fortner in Heidelberg. It is to Fortner, whose pupil I became in 1946, that I owe a knowledge of the old methods of composition, traditional counterpoint, the art of fugue. At the same time Fortner gave me a comprehensive introduction to the realm of modern music and the aesthetic problems connected with contemporary composition.

The music I wrote before my musical education (I began composing at the age of thirteen) was free—and free from imitation of earlier worlds of sound; undisciplined, replete with every possible sign of the untutored. I could neither redress my cumbersome disjointed harmony, nor do more with a melodic idea than jot it down in rough outline. But from the start I had a yearning for those full wild harmonies that I was later to find in certain works of the New Music. To me, in the secluded little Westphalian farming village where I grew up, this was what I had understood as music.

Since the age of fourteen I had owned a collection of the poems of Georg Trakl that had stayed with me over the years. This autumnal twilit verse again and again influenced my poor attempts at composition. Understandably, the rigour and practicality of the compositional training I received under Fortner—the discovery of the arts of counterpoint and of all the remarkable, even mysterious, processes of intervallic tensions—obscured the sound world I had

---

* 'Erste Werke'. Radio Bremen 1953, in *Radio Bremen Hausbuch* 1958.

built up for myself. Indeed I think I even looked back on it with antipathy. As a result it is mainly by chance that something of the lyricism of the later works can still be found here and there in my first published compositions. My first works gave the impression of a hotheaded attempt to outrage the public (which indeed I wanted to do), but as soon as I recognized with my creative imagination the feeling of well-being that arises when one is on the right path and senses new possibilities, the early autumnal mood reappeared in the strongly rhythmical bitonal complexes of my earliest works.

In the summer of 1947, after weeks spent attempting a violin concerto, I plunged into a hitherto unknown realm, dodecaphony. I was hoping that my need for my own means of expression, and equally for a more rigorous technical foundation for the things I wanted to say, was more likely to be filled by dodecaphony than by the methods I had used until then. After I had taken this step— which was like acquiring a new area of freedom (in my violin concerto dodecaphonic methods were not yet systematically employed)—there followed a time of conflict, during which I repeatedly shied away from the unremitting severity of the demands of the Schoenberg school. It was not until I learned more about the rules of dodecaphony from René Leibowitz in 1949, and until Josef Rufer, a friend of Schoenberg's and a leading authority on his music, had now and again criticized my work, that I managed to grasp the principles, and gradually began to adapt them for my own purposes.

In my piece for harpsichord and seven instruments, *Apollo et Hyazinthus* (1949), there are for the first time passages where the music approaches the spirit of the poetry and the subject. Thus, at the beginning of the piece, I imagined how Apollo appeared in an ancient grove. The beating of his wings, the suddenly darkening sky, and then the great luminous silence of grace, accompanied by the strange, gentle, sensuous excitement of all men and animals, were to be depicted by such abstract means as a harpsichord and eight chamber instruments. This might have been an opportunity to work with numerous instrumental effects, or to adopt a baroque portrayal of stylized naïvety. I decided on something I myself recognized to be a hybrid. (The subtitle is 'Improvisations'.) The piece contains elements that (in my imagination) could have belonged to a French chamber concerto of the eighteenth century—rather as Douanier Rousseau used to claim he was painting 'in the Egyptian style'. These elements lead the ear to specific, almost pictorial notions, conjuring up associations, engaging the listener, and thereby making my own contributions more comprehensible and acceptable, especially as I remember that in this piece I sometimes crossed the permitted boundaries of abstraction in ways reminiscent of 'programme music'. That a brief poem by Trakl* appears as an alto solo at the end is no purely musical device either. It is meant as a threnody on the death of Hyacinth—'olympian funeral music'—and at the same time as a symbol of empathy with this poet, who died so young and from whom I have learned the meaning of what he calls the 'Verwandlung des Bösen, Siebengesang des Todes, die Hölle des Schlafs, Sebastian im Traum' (the transformation of evil, the sevenfold song of death, the hell of sleep, Sebastian dreaming).

\*

| | |
|---|---|
| *Wieder wandelnd im alten Park,* | Walking once again in the old park, |
| *O! Stille gelb und roter Blumen.* | Oh! Silence yellow and of red flowers. |
| *Ihr auch trauert, ihr sanften Götter,* | You mourn too, you gentle gods, |
| *Und das herbstliche Gold der Ulme.* | And the autumnal gold of the elms. |
| *Reglos ragt am bläulichen Weiher* | Motionless by the bluish pond |
| *Das Rohr, verstummt am Abend die Drossel.* | Juts the reed, in the evening the thrush is silent. |
| *O! Dann neige auch du die Stirne* | Oh! Then bow your brow too |
| *Vor der Ahnen verfallenem Marmor.* | Before the decayed marble of your ancestors. |

Georg Trakl, 'In the Park', *Sebastian im Traum*

# German Music in the 1940s and 1950s*

My passion for music began when I was about thirteen. From then on I neglected my school work to play music in the afternoons and evenings, and to compose chamber pieces that were sightread once with friends and then laid aside. I did not like practising the piano. Everything was still a game. Just as puddles become lakes for children, domestic cats turn into tigers, and teachers into evil spirits, so my fellow-players became *beaux* and geniuses. But making music with them became a reality that penetrated the secret of the world, and in which there were formulations at last for what had hitherto been inexpressible. The suspended cadences in the adagios of Corelli's 'church' sonatas were ceremonious promises of love, full of renunciation; the allegros in Bach, Vivaldi and Bach–Vivaldi represented sexual excitement. In the closing chorus of the *St Matthew Passion* we, the chosen children, sat down in actual tears after the long evening of lamentation.

Eventually I fled from the Bielefeld grammar school, and in 1942 went to a music school. The Brunswick State School of Music had been my father's last resort; he had believed that there, where I could study at first hand the drawbacks of life as a café fiddler, I would most rapidly get to know what a shabby existence it was. Life was not so bad in this school—and caution made me refuse to learn how to play the violin. Now that I no longer belonged to the elite of

---

* This autobiographical sketch conflates an interview with Hubert Kolland (in *Musik 50er Jahre*, ed. Hanns-Werner Heister and Dietrich Stern, Argument-Sonderband A5 42, Berlin 1980) and the following essays from *Musik und Politik*: 'Nach dem Krieg' (1964); 'Italien' (1964); 'Die Bundesrepublik Deutschland und die Musik' (1967–8).

grammar school pupils, who were to become air-raid auxiliaries and university students, they would soon call me up into the army. Until that happened I wanted to hear all the operas again in the Stadttheater, or even practise the piano if there was nothing 'better' to do. 'Better' meant going for a walk, reading, composing secretly, killing time with the girls from the drama school (feline figures out of mythology, Thespian dollies), by day in the coffee house (where nobody was playing the violin any more) and by night in the air-raid shelter. The only future I could conceive for myself was as what's called a 'practising musician'. Sometimes I saw myself marooned as an organist in a grey little town in the north, very much alone, with my contemplative life enlivened perhaps by a handful of secrets. Fancifully, I saw myself *en route* for St Egidius after a frugal meal, held back by gusts of wind; finally reaching the door of the church; its rusty old key, Gothic interior, frost; in my imagination I heard the austere, hard and enigmatic counterpoint, alien to the uninitiated ear, alien to me as well, but the truth had to lie there, and at the end of its lines something would happen. My profession, I thought, consists of bringing truths nearer to the point where they explode. With such ideas I tempered my inability to conceive of anything real as a future profession.

It was quite clear to me that we, the German people, were living under a dictatorship. For instance, I was aware that I was deprived of the things that mattered most to me, in human and musical terms. And this was on grounds that were, to my mind, just as threadbare and idiotic as the regime as a whole was dark and philistine, evil and dangerous, petty-bourgeois and lethal. What was remarkable was that in this little provincial music school there was an anti-Nazi climate among the students and staff, even though it was a state institution, and the director and several of the teachers were members of the Nazi party. (The director committed suicide a few days before the war ended; no one knows exactly why.) Perhaps it was because people knew that the whole business would soon be over; or perhaps nobody wanted to have anything to do with the Nazis. People had stopped saying 'Heil Hitler!', as was still the custom at the other local music school—Die Waffen-SS-

Musikschule Braunschweig—from where, with drill and discipline, you could be turned out as the smartest musician in the land. I nearly ended up there, thanks to my father, as a punishment for my poor performance at the grammar school. But then at the last minute the music teacher at the school managed to prevent it; he liked me and wanted to rescue me. By contrast, in the conservative music school I then entered, which mainly trained orchestral players, people simply said 'Guten Tag!' This was already a transgression, but that's how things were. People spoke about the suppression of personal freedom, and reminded you in a whisper about the composers who could no longer be performed (you didn't know much about them yourself). For the rebellious, these became names to conjure with; first and foremost, of course, our underground national composer, Paul Hindemith. And Stravinsky.

The twelve-note system made people apprehensive; there was something perverse and decadent about it (they said) that filled you with nervous curiosity, especially Schoenberg—in other words the Viennese School, etc. We knew most about Hindemith, thanks to those people who had known him previously, and were able to talk about him. For instance in Brunswick in 1928 he had played his Viola Concerto, and it had gone down extremely badly. You could still get hold of Hindemith's works under the counter; you could order them from Schotts, for they published Hindemith right up to the outbreak of war, until postal services to the United States were stopped.

All in all people had had enough. The other students and I didn't want to go to war on top of everything else. Former students, who had been wounded, dropped in and told of the appalling things they had witnessed on the Eastern Front. We would have preferred the war to end immediately—which meant victory for the Allies, who made their own desire for a swift end plain enough with all-night bombing raids. Defeatism was a relatively widespread attitude, even if it may not have been displayed openly. For you were literally placing yourself in mortal danger if you expressed doubts about the ultimate triumph of the Reich, let alone said that you hoped for a quick defeat.

*[29]*

There followed a period in uniform, when I was confronted with NCOs, punishment drill, disgust, the glasshouse, shelling, fear, suffering; then with the end of the war, my triumph. When I was drafted into the army in 1944 (to be trained for an armoured division) I didn't kill myself or desert as I had planned, but switched off, made myself invisible, and hid my humiliation and torment beneath an indifferent exterior, enduring everything. One day in early summer of that year the radio was playing in the square of the Seeckt barracks in Magdeburg. I'll never forget that day. We had weapons inspection—all that peering down the barrel, with confinement to barracks if a speck of dust was found; cleaning the steps with one's own toothbrush; punishment drill with a gas mask; the brutality of the NCOs; constant threats of every form of humiliation. Then suddenly we heard over the loudspeaker the news that the Allies, our saviours, had just landed. Next to me was standing my best friend in the company, Walter Kremser, a painter; he nearly passed out with joy. That evening, as so often, there was no going out. But we were happy; we had something to drink— French red wine from the Magdeburg cellar of Walter's father, who was an officer in France—and so we hid ourselves in a dip in the parade-ground and there, in the darkness, celebrated the beginning of the end.

There was quite a lot of rebelliousness among young people, but it was impotent. It took place in the head and in music. Occasionally, if I was on duty as a wireless operator, I could listen to music by Stravinsky, Berg and Schoenberg, even though this was forbidden by military law, as well as the news from 'enemy stations' that sounded so different from ours. I developed a sort of cultural contempt for those of my fellow-countrymen who had permitted the Nazi terror to take place, who had participated in this 'Blut und Boden' pseudo-culture, and who then disappeared from the musical scene after the capitulation, at any rate for the time being.

A notable exception was Karl Amadeus Hartmann, the finest composer of his generation, who lived in Munich and was supported by his relatives. He had always refused to allow his works to be published or performed under the Nazis. He was an anti-fascist, and his compositions, which one could get to know only after 1945, are beautiful, deeply felt hymns of solidarity with the international anti-fascist movement. And they are of international standing from a technical and artistic point of view too. There was for instance an orchestral overture, *China's Struggle*, an extremely fine piece, which has a different title now. Hermann Scherchen performed it at one of the first Darmstadt get-togethers, I think it was 1947. That was how we started off then. Later, things were different, much less 'committed'.

But to return to the Nazi years. Few of us young people had a good knowledge of literature. But in 1940 a classmate in Bielefeld, son of the town's chief librarian, regularly used to smuggle out of the public library banned books which had been removed from the shelves. So we read Wedekind, Hofmannsthal, Werfel, Trakl, Mann, Heym, and Brecht too—whatever came to hand—and were captivated and fascinated by these works, which were about human beings and not monsters. Wedekind's *Spring Awakening* became our bible. My own favourite was Expressionist poetry. A time of learning and contraband culture. Later on, our fathers found out and took the books away from us, as well as the key to the 'poison cabinet' (where the prohibited books were kept), and we got a severe reprimand. Too late! The 'poison' had already entered our ideas, our imagination, and our consciousness.

This music school was full of rebellious young people. In those days even defeatism was a way of expressing dissent. The German music scene as a whole witnessed no violent protests against the regime; no one is suggesting that. On the other hand the pianist, Helmut Roloff, for example, spent years in a Gestapo prison in Berlin because he was suspected of having worked in a subversive organization (which he had). There was much discontent with the Nazis, especially towards the end of the war when defeat began to look likely (though people had not been so critical when things were going well). Repression and violence increased—against citizens of the Reich too—as Germany's military situation deteriorated. The teachers at the music school were mostly the old guard from before 1933. When the Nazis came to power, they didn't like it one bit; but they stayed on, and towards the end found things more and more unbearable, and so their resistance increased. This was no doubt motivated by a homespun conception of justice and freedom, such as one finds in the soul of many a musician. My theory teacher, Hartung, who composed in Thuille's late-romantic style, and to whom I never dared confess that I wrote atonal music, was one of these upright and amiable individuals.

In those years Brunswick had 'reds' again: workers' sons, who moved around in groups, wore their hair long and greased—it looked pretty outrageous—and were known as *Stenze* (teddy boys). Their behaviour and dress totally contradicted the ideas of the Nazi authorities. They had something of that rebelliousness that one later found among the 'rockers', and were no respecters of authority. And one day they were arrested in an SS and police operation, known as *Heldenklau*: young workers, craft-apprentices, shop assistants and music students who did not belong to Nazi organizations and didn't have the good fortune to go to the grammar school were press-ganged. I and several of my fellow music students were hauled in. We were all lined up in alphabetical order in the courtyard of police headquarters, given a medical examination, and were supposed to come out by the back door with call-up papers for the Waffen-SS! However I had the presence of mind to trick the medical examiners and escape from the building without papers. But the memory of the brutality of these Nazis has never left me. They punched anyone in the face who they thought seemed rebellious. One youth had been so savagely beaten up that he was lying bleeding and unconscious on the ground; it was forbidden to step out of line and go to his assistance. Then I saw how these Brunswick 'teddy boys' were publicly humiliated. They were shorn by these SS swine, who kept their gloves on, evidently because they couldn't stomach handling the greasy hair of these proles. You can have no idea how violent and sinister it was, and of course it was supposed to be in order to frighten everyone into signing on. No one who had not gone through it would ever believe it. It was a time of utter lawlessness, terror, fear. The tragedy of fascism left its mark on every individual, either as a source of despair or of resistance and hope. And the Germans showed their worst side. One got to know hatred, deception, betrayal, racism, the loss of human dignity.

I can speak only for myself about how things were after 8 May 1945, as at the beginning I was fairly isolated; but many will have had similar experiences. In that wonderful spring I found myself, like thousands of other soldiers of the defeated German army, a prisoner of war of the British, on the Eiderstedt peninsula on the North Sea. We camped in tents on the meadows; the farmers weren't exactly thrilled at our presence—we disrupted their calm, trespassed on their fields, looked for eggs to steal, and so on. We had nothing to do and nothing to eat, but we went for walks on the dykes and talked excitedly about the past and the future. Many of us still believed that, as rumours had predicted, we were going to be sent to the mines of Siberia or Yorkshire, that we would be castrated, etc. There was one smart lad among us: his name was Jimmy Kellner; he later edited an American cultural magazine in Berlin. He constantly discussed politics with an oboist from Dresden, Willy Meyer—short, bandy-legged, a terribly nice chap—about the way things were going to go. Jimmy talked of the importance of the United States for Europe, about integration and so forth; Willy about the democratic and anti-fascist reshaping of our country. Having grown up in a village, I found all this fascinating, even if more or less incomprehensible. It was then that I first heard the expression 'dictatorship of the proletariat'—it scared me, it sounded so uncomfortable—because of course this oboist from Dresden was an old communist, who was planning to take up again the struggle of the years before 1933.

The annexation of Alsace had turned some of our fellow-prisoners back into Frenchmen, so they isolated themselves, spoke only French, and sang French songs. One of them gave me lessons. I managed to improve my English there too. And I also composed—a whole series of pieces for oboe and wind ensembles (they still exist) for my friend Willy Meyer. On my eighteenth birthday he gave me the last tin of corned beef from his iron rations. About a fortnight later, in mid-July, I was released, went home, and tried to get a job to support my family—six brothers and sisters and my mother. My father had not returned. He had already been wounded in the First World War and at the start of the Second, but at the end he actually volunteered to serve the fatherland for the third time. We had no money and nothing to eat. At first I worked as a transport worker in a British army ordnance depot, and when in October the Bielefeld Stadttheater re-opened, I got a very badly paid job as a rehearsal pianist with the ballet company. I got to know the operettas of Kálmán and others *ad nauseam*. Sometimes I also managed to coach small parts in the operas, and help out at performances, giving cues, usually too late, to offstage flutes or trumpets. I could not have put up with life in this theatre for long; I did not meet a single person there who showed anything approaching enthusiasm for what I was doing. Perhaps it was the hunger that dominated everything. Playing the piano in clubs for officers of the British Army, you could occasionally earn a tin of corned beef and a few cigarettes. Everything was grey: the air, the houses, the faces, the stage-sets; and it was cold.

At that time a young French officer was billeted in our house. He had just come back from a visit to Bergen-Belsen. He was beside himself, absolutely appalled; he simply couldn't understand how anything like that could have happened, and I had no explanation for him either. It was a terrible shock. The world had been shown what fascism was capable of; no more excuses could be made. Everything was worse than people had suspected; and people had, in any case, done more than just suspect. In one way or another, many people knew about the concentration camps, the mass executions and the terror. Although I had had nothing to do with these atrocities, I began to feel guilty (responsible?) and couldn't understand those who didn't. That feeling is still with me today. It wasn't a sense of collective guilt. It was quite simply my amazement that so many people, who had had a hand in things, were now carrying on as if nothing had happened, as if my father's generation had not been the active servants of this barbarism.

If someone like myself, a fifteen-year-old living in the depths of the country, knew about the concentration camps by the beginning of the 1940s, then other people, the adults, definitely knew better than me what was going on. A neighbour's fiancé in our village, Senne II near Bielefeld—and this is just one example—was in the SS and sometimes came home on leave. His bride told me at the wedding reception that her handsome, tall, blond Jürgen had terrible nightmares, ever since he had begun to serve in a concentration camp and had to do guard duty at night on the watchtowers. From there he could see how the prisoners would deliberately kill themselves by clambering on to the electrified barbed-wire. He couldn't bear to watch it any more. He was hoping for a transfer. While Jürgen's bride was telling me this I could hear my father, in his Nazi uniform, roaming drunkenly through the woods with his party cronies, bawling out repulsive songs: 'When Jewish blood splashes off your knife'. These are traumatic memories.

When all this came out into the open, most people denied all knowledge. This is of course connected with the *innere Emigration* (inward emigration) which you might say was fashionable in the preceding years. People had withdrawn from the Nazis into an intimate circle of friends, and had continued to play Baroque music on cosy evenings in their cosy drawing-rooms. Anyway, that's what it was like in the bourgeois world of Bielefeld, to which I had been admitted, thanks to my being musical. Here the Nazis were considered unseemly; people tacitly rejected them, and found that Hitler fellow more and more of a nuisance, especially now that he was losing us the war and had landed us with air-raids. And afterwards, things weren't really so difficult because one had after all always been against the Nazis! A great many people said this, and many arranged things so that they were in a position to say it.

This 'I was always against the Nazis' represents a banal and frivolous stance (created on the stage by Auden in the last scene of *The Bassarids*) and those who used this catchphrase were merely saying that they had remained silent and hadn't lifted a finger; they had been accessories. But let's not forget that anyone who did lift a finger had to fear for his life. The Germans at that time were not just a race of judges and executioners, but also of informers. The network of secret police and informers was faultless and ruthless. Indeed people continued to inform after the end of the war; it had become second nature. The English commandant of Bielefeld had to put up a notice at the town hall door saying that informers would not be heard.

In their very first concert after the Hitler period the Bielefeld orchestra played Hindemith's *Mathis der Maler* symphony. It went down with a discreet cultural *frisson* of 'We're permitted to, we're able to, we have the freedom to play Hindemith, we can listen to *Mathis der Maler*, even if we hadn't actually missed this music.' But there was also an undertone of 'Now that Hindemith can be played again, our guilt is removed, everything is right with the world again, isn't it?' Fascism had been no more than a bad dream.

I was thrilled to have survived. In 1946 I wrote the *Chor gefangener Trojer*, based on a text from the second part of Goethe's *Faust*, where there is a chorus of captured Trojan women who look upon the destruction of their city and curse the god of war. This, by the way, was my first major public piece. I wrote it for the Bielefeld music society, who put on one or two concerts a year. It was beautifully performed in 1948, under Hans Hoffmann, the General-Musikdirektor; it was a great day for me. In this piece I identify myself with the captured women, and curse everything that had made me so unhappy till then, that had placed such burdens on me and had only just come to an end. I had survived, come through it all, in order to be able to write and to live. I had managed this, so I thought, with some skill—rather like a cat. Now the time had come when I was free, when it was possible, and indeed necessary, to create wonderful new things. And a great spirit of friendliness would grow up among people—those were the naïve notions I had in those days, like other young people, the few survivors of my generation.

One night in early 1946 I crawled across the railway tracks at Cassel from the British into the American zone with false papers, and after some difficulty reached Heidelberg, to start studying music properly at last. Friends had helped me on the journey; now I made a living as private tutor in maths, Latin and music to three children, and had no problems apart from the fact that in a short time I had to catch up with a syllabus that normally took years. I loved Heidelberg and my studies, the logic that resided in the traditional rules; it became clearer to me than it had been before that I wanted to be a composer.

After I had gone to Heidelberg a vital source of music sprang up in the shape of the Südwestfunk in Baden-Baden. Here Dr Strobel, a bad-tempered eccentric who had just returned to Germany and was to become high priest of the music scene, imported modern music with the help of French cultural officials, including Pierre Ponnelle, father of the opera-producer Jean-Pierre Ponnelle. Strobel broadcast a great deal of the music that had been composed abroad between 1933 and 1945, and much that had been banned under the fascists. I heard for the first time rehearsals and performances of pieces by Berg—they made a strong impression on me—and then pieces by Schoenberg, such as the Serenade op. 24 and *A Survivor from Warsaw*. Painstakingly, the orchestras learned Stravinsky's *Rite of Spring*, as for instance in Frankfurt under Winfried Zillig. Each encounter with one of these new works was a revelation, something like a blow waking me from sleep.

The Darmstadt summer courses were extremely important in promoting knowledge of modern music, at any rate during the first few years. It was the idea of the chief cultural administrator there, Wolfgang Steinecke, to bring congresses and conferences to the blitzed city of Darmstadt. The first summer course was in 1946. We put on Brecht's *Lehrstück vom Einverständnis* (I conducted it), and there was a great deal of discussion about the text and its meaning, but nobody discussed Hindemith's music. At the beginning none of the composers who were later to become famous was there. I was the only young composer among instrumentalists and singers of my age. There were also a few senior composers who had more or less collaborated during the Third Reich—I've forgotten their names—but nobody wanted to know about them; their music was no good, and they quickly vanished from the scene.

Darmstadt's development was dynamic; decisions were swiftly taken and guidelines laid down. As early as 1947 René Leibowitz took a class analysing Schoenberg. He was a marvellous teacher and, what is more, a delightful man; he taught me a great deal. We wanted to know in more detail what twelve-note composition was all about. But there were hardly any scores or recordings, let alone theoretical works, and my teacher, Fortner, had informed me in Heidelberg in 1946 and 1947 that twelve-note music had gone out long before 1930. That was his verdict. And then suddenly one heard Bartók's Violin Concerto, which contains some disconcerting twelve-note passages. Was the dragon not slain after all? So we very quickly realized that dodecaphony and serialism were the only viable new techniques: fresh, and able to generate new musical patterns.

When I say that decisions were taken and guidelines laid down in Darmstadt I have in mind the technocratic conception of art, dodecaphony's mechanistic heresy, which became official doctrine there at the beginning of the 1950s, and which for many years dominated radio networks and composers. In so far as it is at all possible to speak of a market for modern music, dictatorial control over it was exercised from Darmstadt, and also from Donaueschingen. The radio stations were behind this, as their producers scrambled for new works—in other words, for the prestige of a first performance. Along came Karlheinz Stockhausen, amid much pomp and circumstance, with claims that were immediately acknowledged. He said out loud what he thought: there was nobody around who knew anything about music apart from him. This marked the end of the solidarity that had previously existed among young composers. At the beginning it had looked as though we were all working together on a humanistic project, as if we were all brothers, comrades, allies. That was now gone. Slowly but surely we became, or were made into, competitors in the same market.

As a small boy Karlheinz must already have possessed a boundless sense of mission; at any rate his behaviour always indicated something of the sort. He was always in a fever, on cloud nine. I remember a music festival in Vienna at the beginning of the 1950s. We were driving back to the city with publishers from Universal Edition after an evening's drinking in Grinzing, when

Stockhausen said, on seeing the still somewhat sparsely lit city: 'Look, down there you can see the ocean of light that is Vienna. In a few years' time I will have progressed so far that, with a single electronic bang, I'll be able to blow the whole city sky-high!' I pointed out that there were already perfectly adequate explosives for such purposes, and that musicians might therefore do better to turn their attention to other matters.

At the first Darmstadt 'summer school' in the autumn of 1946, a work of mine for flute, piano and strings was played publicly for the first time; it immediately found publishers, who are still printing my works today. All this so much encouraged me that I now vehemently threw myself into composing.

A feverish struggle against my own inadequacies. It had been an indescribable feeling to hear my music played by professionals, cleanly in tune and absolutely faultless from beginning to end. It was as if a problem had been got out of the way, a misfortune banished, a riddle solved. So from now on everything, dark and bright, as soon as it touched the psyche would be written down in the sign-language of musical notation, like a question. The answer would come from the sound itself once the music was played. That was my expectation, in fact things worked out rather differently, the first surprise being what happens when you get taken up by the professional music world.

So guardian angels appeared. Everyone knows who they are, everyone needs them. They need us. It is all a question of personal connections. You must be noticed, you must please, be sympathetic, amenable, and must justify hopes. Being 'nice' is everything; you may be scheming, but not impertinent. A good listener, one who gratefully takes up hints (woe betide those who don't!); modesty is in order; the angels (later also playing the roles of functionaries, managers, impresarios, departmental directors and presidents) are paternalistic friends, who know what you ought to do. Generously, they distribute their gifts in the form of contracts; calmly, they indicate their temperamental *penchants* for one or other style, artist or up-and-coming composer.

Occasionally it becomes difficult to find your way around: does

[39]

what you do still belong to you, or is it already what the entrepreneurs want? Perhaps slowly and without your recognizing it you begin to repress from your music what you wanted but which others thought inappropriate.

During these immediate post-war years no one believed how it could have been possible for a nation to have sunk so low—into a disgrace that centuries could not wash clean. We were assured by senior composers that music is abstract, not to be connected with everyday life, and that immeasurable and inalienable values are lodged in it (which is precisely why the Nazis censored those modern works which strove to achieve absolute freedom). Was not Stravinsky right when 'between the battles' of the last years of the Second World War he wrote ballet scenes for a revue, circus polkas, and such like? For even if the inferno and carnage in Europe and Asia burdened his soul, the purity (*Reinheit*) of art gave no quarter, its laws admitted of no exceptions. And Stravinsky believed that music could raise the general moral tone. His works are particularly good examples of the Apollonian stance.

Everything had to be stylized and made abstract: music regarded as a glass-bead-game, a fossil of life. Discipline was the order of the day. Through discipline it was going to be possible to get music back on its feet again, though nobody asked what for. Discipline enabled form to come about; there were rules and parameters for everything. Expressionism and (left-wing) Surrealism were mystically remote; we were told that these movements were already obsolete before 1930, and had been surpassed. The new avant-garde would reaffirm this. The audience, at whom our music was supposed to be directed, would be made up of experts. The public would be excused from attending our concerts; in other words, our public would be the press and our protectors.

The existing audience of music-lovers, music-consumers, was to be ignored. Their demand for 'plain-language' music was to be dismissed as improper. (A wise man does not answer an impertinent questioner.) On top of this we had to visualize the public as illiterate, and perhaps even hostile. If it was our fate that we, the elite, were exposed to these philistines, we were to arm ourselves with contempt and the smug feelings of martyrs. Any encounter with the listeners that was not catastrophic and scandalous would defile the artist, and would mobilize mistrust against us. At best one could approach the public with enigmas, without providing solutions. As Adorno decreed, the job of a composer was to write music that would repel, shock, and be the vehicle for 'unmitigated cruelty'. At the same time the composer had to allow himself to be guided in his idiosyncrasy by taste, the truest seismograph of historical experience. Thus spake Adorno; this was supposed to be the point of departure for the new international generation of composers.

In his critique of Futurism in *Literature and Revolution* Trotsky says:

The class of intellectuals is extremely heterogeneous. Every recognized school is at the same time a well-paid school, at whose head stand mandarins with many decorations. The artistic mandarins as a rule bring the style of their school to the highest level of refinement, but at the same time they shoot off their entire store of powder. Then some kind of objective change, a political upheaval or a minor social breeze, brings the literary bohemia on to its feet— the young, these geniuses of military service age, who customarily accompany their curses against satiated and tasteless bourgeois culture with the secret wish for their own medals, preferably golden.

The guardian angels meanwhile became agents and entrepreneurs, benevolently accepting dedications of works by other and younger composers, no longer contenting themselves with whims and preferences, but exerting influence (often steered by the groups), plotting strategy, electing themselves spokesmen, and furthering their own social careers at the same time. And why not? Small-time Diaghilevs reprimanded grown composers for writing too dissonantly or too consonantly, issued decrees about what was 'in' and what was 'out' and knew exactly what one could and couldn't write. 'He's had it. He's finished. You can't do that any more. In the age of structuralism you must write structures. A young composer

shouldn't come up with a score like that. Well, after Webern the
only thing you can do is this. . . .'

The year 1952 was particularly eventful for me: *Boulevard Solitude*
in Hanover, the ballet *The Idiot* in Berlin and Venice, *Pas d'Action*
in Munich, Second String Quartet, the 'choreographic fantasy'
*Labyrinth*, the radio opera *Ein Landarzt*, trips to Paris, inventing a
persona for myself amid *enfants du paradis*, masks and disguises.
Romanticism and *Schwärmerei*, my close companions,
had disported themselves against the lunar landscape of Berlin
as seen in paintings by Werner Held, and in the snowy
Dostoevskyan nights of a destroyed Munich. Everywhere the old
was not yet old enough, while the new pointed towards a future that
no one was prepared to expect too much of. I travelled ceaselessly
up and down Germany, without managing to find a capital city;
such cities as survived were places where, in the heat, the wind
swirled the dust of the rubble up into the air, and in winter the mist
concealed the non-existence of a centre. From the autobahn, that
endless strip of death, you could see these places, in the middle
distance or on the horizon, the first hideous neon tubes on new
buildings, mass-produced furniture, ignoble dwellings of reinforced concrete in which the new society was growing up, places
of calumny and suspiciousness. There was no communication;
people remained silent or talked past one another. All one heard was
the murmur, even the tumult, of innumerable monologues.

I had a rough time. I was subjected to reproaches, admonitions
by the police, shown my place; trees, they insisted, were *not* to grow
towards the sky. This was an industrious country, where the
diligent, forgetful of the past, were already striving for the
reintroduction of military service and general rearmament. What
did they want? Where was it all supposed to lead? Which way
should one turn?

Renewed or first encounters with the works of the Viennese
trinity Schoenberg/Berg/Webern had made a particularly strong
impression on me. The freshness and beauty of some of these works
had a great impact on us young composers, while others were

especially attracted by the possibilities implicit in those scores, of the total rationalization of musical creation. In the following years it was, indeed, chiefly this aspect that served as a model, and pointed towards the new types of serial composition. The formation of a new musical bourgeoisie was important and necessary, not least because without it one would not have been able to measure how far one was away from it. It is thanks to its influence and efforts that the specific disposition of this new musical world moved further and further beyond its own horizons; that I felt myself less and less tied; that I saw more and more clearly that there were also other things that were going to be significant, but I would have to discover them for myself.

When I came back to Darmstadt again from Italy in 1955, to give a composition class with Maderna and Boulez, things had become pretty absurd. Boulez, who saw himself as the supreme authority, was sitting at the piano, flanked by Maderna and myself—we must have looked like reluctant assistant judges at a trial, as young composers brought their pieces forward for opinion. Anything that wasn't Webernian, he brusquely dismissed: 'If it isn't written in the style of Webern it's of no interest'.

My antipathy was directed not against Webern's music, but against the misuse and misinterpretation of his aesthetic and, indeed, of his technique and its motivation and significance. Thanks to the initiative of Boulez and Stockhausen this had become institutionalized as official musical thinking, whose maxims the body of lesser mortals now had to put into practice (allowing for seasonal variations) with religious devotion, *esprit de corps* and slavish obedience. The old Webernians, people who had known him and worked with him, and who were now to witness the spectacle of this aesthetic error, began to feel more and more redundant, went down in the estimation of the technocrats of Darmstadt, and were no longer 'in' but 'out'.

I found this entire development regrettable. In those days, everything that did not fit into this scheme was rejected; the whole thing was run according to rules and principles, without a trace of humour or humanity. The music of Mahler was regarded as Art

Nouveau kitsch, suited at best only to provoke laughter. With the coming of the first strict serial compositions the least glimmer of any political spark was finally extinguished in the minds of their creators. It is true that the tendency towards depoliticization had started early on, in Darmstadt as elsewhere in Germany; but with the production of music that was totally mechanized and incapable of expressiveness, it reached a peak in the mid-1950s.

In Western Germany art had become a question of power, of influence, of contacts, of political and moral conformism. The personal taste of a department head and his wife determined the fate of works, the fate of their composers, and whether their products were going to reach the market or not. These people behaved like princes and patrons of feudal times. They became prelates, who greeted you with a ceremoniously raised hand that was then lowered in benediction.

There was one frustrating thing about the so-called 'night studios'—hardly anybody listened to these broadcasts around midnight! The music thus never reached the majority of listeners— for whom a composer should after all be writing—and as a result there was no interaction with the public. This led to isolation, and hardly any attempts were made to minimize or overcome it. On the contrary, this hermetic production process carried with it a certain aura; these 'night studios' took control over music, and composers acquiesced. The line of least resistance had been found: the possibility of complete agreement between composer and func-tionary. This did a considerable amount to promote the 'Darmstadt style'; naturally it also developed in line with the prodigious orchestral and financial resources of the radio stations—in the sense that pieces that did not require at least sixty rehearsals were regarded as dubious, superficial and frivolous. Things were pretty strict. The atmosphere was that of an—admittedly well-heeled— early Christian sect, and people even talked of an 'Ars Nova'—a crass example of the unhistorical thinking that prevailed at the time. And there was constant talk of law and order. Just imagine: it was being bureaucratically determined how people should compose, in which style and according to which criteria. It was a winter's tale.

The Germany that Heine had satirized a hundred years previously held sway again, ever mindful of its ceaseless aspirations to hegemony.

After all I'd been through with fascism I believed that music could be a powerful healing force. I was not alone; others, such as Luigi Nono, who came to Darmstadt in around 1950, and Bruno Maderna, both of whom were influenced by Hermann Scherchen, thought and worked along similar lines. We believed that through music it would be possible to bring about intellectual and moral change, and democratic musical thinking.

As things turned out, Nono left Darmstadt in a rather spectacular way, when Cage—after considerable delay—made his entrance. I think it was in about 1958, and the whole world—and in particular the worlds of Stockhausen and Boulez—was thrilled by the glad tidings of structureless and aleatory music, which contributed substantially to the demise of strict seriality. Nono delivered a lampoon against Cage and his ideology, and turned his back on Darmstadt for good.

My aesthetic and social views of that time are most clearly expressed in my music for the theatre. For instance, *Boulevard Solitude* (1951, the third operatic version of *Manon Lescaut*) incorporates popular music from various sources in a dialectical interplay. It quotes Parisian music-hall, and the then fashionable brutalistic 'symphonic' jazz of Stan Kenton, and it alludes to socio-critical operatic themes such as that of *La Traviata*. The bourgeois capitalistic world is tonal; that of love (unhappiness, despair) atonal. At all events the piece still makes an impact in the theatre today, and it was at the time regarded as an outspoken attack on bourgeois values. To *épater le bourgeois* came quite naturally to me. At the Hanover premiere in 1952, I had a packed live audience for the first time. They were interested in my music, just as my music was interested in them. I realized that I could get people to listen to me—make them happy or angry, make them laugh or cry.

This was an important and decisive experience. Music as speech: a discourse, a syntax, a means of communication and instruction.

Since then I have tried, to an increasingly conscious degree, to write 'public' pieces. This tendency had already been anticipated in my symphonies. The first was premiered in front of a large audience in Bad Pyrmont in 1948; the second was performed in a cinema in Stuttgart in 1949, and it too had a marked impact on the large audience. In the same year the Third Symphony was played at the avant-garde festival in Donaueschingen, where some people were not best pleased that the work failed to follow the modernist eclectics of the Darmstadt School.

A few years later, in 1958, I had an unusual experience at a performance in Donaueschingen of my *Nachtstücke und Arien*, which consist of four orchestral pieces and the settings of two beautiful poems by Ingeborg Bachmann—one of them a love song full of myth and mystery, the other a polemic against war and nuclear weapons. Gloria Davy sang magnificently and the work, conducted by Hans Rosbaud, was very well received. But from my seat I could see that, after the first few bars, Boulez, Stockhausen, and also my friend Nono, got up together and left the auditorium, making sure that everyone saw them. They weren't even prepared to *listen* to this music that sounded so different from theirs. There was something symbolic about the sight of these three colleagues walking out on my music. It gave me food for thought. What must have shocked them and made it impossible for them to stay were presumably (I have never bothered to ask them) the light cadences of Neapolitan or Spanish *café chantant* music which the piece incorporates at certain points. That must have been it, and it seems fitting, because these and similar influences from popular culture and everyday life were the stuff of my music in those years; they can also be found in my ballet *Ondine* and in the opera *König Hirsch*.

The accusation that my efforts to reach the public were an accommodation to public taste came—and still comes—from not a million miles from Darmstadt. Or if it is no longer heard, that is because today the whole world is writing tonal music—to a far greater extent than I consider desirable—even Stockhausen and Kagel! This all goes back to the fact that the developments of the early 1950s resulted in a sort of division of labour: *they* got the electronic studios and the late-night programmes, *I* got the symphony concerts and opera houses. That was how things turned out. But it was by no means easy for me to develop a musical language independent of the 'public taste' that then allegedly existed. Is there in fact any such thing? Does it not rather have to be modified and re-invented over and over again? Is it not a prime function of the composer to influence, and indeed educate, habits of listening?

I was practically the only composer—or at least one of the first— to break free of the Darmstadt manner. I have never been able to go along with all this acoustic research, this technological and electronic hunt for new sounds, which is undertaken in the new laboratories. I do not have the impression that any useful advances have come to light. But perhaps they are still to come—now that in Paris Boulez has had installed that fantastic new computer from Stanford, California.

In the 1950s I had anyway to overcome considerable resistance on the part of the public and a large part of the press. There was still powerful prejudice against modern music; people talked of 'decadence', 'cultural disintegration', etc., just as they'd done in the 1930s. Year after year I was booed and whistled by the public to whose taste I was supposed to be pandering; for instance in West Berlin, where it became something of a local custom. It happened at the premiere of *König Hirsch* at the 1956 Festival. That turned into a full-blooded theatrical scandal which was also directed against the conductor, Hermann Scherchen. The audience rejected the 'red dictator', as he was called by the orchestral players; he once even had his tyres slashed in the car park next to the theatre. Needless to say, that couldn't happen in a 'night studio'.

The arguments used against *König Hirsch* were: 'written against the voice', 'crazy', 'too loud', 'too many dissonances', 'no melodies', 'we want *Lohengrin*'—yes, that too, because what people had really been looking forward to was a new production of that opera. The performance had been interrupted by cat-calls and shouts; the quiet ends of the acts had been ruined, and the performance was interrupted twice in the third act.

A year later there was another uproar at the Berlin Festival, and this time it was my ballet *Maratona di Danza*, staged by Luchino Visconti. The audience was incensed at a ballet with a realistic plot and production; 'abstract' ballets had just come into fashion. For all that, it was splendidly performed, Renzo Vespignani's sets were brilliantly lit, it was superbly danced (Jean Babilée) and acted. But the audience and the critics didn't see that at all. They were only prepared to hail works staged in the dismal neo-Expressionism characteristic of post-war German theatre. I remember someone calling out to the city's cultural administrator: 'Tiburtius, is *this* your sort of thing?' (To my mind Visconti's production would be extremely well received today.) That was how things went until the mid-1960s, when the attacks relented, albeit only temporarily. Then they started off again in the 1970s; there was a furore in the West Berlin Deutsche Oper over *Natascha Ungeheuer* and *We Come to the River*. A great part of the hostility against modern music was unloaded on to me; for I was no longer a night-studio composer and was more or less the only one they could get their hands on in public.

At the time of these scandals, widely reported in the international press, I was already living in Italy; I could always return there as if it were home, until it did in fact become my home. (By the way, *Boulevard Solitude* created two memorable scandals there too in 1954, in the S. Carlo theatre in Naples, and especially in the Teatro dell'Opera in Rome.) But this period before I moved to Italy was certainly difficult. At the end of 1949 my job with Heinz Hilpert's Deutsches Theater in Constance finished because the theatre went bankrupt. This was because Hilpert stood out against concessions to popular taste, insisting on presenting only pieces of classic status.

I found myself in West Berlin without a job; I literally didn't have a penny to my name, and as I didn't know where to go, I simply stayed where I was. I was fascinated by the city, the first metropolis I had been to in my life. I fell in love with it, and it was and still is very important to me to be recognized in this city as a German composer. A performance of my short opera *Das Wundertheater* in the winter of 1949/50 at the Städische Oper helped me to meet people from the music world, and they tried to get jobs for me. For instance at the beginning of 1950 I conducted a radio performance of my ballet *Jack Pudding*, with members of the Berlin Philharmonic; it went badly, as I had had little conducting experience. Things started to go wrong. I had to borrow money which I couldn't pay back. Nothing was working out. Then, on top of everything, I had personal difficulties and didn't know how to go on. It was a terrible confusion, a great despair in the midst of that icy winter, a moment of darkness. I became ill and was in the Westend Hospital for weeks. The only person who visited me regularly was Paul Dessau. Almost every day he made the long S-Bahn journey from Zeuthen-Königswusterhausen, bringing with him some oranges, apples, books (for instance, the Adorno/Eisler *Komposition für den Film*), and then we talked about music, theatre, politics. He treated me like a colleague of his own age; he was never patronizing. We became great friends and remained so for many years, right up to his death; we used to see one another often. I owe a great deal of my political education to him, a Marxist and humanistic moralist. After leaving the hospital my financial situation was worse than before, and then Dr Adolf Schüle, a professor of law at Heidelberg, and father of the children whom I'd tutored, came to my aid. I spent the summer of 1950 in his home in the Mozartstrasse writing—apart from the instrumentation of my Whitman songs—nothing but letters, in an attempt to get some kind of work. Finally I obtained a job at the Wiesbaden State Theatre, arranging, and conducting ballet scores and incidental music. But because I was working for and in the theatre from morning till night I had very little time for writing my own music. Every young composer knows the situation: if he has a job he has money but no time to write; if he writes, he has no money.

On reflection, I can begin to understand my differences with the Darmstadt School. It may seem a bit far-fetched, but I have often thought that their attempt to make music non-communicative had something to do with the ruling class's belief that art is a thing apart from life, better kept that way, and without any social dimension.

The reason why this 'non-communicative' tendency, which possessed a mystical, indeed an expressly Catholic element, was so vigorously promoted was, I think, the desire to prevent people from seeing music as simple, concrete and comprehensible communication between human beings. The former Bauhaus painter, Werner Gilles, whom I often used to visit in Munich and also saw in Italy, was an acute observer of the times. As is often the case with painters, he was deeply familiar with the reality of the natural world. He took a negative view of the development of the arts in post-war Germany. The worst thing, in his eyes, was the kind of pressure that made young artists dependent on the official line in modern art, thus preventing them from discovering their own way.

But this was only one phenomenon. The period of political reconstruction around and after 1950 was also that leading up to the banning of the KPD (German Communist Party); old comrades, who had been imprisoned by the Nazis, were locked up again. I have never heard anyone mention this in musical circles. Music is, after all, unpolitical! The ban, incidentally, also killed off workers' music and the democratic tradition of folk song. The poet Enzensberger was one of the first intellectuals in the Federal Republic who spoke out publicly against these arrests. The newspapers began to resurrect the idea of the 'German soldier'. People asked themselves: 'Are we going to have an army again?' The answer was: 'And what if we are?' I remember effusive articles that appeared—it may have been in the magazine *Stern*—proclaiming: 'It was wonderful to be a German soldier' and suchlike, everyone conveniently forgetting that the war had cost 50 million lives. The result was a rehabilitation of German militarism. All this was extremely skilfully engineered, and one day there it was: this new army for peacetime and defence, the Bundeswehr—something which in 1945 no one would have thought possible. It looked to me like a gradual return to the recent past, under which its appalling conditions once again became conceivable.

In addition there was my social isolation as a homosexual. For it was then socially impossible to be a homosexual as this was considered a pathological state, an affront to the feelings of a healthy community (*das gesunde Volksempfinden*) and to those of the concert-going public. For instance, according to a West Berlin lady who telephoned me the following day, I really shouldn't have taken Fernando, my friend from Calabria, to the party for Stravinsky in Blacher's house—even though he was much better looking than everyone else there, apart from Stravinsky! Or, at six o'clock one morning the police arrived to haul off my friend and myself. We were questioned separately, and in those days (when the law still took an inflexible stance on the subject) there was no alternative but to deny one's inclinations if one wanted to avoid a trial and imprisonment; one had to behave like a criminal trying to slip through the net of justice. For this elevating patriotic experience, granted me in the winter of 1948–9 in Constance, I have to thank an informer, a landlady. Small wonder that I was already thinking of emigration as early as that.

Such experiences were part and parcel of the climate of the 1950s, as was the constant pressure to achieve, to attain status. One also had to learn how to survive the scrutiny of the press, and to win its favour. This meant that one always had to have a new idea to sell. A composer in the late-capitalist world is more or less a small industrialist, an entrepreneur, a self-employed producer whose products can't afford to be forgotten. During those years I was on more than one occasion 'out'. One had the unmistakable impression that one was always expected to produce something sensational—like a tightrope walker, professional boxer or magician.

These pressures prevented you from articulating your own hopes and point of view, and from seeing what was really going wrong in the world, from getting to the bottom of social questions. So it happened more and more often that I would switch off the news on the radio and stop reading the newspapers, for together with all these other 'obligations', such things didn't really seem to concern one that much. We were repeatedly told: 'Create, artist, and hold your tongue!' Or: 'Music has nothing to do with politics!' I think that the most important thing for someone in my position was, and is, to arrange matters in such a way that he does not constantly have

[51]

to meet these obligations. That is the only luxury that an artist under this system can earn for himself.

When I crossed the Alps to Italy in early 1953 in my car, which I had bought on hire-purchase out of my earnings in the Federal Republic, and which was loaded with a couple of suitcases, some music paper and a few classical scores (I'd had to sell everything else, even my books), I felt a bit like someone who had been rescued from a disaster. In order to start afresh, I was now turning my back on post-war Germany, where the old guard again, or still, had a considerable share of the say. I felt I had the chance to do something real, to forget what I had suffered, and to listen to what was around me; to study people's interests in a revolutionary country with a classical culture.

The first evening: Venice. Sitting for hours in the unfamiliar, wide squares, walking in the labyrinth of deserted *calli*. All that has been should now be forgotten; everything will be different, the sun will transform everything. Crossing Tuscany, a broad and immense receptacle of grace and proportion; a few days in Quinto near Florence. '*Les nourritures terrestres*', much silence, more forgetting, great expectations.

Then began the years on the island of Ischia, which the Greeks had called Pithecoussa. The small two-room house was in my eyes a Saracen fortress; high whitewashed walls offering protection from the sun and from the salty sea-winds of the winter. Lucia and her sons defended it against intruders or the evil eye, and they watched over my growing opera *König Hirsch* (*Re Cervo*). In the inner courtyard of the house wild cats perched in the splendid fig tree; a crown of agaves grew out of its wing. Volcanoes spewed fresh wine, friendly lizards dropped by for an apéritif. On the horizon the sky and the sea celebrated their union, making the light quiver; the scirocco made music amid the reeds. I came to know Italian as a ceremonious and dark tongue; I tried to hear with Neapolitan ears, and took history lessons in the depths of unfathomable almond eyes.

I came under the spell of Italian folk song, in particular the songs of peasants and fishermen that seem to come from North Africa and Asia Minor. In fact one can trace in them the development of the music of southern Europe right down to popular Neapolitan song. Subsequently I have attempted in almost every new work to make a synthesis between popular musical traditions and the fully evolved style of our own age. In the first stage work undertaken in Italy, *König Hirsch*, this can be heard clearly in Checco's *canzone* in the second act. Then again in the *Fünf neapolitanische Lieder* (1957) and in the *Nachtstücke und Arien* with the Bachmann poems, already mentioned. One finds something of this Neapolitan *languore* in the ballet *Ondine*, and it would be true to say that my musical syntax became de-Germanized, and Neapolitanized instead. *Kammermusik* (1958) signals a change, as there are once again more austere elements in the octet movements, amid the Neapolitan-inspired textures of the voice and the guitar. *Antifone* marks a sudden return to dodecaphony (the piece is inspired by Ginsberg's poem 'Howl'), followed by an austere piano sonata (with a strict fugue for its last movement) and the opera *Der Prinz von Homburg*. In this work nearly everything is linear and polyphonic; the newly found rich sonority gives way to counterpoint. The result is an interaction between homophony and polyphony, between free music and strict composition. It is also a result of the subject-matter. The work is about dream and reality, and the infinite contrast between them. But there is another shift that explains my return to stricter forms. I no longer wanted to stay in Naples; it had become too seductive, too lyrical for me, and during the last year there I knew that I would leave. I was in the wrong social setting; I had gone to the wrong address in 1955 when I had moved from Ischia to the mainland. In Ischia I had lived in relative seclusion, and apart from my neighbours and the local people, I rarely saw anyone—only Werner Gilles, W. H. Auden and Chester Kallman, and later William and Susana Walton as well as the Munich artist, Margherita Utescher, of whom I was extremely fond (she was incredibly attractive and funny) and was married to Carlo Ferdinando Russo, a professor of

*[53]*

Greek literature at Bari university. I spent most winter evenings on Ischia with them, and our conversations were virtually my first real lessons in Italian politics.

In 1956 I moved from Ischia to Naples, where I lived until 1961. Naples still had its aristocrats; it was very traditional. If you received any invitations at all, say to a musical afternoon, it was usually in the dilapidated *palazzo* of some *principe*, usually a tradition-conscious Spaniard from one of the Aragonese families. This was not without a certain historical interest; I managed to see a little of what the ruling class of Naples had once been (six hundred years ago, not three hundred), relics of which still survive in the shape of the society of *Nobili Spagnoli in Napoli*. Strangely enough, they have a culture that is German-influenced; they read Nietzsche and go to Bayreuth. But they are old, and their sons are born old; everything is stamped with pessimism and a strange weariness. What I liked about them was a certain awareness of their own negativity, but that is perhaps not enough for one to be able to live off it for hours at a time, let alone years. The artistic friendships I made then were in Rome, not in Naples, whose young intellectuals fled the crumbling metropolis and the dangers of lethargy, surrender and resignation, by moving to Milan or Rome.

I went to Rome in 1961, to that ancient African citadel with its modern appendages, its golden light, its atmosphere of medieval superstition, vulgarity, aggressiveness and corruption. In Rome, whose prelates had once burnt Giordano Bruno, the first work I wrote was the cantata *Novae de Infinito Laudes* on texts by him, in brittle tonal contours and madrigal-like polyphony.

In Italy you are repeatedly confronted with German history. Around 1950 I felt this in a concrete way, in my everyday dealings with people: for instance in the morning when buying my rolls in the little piazza near where I lived in Naples. During the last days of the occupation—the famous *tre giornate di Napoli*—Wehrmacht soldiers shot six young men, sons of the tradesmen from whom I, recognizably a German, was now buying my food. But the people were friendly, and I felt ashamed and bewildered.

I had known from the outset what I like and dislike about people, what I want for them and what I don't. This attitude is accompanied and energized by a contradictory career and learning-process. Aristocrats, capitalists, bourgeois are no empty abstractions for me; I know such people and their circles, and not just from Naples. I know people from German industrial firms, and I know why I have no sympathy for them. What I mean is that it is valuable for an artist to have first-hand experience of a wide range of backgrounds and ways of life, especially if he wants to write for the theatre. For instance, during my time as a student in Heidelberg, I frequented not only the railway station to sell American cigarettes on the black market, but also the local Stefan George circle. All this is part and parcel of my slow, hesitant development, including that of my music. I learned to operate on different levels, to keep my eyes open, to acquaint myself with human reality, to accept nothing that was purely theoretical, but always to be doing and creating.

My friendship with Visconti was an important element in my development. We got to know one another in 1956 in Milan. He was a visual artist, a communist, with a clear Stanislavskian conception of theatre and music drama. In his work I detected a relationship between art and politics fundamentally different from Brecht's.

With the 1960s came the period when the Vietnam War escalated, and the movement opposing the war continued to grow. In the summer of 1967 I looked out of an aeroplane window down on to the flames and black smoke of the riots in Washington and Newark, and asked myself what my role, my function, was in these times of conflict, of a new emergent society. What was I doing? Who was I? What could I do? What could music do? In New York I was deeply struck by the problems of the blacks—to which I returned in 1979 in a work entitled *El Rey de Harlem*—and I saw the bitterness and the humiliation in the lives of my black friends. I suffered with them but didn't know what I should do. I was worried and ignorant.

Finally, I began to read systematically, stealing time in order to do so. I started with Marcuse, and read some Adorno; Marx and Lenin were to come later. This marked the start of a period of theoretical study. I also managed to read Brecht's writings on the theatre, which were now published and available. Brecht's writings as a whole have exercised a lasting influence on me. During this time I went often to Berlin to meet and talk with the radical student group, the SDS, and Rudi Dutschke in particular. I now and then still see someone from those days, and the experiences of the late 1960s—my involvement with the young left in the Federal Republic and West Berlin—were significant for my subsequent political development. As things turned out, that was to take place not in Germany but in Cuba and in Italy, where I had settled. There, with ever-increasing confidence, I began to learn how my music and my political beliefs could support and strengthen each other.

# König Hirsch (Il Re Cervo)
## (1) The Spirit of Italy *

*From a letter to Josef Rufer:*

'I have been working for a year and a half now on this opera, which Heinz von Cramer has adapted freely from Gozzi. The second act is just finished. It contains a multiplicity of forms: arias, duets, ensembles for several voices, hunt music, cabalettas, *canzoni*, mime. The finale is a symphony in five connected movements (my "Fourth"). The sections in the opera are self-contained, but have bridge-passages, which gives the impression of a through-composed score articulated principally by changes of tempo and colour. I have not yet timed the first two acts, but there is already an enormous heap of music manuscripts piling up on the desk.

In each scene a particular musical category is investigated, whether by design or spontaneous discovery. I have not used a tone-row, nor are there any central themes or leitmotifs (except for a sequence of notes that crept in some time ago, a little tag that has started to spread; I don't yet know where it will lead). So each scene has a self-contained form, as the dramatic situation demands. Several elements of Italian opera, which I discovered here for the first time, occur in a manner that is more or less transformed; similarly conventional idioms and sonorities of the "music of our time" have vanished from the score. . . .

I feel well here, and am interested in nothing except this work,

---

* 'Über *Re Cervo* (*König Hirsch*).' *Musiker über Musik*, Darmstadt 1956 (part); *Melos* vol 23 no 9 1956 (part).

and how I can make something suitable and usable out of this somewhat wild excursion from my previous musical environment. What seem on the surface the simplest things still present the greatest problems. For instance, in the second act someone has to sing a brief song, half from love, anxiously, and half from fear of loneliness. The form of the words and the setting of the action suggest a Neapolitan *canzone*, the type of song you hear in this place day and night, near and far, shouted incoherently, or softly merging into the landscape. For the most part these *canzoni* are extensively improvised in text and melody, to the point where the originals are no longer recognizable; they are variants of poignant, enigmatic compositions, dating back a hundred or a thousand years, made up of quartertones—magical intervals that can hardly be captured in our notation. To create something of this kind oneself—something that sounds neither artificial nor clever, but leaves its imprint on the world (like graffiti on a prison cell wall), accompanied by no more than a few plucked guitar notes that are scarcely meant to leave the empty strings—this turns out to be a singular adventure. The first experiments were insipid and quite ludicrously primitive. Mrs Polyhymnia was in the way, and *cultura settentrionale* (northern culture) too.

After I had given up trying, something actually succeeded, more by accident than anything else. (Perhaps I had left my cigarettes in the study and inadvertently brushed against the desk when looking for them, or something like that, saw the sketch, discovered a solution.) But I have had a fair amount of time to measure the gap between *musica da camera* and *musica da piazza*, whether or not this appears regrettable, capable of sociological explanation, true or false. I myself found (and still find) this gap pointlessly great and unsatisfactory, and as an inhabitant of the *camera* am not at all sure whether the *piazza* is not far more real, and closer to that "smallest size" which Brecht spoke of in the Baden *Lehrstück** and which it is one's job to seek.

Perhaps by moving towards it one might also stand a better

---

* 'When the thinker came to a great storm, he sat in a large vehicle and took up a great deal of room. The first thing was that he got out of his vehicle, the second was

chance of reaching that physical substance of which music is composed, that warmth that attracts people because they need it.'

It was in Berlin at the end of 1952, while *Ode to the West Wind* was still in progress, that Cramer and I had begun to discuss Gozzi's *Re Cervo*. This Venetian *fiaba* full of miraculous events, inspired by Indian legends, and replete with magical scene-changes and exuberance, had begun to exert a powerful attraction on us. Eccentric robust buffoons—droll fellows with a propensity for the mythical; a bygone baroque Italy, fantastical and bizarre. We wrote our scenario for the opera slowly and not without difficulty. At several points it parted company with the original. Whereas with Gozzi, improvisations, mystifications and the formulas of *commedia dell'arte* are preponderant, Cramer's new version embodies a broadly conceived psychologized plot, reduces the comedy to decorative trimmings, and conjures up the benevolent spirits of Italy, introducing also new ideas and images.

The gentle and simple music of the first sketches for the opera was the point from which a score developed over the years, amid restless labour that filled day after day, month after month, like a diary in which one records observations and reflections. Here is the shattering sound of the *banda* during the evening feast of S. Vito, mingled with the frenetic singing of the procession; the twinkling high notes of the mandoline, insistently and lasciviously hanging in the air like a scent; the darker tone of guitars, from distant centuries; here is the street cry, with infinite coloraturas and variations, insane, piercing noise and soft vowels, murderous screaming, a litany, the faint tinkling of the angelus bell. The people of this southern city, "Napoli nobilissima e gentilissima", are so enigmatic that you think you will never understand them; but that is good, and their mime and strangeness are themselves an inspiration; their marvellous proximity demands a response.

---

that he took off his coat, the third was that he lay on the ground. That was how he managed to overcome the storm in his smallest size.'

Bertolt Brecht, *Das Badener Lehrstück vom Einverständnis*, scene 7

I tried to develop a vocal style that, without leaning too much on existing models, corresponded to the dramatic conception. Each singer should be able to portray his or her own persona merely through "vocal behaviour", and it was to be the singers who determined the direction of the work, its expression and its meaning. The melodic dimension is not problematic when regarded as an indispensable element of music, capable of change and development. But as it is no longer a matter of course in the music of my generation, it raised a number of stylistic questions with unexpected pungency. Added to this were formal problems. Among other things, Cramer's libretto required finales of over twenty minutes' duration, which had to be solved individually, with the predominant idea of avoiding old and (especially) contemporary models, particularly where they most obviously suggested themselves. Each "piece" (there are no "numbers" in the traditional sense) is the length of a scene, each scene is a form. In one case the form develops widely like 'automatic writing'; in another it is the result of planning, or derives logically from the structure of the scene. Thus, for instance, the second act (in the original version) consists of only the following superstructure-like elements: (a) a dream in three sections; (b) hunt music; (c) a scene for tenor and ballerina; (d) a *canzone*; (e) three consecutive scenes in *vivace* $\frac{9}{16}$; (f) metamorphoses; (g) finale.

The elaborate orchestration is treated differently from (for instance) *Boulevard Solitude*, where small solo groups in fragile note-clusters determined the timbre. Here everything is hard and robust; *molto vivace, senza complimenti*, qualities that I have admired so much in Bellini, although the sound of his *banda* may be detected at only a few carefully chosen moments.* At the time of writing I have not yet heard the orchestra of *König Hirsch*, but if something of my ideas were to succeed, you should be able to recognize in its timbres the adventures and agitations amid which the score grew up.

* '*Les souvenirs sont cors de chasse
  dont meurt le bruit parmi le vent.*'

Guillaume Apollinaire

Street singing is, as it were, continued without interruption on the stages of the opera houses, which explains why for an Italian audience there is not the least suspicion that opera might be something artificial, antiquated, in need of updating, a monster. It is right and natural to give emphasis to a heightened moment of life by singing, and it is "realistic"! The problems that face composers are of purely dramatic and above all purely musical nature. To these are added today (as in the past) the "struggle with the material", a struggle that could be kept under control only by restricting it to the sharpening of the means by which the work is intended to communicate.

Admittedly, the experience gained from my serial compositions has been most valuable. At the beginning of the opera, rudiments of serial technique can still be found. They seem to mobilize the harmony, and rhythm, in order to release the material with greater freedom. Themes or their constituent parts, in so far as they recur, do not serve as leitmotifs in the old sense, and are thus connected only indirectly with the events on stage; but thorough analysis could perhaps lay bare and illuminate the extent to which the melodies are interrelated, and their connection with the action.

The miracles that take place in the legend of *König Hirsch*, the idea of metamorphosis, thoughts of a freedom that transcends the tolerable, the tyrant's death, peace—all these themes must be portrayed without the slightest distortion, without parody and without artifice. The piece is conceived neither as a fairy opera nor as a dream play, nor even as a modern *commedia dell'arte*, whatever elements it may have of all of these. Its simple title 'opera' suggests the discipline that has been striven for. The scenario filled with miraculous happenings at first steers away from the intended goal of realism, only subsequently to work towards it and ultimately reinforce it.

Everything that constitutes music, and for which it is loved, has here appeared to me as completely new, beautiful and spacious. My work can be nothing other than an attempt to approach an ideal, the discovery of beauty—albeit an ideal that appears more distant, the more of its dimensions one can perceive with one's own eyes.'

# König Hirsch
## (2) Two Performing Versions *

Rome, 3 January 1973

Dear Jo,

It is true that in conversation with Klaus Tennstedt I didn't actually discourage performance of *König Hirsch* in the form you would like to employ, more or less your 'Bielefeld version', in other words cut once again, and different from the printed shorter version, *Re Cervo oder Die Irrfahrten der Wahrheit*, which I made in 1962–3. But I did not say that such an enterprise would please me.

I don't know your arguments against the new *Re Cervo*, but they must be weighty if you prefer a mutilated version to the original. I do agree with you about one thing: I too prefer *König Hirsch*, the original version. But only if it's uncut. After painstaking investigations I have come to the conclusion that it is impossible to find a really satisfactory solution if one insists on cutting. No matter what you do, the result would inevitably be experienced as wrong or weak by the listener. Something happens to the form that it cannot stand up to; its breadth, pathos and baroque quality demand time. Things can't be fanned out any more; the fan has holes in it, the mechanism no longer functions properly. This work is deliberately through-composed (not at all aleatory or indeterminate in form), so like a novel, that nothing can be left out. I think we already knew

* '*König Hirsch*—Brief an Joachim Klaiber.' First published in *Kieler Theaterfestschrift*, n.d.

[62]

that back in Bielefeld, even if our pleasure at the success of the performance clouded our judgement for a while.

For *Il Re Cervo*, the new version by Cramer and myself, we removed whole blocks of material and replaced them with abbreviated forms. We inserted a speaking part, the magician Cigolotti, who ensures that the plot remains comprehensible even though it is compressed. I wrote a few new numbers and put them in place of larger ones. The finale of the second act became my Fourth Symphony. The orchestra was reduced in size. The whole piece is practicable—a compromise we made to render further 'versions' superfluous.

Meanwhile the premiere of the original *König Hirsch* has yet to take place. To be able to see, hear and comprehend the piece correctly, you must hear it whole. Only then can the connections be grasped. That has not been done yet.

It requires a fairy-tale and mythical pomp of a popular kind, as in the Viennese or Venetian popular theatre. Perhaps the performance should be spread over two or three evenings, or over a whole (Sun)day—it was after all also inspired by Chinese opera and Japanese Kabuki theatre, and we envisage the audience like this: you come when you like, go when you like (How can one grasp the connections in that case?—a justified objection), bring along the children, have a picnic. It must be entertaining; apart from primadonnas and heroes there are also conjurors, acrobats, actors and clowns. And a conductor with a large orchestra.

It was planned, after all, as a new form of theatre (or circus); there is nothing psychological or Adornesque or fashionable about it. Indeed it completely sets its face against 'Fashion' by ignoring it altogether.

I have worked on it for years, with the moon as a chronometer. It should be seen as a diary, an autobiography, which tells how I discovered music. And then it wasn't possible for me to secure a premiere of the original version. No one thought it conceivable that Cramer and I could possibly have been right in our arguments, which I have set out above. (We were, after all, so young and inexperienced.) Before I got to the rehearsals for the Berlin premiere Scherchen, the conductor, had run riot with his blue pencil: his favourite victims were the arias (to which I had devoted particular attention during composition) because he felt that 'we' didn't write arias any more nowadays. He didn't want to recognize *König Hirsch*. But that isn't all that happened. And since then we have had a problem, one that is unsolved.

# The Bourgeois Artist[*]

By the end of 1955 *König Hirsch* was complete. The *Three Symphonic Studies* had been composed, like a reverberation from the opera; they, and the *Quattro Poemi*, composed between the second and third acts, contain thematic material from it. In the summer of 1956 I was on Ischia, preparing the scenario for *Ondine* with Ashton. In the autumn the turbulent premiere of *König Hirsch* at the Berlin Städtische Oper. Winter in London, composing *Ondine*. In early 1957 I moved to Naples.

The bourgeois artist, or one who feels himself to be socially secure, tends to disintegrate the material at his disposal while he is creating, whereas the alienated one, the outlaw, puts all his energy into achieving the opposite with the same material, namely to try to integrate himself at all costs. This is something that has occurred at all periods and in all the arts, though it should be added that the longing for integration is peculiar to the alienated artist, who strives for a social form that corresponds to his isolation—one or other form of minority with which he sympathizes, and which moves his sensual and spiritual substance. He will not aim to reconcile himself with the fundamental tendencies of the ruling ideas of his time. He looks for understanding not among *nouveau-riche*, middle-class consumers, but among individuals or minorities with whom he believes he can communicate. Thus both his behaviour and the form of his works are implicitly provocative, and more or less consciously he makes this provocation his goal.

* 'Künstler als Aussenseiter.' *Essays* 1964.

# Naples *

With the faded melancholy elegance of a former capital, an incredible mixture of metropolis and village, Paris and Chicago, an architectonic trauma, a stage for the most sensitive but also the most sentimental human behaviour, the most delicate and the coarsest, the wisest and the most impertinent, Naples seemed the appropriate environment for jettisoning all possible convention and caution, and any excess of counterpoint and esotericism, and for responding with a similar openness to the spontaneity and directness to be found in everything Neapolitan. The melodiousness of the language, faces, and the colours of the sky and sea lead to transformations in the psyche without one having to do anything except let it happen.

What I see and hear in Naples: it is winter, and the sun has been dazzlingly white all day, though not very strong; the shadows have preserved a damp coldness in the long crooked streets even at midday, when the distant light attempts to enter the backyards for a few moments. In the dusk a few people are treading gingerly along the steep Via Constantinopoli (damp, scraps of fish, cats), where sawdust has been spread to prevent passers-by from slipping on the old smooth pavement. The street is lined on one side by a high wall.

This wall was built in the eighth century BC; it is part of the city wall of Parthenope, one of the first Greek settlements in Italy. The other side of the street consists of houses built in the eighteenth and nineteenth centuries. The doors to the *bassi* are open. One step would take you into the room where the whole family lives; there is

---

* 'Neapel.' *Essays* 1964

[66]

the bed, the wardrobe, the Madonna beneath her glass dome. Children sleep on the floor, behind the curtain, in the darkness at the end of the room. At this time in the evening little fires have been lit in the streets; crates and cardboard boxes feed the flames, and in front of them, on the damp ground, squat little barefoot boys. Quite still, almost motionless, without a sound. No one pays any attention to them. Cars execute elegant arcs to avoid them. Out of the pallid faces gaze the eyes of Romans, eyes of Grecian blue, Byzantine eyes, questioning Spanish eyes, the inquisitive eyes of the Neapolitan. Around the wretched warmth of these little pyres hovers the infinite melancholy of the Mediterranean; more clearly expressed in the faces of these children, which hide nothing, than of adults, who have already become accustomed to living without hope. Amid the motionless groups warming themselves, one child reaches out a hand that has become quite numb, and holds it over the flames: a delicate brown hand with sickle-shaped fingernails, a hand for talking with, for swift theft, for a tender embrace, for begging, for defence, the avenger's hand, the alien hand of the Arab.

In the twelfth and thirteenth centuries the troubadours came from France in the wake of the crusaders, and many traces of their songs are to be found. (Dante mentions the troubadour Sordello in the *Purgatorio*.) As a result of repeated barbarian invasions from the far north and the far south, the most remarkable transformations and innovations occurred in the music and language of the period. Frederick II of Hohenstaufen, the founder of the university of Naples, ordered the establishment of a faculty to foster the new language. Towards the middle of the fifteenth century Neapolitan was declared the official language by Alphonso of Aragon. I know of no authentic musical works which have been preserved from the period of the late antique kingdom, the time of the maritime city-state and the empire of Constantinople, but it is possible to get an idea of them; one has only to think of the Moorish elements that still dominate the entire corpus of the *canzone napoletana*. This influence is the essential and most characteristic trait, not only in the kind of singing, but also in cadences and the relationship of intervals, and even in the later songs it is possible to recognize their origins through their colouring and expression. This produces a unity made up of several centuries of turbulent history—musical history, condensed in the little rhythms of the ritornello, wafted by the wild fragrances of Arabia, Spain, Portugal and Sicily, together with the modern-sentimental feeling of the nineteenth century—all this is transformed, reshaped into the rough recitative of a vigorous, demotic reality.

The earliest signs of the independent existence of the *canzone napoletana* date from the first years of the fifteenth century. A volume has been preserved entitled *New Opus, containing most beautiful songs on divers subjects composed, in order to arouse affection and love in beautiful and young ladies, a la napoletana.* This was music of a polyphonic nature, such as Antonio Scandello's 1565 *Canzoni napoletane poste in musica a quattro e a sei voci* which, as it became popular, ordinary people reduced without scruple to monody. Two other still earlier forms were the *strambotto* and the *ottava siciliana*, of which nothing survives apart from a few fragments of texts. During this time arose the madrigal, which consisted initially of rather uncouth love songs that soon, however, began to inspire the musicians, in whose hands they grew into artistic compositions (Philippe de Vitry). Simultaneously, and untouched by musical developments in the court sphere, new shepherds' songs, the *pastorali*, were ceaselessly created; their rhythm, their flow, and their tender mood exerted a powerful influence on music throughout Europe. There began a friendly exchange between the shepherds (with their rough voices, the 'pedal' fifths of their bagpipes, and the frenzied drums that rise and grow to the moment of excitement where the *tarantella* begins), and the noble delicate spirit of Domenico Scarlatti (who discovered a new harmonic sensibility, and incorporated these inspirations in his harpsichord sonatas).

The city is filled with sounds, piercing din and disturbing noises, and it seems that everything is connected with, comes from and ends in singing. But it begins with speech. Not speech in the Central European sense; this speech traverses all conceivable timbres, always with the tendency to break into song. It is tenderness, softness, the rough heavy tones of the language of fishermen; the nimble urban accents of the *lazzaroni*, swift excited *staccati* and mild assuring *legati*; the grandiloquence of the *commendatori*; the sighing, flattery, slander of the *cavalieri*; there is the whispering of whores, and the warm good converse of lovers; and then it is transformed into shouting: from vocal chords taut as bowstrings, shouting springs up into the air. Like shots from a revolver it pierces the milky viscous layer of simmering noise produced by the speech of thousands of people. It is the cry of birth, the cry of distress, the cry of the market-place, the groan of hunger, the moan of death. The jeering street-urchins, the scolding mothers, the street traders, each with their own calls, their own three or four notes, literally taken over from the Greeks and Moors. Trills, cadences; here articulated clearly and almost refined; there enraged and angry, as if from the victims of some disaster. Then again imaginative modulations, hot-blooded, caressing, the yearning tremblings of life, of the times, voices vying with one another and overlapping. By night, when the shouts and cries are stilled and occur only in isolation, when the silences, which are very audible, lengthen like the breathing of someone deeply asleep, the sounds that manage to reach the uppermost floors from the lanes below are reminiscent of the forlorn calls of migratory birds, oppressive in their sadness, or of the sounds of a murder or a sudden death. When this is once again succeeded by song, it sounds like the apotheosis of speaking and shouting—the third stage, which could be followed only by silence. A psychic necessity, singing stands for all nuances between laughing and weeping. Even when the text of a *canzone* is burlesque, it still contains the dark, melancholy tone of the East, the parting of Tancredi and Clorinda, *melismata* elaborated in the popular manner and yet supremely sensitive.

Spanish, Greek, and Arab blood, jealousy, fidelity, superhuman love, sudden hatred, light-heartedness, frivolity, sentimentality, elegance, pride and arrogance . . . the dark beauty of the women, their calm gaze full of certainty and without illusions. The Neapolitans are a people about whom it is said that they are always cheerful, but also languid, sleepy and indolent. Yet there is no city so dominated by grief, the frenetic noise that makes one think of despair, a deep buzzing in Hades. The much-vaunted cheerfulness is merely swiftness, haste, running away, wanting to get things done, or it is a playful façade for strangers. The wretchedness of the lower classes, which so horrifies anyone who is not prepared for it, is allied with pride and fatalism; it forms the heavy and bitter foundation of this gloomy metropolis beneath the all-scorching sun, beneath the dark red, much-travelled North African moon.

You walk on lava from Vesuvius. Narrow alleys climb into the distance beneath the white, pale red and violet banners of washing, which stretch from one window to its opposite, as in a triumphal street decorated for a festival. Walled-up streets that can be reached only on foot, where in dark corners, behind rusty railings, yellowish lights dimly illumine the fixed smile of a Madonna. Dilapidated churches in the Spanish style, the rustic vigour of early Baroque in romantically decaying stairwells. Noisy children, as innumerable as the very fat and very thin predatory grey cats, on every floor. The children, barefoot in winter too, often wear pieces of string tied round their shins, perhaps as symbols for the absent shoes. Pianolas strum on barrows. The teeming stench of the markets, with the gleaming, gruesomely slit carcasses of animals, and the silvery sparkle of the fish. Swarms of flies hovering over the green blood which runs down the streets. Women, always pregnant; fat men. Nine out of ten conversations are about money—a characteristic of poor countries. In the Via Caracciolo, a handsome street with elegant hotels and fashionable people, a herdsman is driving goats along the pavement. War against dirt is waged tirelessly with enormous brooms, on the squares, in the *gallerie*, after midnight: a hopeless struggle.

Pulcinella, with a shrill amplified voice, thrashes the civic guard. Heroism, faith and honour are the themes of the *opere dei pupi*: plays for lifesize marionettes, episodes from *Jerusalem Delivered*, very freely adapted from Tasso, and full of heroic duels and noble love-scenes. But there are also revenge melodramas from the nineteenth century, three acts per evening, dramatized serials, as it were; the performances last for weeks. The people live according to the moral precepts and ideas portrayed in these works, and earnestly discuss the good and bad traits of their wooden simulacra.

Towards midday there are always a few poor poets standing about by the entrances of schools, waiting to ask the pupils for modest donations in the name of the muses, or the saints. The schoolboys stand round the poet in a circle, and listen open-mouthed while, for a few cigarettes or fifty lire, he recites hundreds and hundreds of lines of verse, which always have the same theme: chivalric honour and morality.

On the streets, in ragged Jacobin costume, a trumpeter, a dancer, drummers. Groups like this can be seen throughout the city. It announces the programme for the next evening festival, with fireworks and wind music, that is being prepared for the feast of a local saint.

There are percussion instruments that must have their origins in ancient folklore. A *putipù* consists of a tin can, across one end of which a goat's hide is stretched like a drumhead. A reed cane is jammed into the centre; the muffled sound, which might belong to a muted bass tuba, is produced by using a moistened hand to thrust the cane towards the bottom of the can with a jerking movement. A *scetavaiasse* is a cross between a tambourine and a fiddle: a wooden board on to which six little rods have been diagonally screwed, with the bright metal strips of the tambourine attached to both ends of them; the player moves the strips by drawing a wooden bow across the board. A *triccaballacche* looks like a fan, but is made of wood; its four or five arms, held by a screw, with their ends covered with tin, are rapped together.

Pulcinella, sly but suggestible, an uncouth brother of Pierrot, Harlequin and Charlie Chaplin, constantly asserting himself, is a true likeness of the vulnerable soul of his people, and they love him for it and remain faithful to him. His *tristezza*, his heart-rending popular farces, are as full of life as ever; the tradition of the Pulcinella role is kept alive: Eduardo de Filippo has already found a successor, Achille Millo.

Opera premiere in San Carlo: beneath the entrance arches of the opera house, and on the piazza in front of it, stand elegant policemen decked in tricorns and feathers, swords and white gloves, directing the traffic, an immense mass of Fiats and Alfa Romeos. Like the carriages in days gone by, they drive into the theatre along a proper roadway that leads right through the building. Red carpets are rolled down the steps from the foyer to this street. Liveried attendants open the door, and the ladies and gentlemen who climb out of the cars to assemble in the foyer, before occupying their private boxes, seem to possess the same affable exclusiveness as their Spanish, Bourbon and French forefathers. Hundreds of fans murmur and rustle. The stalls and the boxes pay only the most discreet attention to the opera performance—hands barely moving to offer applause; but in the gallery, and in the upper tiers as a whole, the real audience is to be found, with a fine ear, sceptical gaze, and critical comments, ready at all times for protest, praise, condemnation or encouragement, but also easily carried away by enthusiasm. Here are thin, pallid music students, impoverished lawyers with a glint of expectation beneath their half-closed eyelids, marines, *bersaglieri*, bootblacks, plump petty-bourgeois couples, and diverse representatives of indeterminate trades with elegantly knotted ties and careful suits. These are the great connoisseurs. At this level of the auditorium, where the expensive perfumes of the stalls mingle with the smell of brilliantine and cheap scent, the singers' *pianissimi* fade away, inhaled by open mouths in bewitched faces; here the human drama on the stage is mirrored in moist eyes, the truth and tragedy of life are exorcized into beautiful forms. Strange and lovable life of the San Carlo gallery! What would Verdi, Puccini, Bellini and Donizetti have been without this audience sitting and even standing up there in the dark, and how well they knew the significance of its reactions, its opinions. From here, from 'the gods', fame and love were borne, as if on wings, as if spread by birds' tongues, to the most remote corners of the city; from here the arias were made immortal; simplified, perhaps to the point of unrecognizability, only to rise again from the hot volcanic soil as a new song.

At night, when the opera is over and you are going home, in

thought perhaps still in the *belle époque* or with Taglioni or Grisi, those children are still squatting around the wood fires. It is raining slightly, the fishermen of Mergellina have put up their sad old umbrellas. The neon light in the virtually empty *pizzerie* and *trattorie* gleams pallidly out on to the damp streets. Inside, old musicians are playing dejected tunes on fiddle and mandoline. Everybody is freezing, all the guitars are out of tune. A belated whore hurries by. The fruit barrows for tomorrow morning's market are already in place on the piazza; an old man is guarding them, wedged into a niche, a picture of misery. Humidity rises, cats screech. Beneath the black clouds is a fiery reflection from the blast-furnaces of the Bagnoli industrial works, and the American warships in the harbour cast threatening shadows, or a flashing light blinks an unintelligible warning across the jetty. The sea's calm breaths beat against the walls of the Via Partenope. Everything seems good and still, subdued by the cold, muffled in the heavy mist.

Yet there is a small group of people. A young man squats on the pavement, a guitar on his lap, numb fingers plucking the jangling strings. The youth is singing. Next to him, on the road, stands a Topolino whose door is open, and from the darkness within the car emerge the arpeggios of a second guitar. If it was not for the singing and the strumming you would think they were all asleep—the singer, the invisible player in the car, and the people standing around this scene, with turned-up collars and hands buried in their pockets. Their eyes are closed, no one moves. The light from the street lamps plays on the damp fabric of their suits, amid the raindrops on blue-black hair. Old, and ageless, bitter and tart, a quivering tune floats through the Mediterranean winter's night.

# *Ondine*
# A Bridge to the Nineteenth Century<sup>*</sup>

> . . . to accept space, to own
> That surfaces need not be superficial
> Nor gestures vulgar, cannot really
> Be taught within earshot of running water
> Or in sight of cloud.

W. H. AUDEN, *Good-bye to the Mezzogiorno*

The first discussions about *Ondine* took place in Forio on Ischia. The focal point of the village was 'Maria Internazionale', the proprietress of a café, whose chairs and tables on summer evenings had to be set out far across the piazza to accommodate the numerous Neapolitan families and foreign writers and painters who found their way here for an apéritif, or for midnight conversations that do not come to an end until just before dawn. She had given up her own flat in the centre of the village to Frederick Ashton, who had arrived just in time for the beginning of the Festa of San Vito. The flat was relatively cool, and the noises of the festa were muffled. But I can recall one of the many bells that rang at the most extraordinary hours, continuously and wildly; this one was quite close, and so managed to interrupt the conversations about *Ondine* for a quarter of an hour at a time. The basis was the story by De la Motte Fouqué. This also inspired the *Ondine* ballets of the nineteenth century, and provided Giraudoux with the source for his play.

---

\* A conflation of '*Undine* 1957' (from Henze's *Undine: Tagebuch eines Balletts*, Munich 1959) and '*Undine* 1972' (from *Programmheft der Hamburgischen Staatsoper*, vol 5 1972–3).

## Ondine: A Bridge to the Nineteenth Century

Ashton had Fouqué's book (a 1909 edition translated by W. L. Courtney and illustrated by Arthur Rackham) with him from morning till night, even on the beach, where it became covered in sand and salt, and grew more and more bent under the influence of the sun, as if to hint at the subsequent development of our *Ondine*. It was difficult to extract a simple linear narrative from the story, with its ramifications and wealth of precise detail, and then to translate this narrative into dance, into ideas that could be danced. The simpler and more transparent the plot became, the easier we would find it to prepare the ground for purely choreographic forms. A first suggestion rested on the idea of dissolving each thought into absolute dance, and thereby completely excluding the explanatory, allusive medium of mime, with its frozen rituals. But it soon became apparent that this was not possible and, in the case of a complete evening's three-act work, by no means desirable. So, contrary to the original conception, mime was introduced here and there, effectively in the new light that is shed on its old-fashioned formulas today: brief fleeting communications with the audience, which then make it possible to enter into the pure fantasy world of absolute dance with all the more freedom.

'What is *Ondine*? Who is Ondine?' we asked ourselves. 'Is she the soulless mermaid, obsessed by the desire to gain a soul, without being able to measure the advantages or disadvantages of such a possession? Is it possible that she can yearn for love without comprehending love? What drives her to go among mortals? Is it curiosity, playfulness, or is it the wish of the human being who summons her?' We kept coming back to these questions. On their answers depended whether our Hulbrand would become a dreamer pursued by visions of Ondine; a victim of romantic hallucinations; an inconstant medieval knight; a troubadour; a pathological case; or simply the typical fairy prince of all ballets. To this was related the question of Berta, Hulbrand's earthly beloved, the earthly counterpart of the mermaid. Was she merely a proud young German lady of the castle, or would it be possible to put her in a more interesting and weighty position, as the counterpart to the nymph? Why does Hulbrand relinquish Ondine for her sake?

*[75]*

## Ondine: A Bridge to the Nineteenth Century

How far could we avoid falling back on nineteenth-century types of ballet scenario? How far could we resist clichés of the ballet and at the same time make use of the advantages of the old *grand ballet*? Even more urgent, how far, on the other hand, could the clichés of Modernism be avoided—clichés that surround us and can be employed so easily and ubiquitously—the vibraphone's magic, ostinato rhythms, electronic sounds to denote the supernatural, twelve-note chords, the alienation effect on stage, and the countless tricks born of the Surrealist legacy? Will Ondine be totally transformed by the power of the Mediterranean summer? Should one work against this transformation, or let it happen?

Amid these questions, interrupted by trumpet blasts from *La forza del destino* from the local *banda*, the days passed.

The nineteenth century, which especially during its first half was an age with clear Romantic ideas, brought with it a flowering of ballet that only Diaghilev would conjure up again on a comparable scale, albeit with different content. Ballet in the mid-nineteenth century, at the 'court' theatres of Moscow, Naples and London, revealed in its interpretations of Romantic ideas how fully it was in tune with the feelings of its age. *Giselle*—the transformation of Heine's *Wilis* by Gauthier and Coralli, and Adam's hard music, which in this context loses all foreground quality—is a work of art of considerable stature; unsentimental, full of awe and, especially in the second act, of genuine poetry. It affords an unusually clear picture of a spirituality that unites seriousness and depth with something for which in German we have the somewhat condemnatory word *Gefälligkeit* (complaisance), but which is much more, namely elegance, attained by a mastery and reserve of expression. The fairies' teasing in the third act of *La belle au bois dormant* (to give a further example), when the prince tries in vain to capture his dream image, has nothing of that silly provincial fairy magic that emerges in later decades, but provides an ironic, transparent picture of the painful confusion in which lovers are caught up. Our *Ondine*, or so we intended, should also capture the 'inverted' sensuality contained in such tender scenes. To ensure that the bridge to the nineteenth century did not remain a mere gesture, new formulas had to be found, a flexibility without concealments, explicit and restrained in equal measure.

Palemon (as we renamed Hulbrand) is in love with a dream image. Even if Ondine actually exists as a real nymph, about which we are left in doubt; even if she can be touched (Do the others see her, Palemon's friends, and Berta who has to question Palemon's constancy?); even if in the depths of the forest Palemon, surrounded by tritons and nymphs, holds 'his' Ondine in his arms (or thinks he does); and even after a 'ghostly' wedding with little fauns officiating, this union seems impossible. Instead of a human heart, the mermaid possesses only charm, grace, perhaps ineffable qualities, floating and ageless, like music. Like nature itself, she is without consistency; her thoughts are without consequences. If Palemon is in love with Ondine, he is equally in love with art. Palemon is not granted union with a dream image or work of art (that highest union, attainable only in madness or in death); he is not granted the oblivion he craves; the transformation he longs for does not take place; again and again his human inadequacy drives him back among mortals. Infatuated with the often imprecise and almost unrecognizable image until his very last heartbeat, he is granted a death that he has approached unwittingly, and whose redeeming beauty he has deserved only through his pain, not through faith.

When I was working on the score of *Ondine* in 1956, I saw the Royal Ballet production of the second version of *The Firebird* (Goncharova, Grigoriev). This made an impression on me seldom achieved by music in the theatre, and it no doubt contributed to the creation of the music for *Ondine*, and to the formation of my views on dance drama and on music for the theatre.

During work on the 1972 Hamburg production, even though the emphasis was on areas other than the fairy tale or pure dance, we did much that was operatic to portray Palemon's sickness; you sometimes had the impression that the dancers were singing; you saw and heard dance-arias; it was as if *Ondine* were another opera, a lyric drama about introversion which, as Walter Benjamin has remarked, in the degeneration of the middle class became a school for asocial behaviour.

Faithful to the score, we brought out the irony and parody necessary to justify such an interpretation. Everything was treated lightly and fluidly in order to distance it from Expressionism and its legacy. There was also something of Schoenberg's 'on revient toujours' to be found in every aspect of the production: attention drawn to quotations and anachronisms; changes of scene, gesture and sound used to establish links with the myths which lie behind them. Palemon's sufferings, dreams and fantasies unfolded amid false perspectives, like Italian Renaissance stage-sets, but a late-nineteenth-century setting was painted on to them.

This landscape was governed by the aesthetic of Vincenzo Bellini, that spare refinement rooted in Sicilian art, back to antiquity, a knowledge of which is more telling for a reading of the score of *Ondine* than the quotations it contains from music for the Ballets Russes, and the associations with Symbolism, Max Ernst, Freud and early Hofmannsthal. Elements of heroic epic, as it can be seen in Palermo marionette theatres, are mingled with the German world of fairy tales, which surreptitiously intervene in human reality and desires.

Paradise lost, *paradis artificiels*. Ondine is a crystal from E. T. A. Hoffmann's mines at Falun; she is lethal and thus symbolizes the exaggeration inherent in all fantasy: she is the object of that absurd desire to return to childhood, the innocent world of animals, the womb. The conflict of Palemon, who is frightened of reality, is also represented in the tension between the northern world of De la Motte Fouqué and—introduced by Ashton—the ageless South with its inconsistent promises, which Büchner satirized in *Leonce und Lena*. Apart from the question of style, in that production that aspect was shown only spasmodically, with weeping Pulcinellas as heralds of death, bearers of sickness, avengers. These were masks beneath which the beasts and demons which would destroy the dreamer Palemon were concealed.

I began the sketches for the composition in autumn 1956. I chose a largish chamber orchestra and tried to take into account the resources of a touring ballet company (such as the Royal Ballet) which changed its orchestra from town to town; in other words, the music had to be capable of being performed with a minimum of rehearsal. This led to a further technical limitation, which however also presented a stimulus. The two harps are often employed as solo instruments, almost completely avoiding their characteristic glissandos and arpeggios; their sound represents the ethereal Ondine and her people, and sometimes hardens when it transfers to the piano—as in the third-act divertissement (variations on Scarlatti's 'Cat's Fugue')—or evaporates into string harmonics and celesta. The aim was to produce a weightless sound quality, in contrast with the dark elements of the rest of the orchestra that stand on the earthly side of Palemon. If the dark and light elements were to meet, powerful tensions would result, and pain. Tirrenio, the King of the Tritons, has his own calls which the spirits of air and water follow, just as there are distinct musical intervals for Ondine that here and there expand into melodic figures. Palemon too has his own realm of sound, generally manifested in the lower strings and in solo woodwind *ariosi* that are characterized by often 'speaking' in an operatic recitative-like manner. The music is governed by the variation principle, which is given a dramatic function, generating the twists and changes of direction of the action on the stage. In a sense, the ballet is an opera without singers, the orchestra of instrumental soloists contributing the arias and recitatives.

Several years ago the discovery of melody brought about an enrichment of my expressive means. The difficult process of simplifying my musical language was accelerated by the discovery of the remarkable vigour and immediacy of street cries and canzonetti resting on simple intervallic relationships. In place of serial melody, which outwardly guaranteed a certain 'contemporaneity', came the most simple sequence of notes—the basic intervals that were naturally related to song were to contain everything that was to be said.

## Ondine: A Bridge to the Nineteenth Century

Who is Ondine? De la Motte Fouqué relates that she herself once said to him: 'You should know that in the elements there are creatures who look almost like you, and yet only seldom allow you to see them. The mysterious salamanders glisten and play in the flames, deep in the earth the thin mischievous gnomes reside, through the forests roam the forest people who belong to the air, and in the lakes and streams dwells the large family of water-sprites. It is beautiful to live in echoing crystal vaults, through which the sky peers in, with sun and stars. Tall coral trees, with blue and red fruit, gleam in the gardens, you wander over pure sea sand and lovely coloured shells; the beauties that the old world possessed, such that the present world is no longer worthy of taking pleasure in, these the tides have covered with their secret silver veil; and down below are the noble resplendent monuments, tall and serious and gracefully bedewed . . . but those who live there are charming and beauteous to behold, often more lovely than mortals are. . . .'

The last meeting of Palemon and Ondine is composed as a passacaglia, a simple *canto* in the strings over the always increasingly strong theme in the bass. The music is already filled with awareness of the end, as this last dialogue between mortal and spirit begins, and with perfect logic at the conclusion of the passacaglia comes the lethal kiss. The sound of death has already been anticipated in the prelude to this final act: a loud painful cry that here dies quickly away, preparing for the concluding soft eclogue—a motionless music on whose horizon Palemon and Ondine hover in sounds that are only distantly related, becoming softer, floating away.

# 'Wavering and Positionless' *

During the preliminary work on *Ondine* my main concern was to get the stylistic ambience right. In the 'wavering and positionless' (*schwankenden und positionslosen*) manner for which certain distinguished experts have recently been pleased to reproach me, I then began to discover a form in which the world of this ballet might perhaps unfold. As so often at the beginning of a work, it had at first seemed quite impossible to capture the right tone; so much so that for a while I wanted to abandon the project. It was only slowly that a language evolved, in whose discovery Ashton and Lila de Nobili helped. During last winter (1956–7) I attended the performances of the Royal Ballet almost nightly, to observe my soloists, their idiosyncrasies, their capacity for reacting to music, and the musicality of their movements, primarily in performances of nineteenth-century works, which are a speciality of this company.

Charles X style, Caserta, tritons and nymphs, the *galanterie* of De la Motte Fouqué and mock gothic elements all combined to form a background against which the dreams of our knight unfold: echoes of a timeless romanticism reach us from the remoteness of that age. The tragedies of *Lucia di Lammermoor*, *Giselle*, *La Sonnambula* all possess something of that tender enamoured spirit, of a Heinean proximity to death, steeled by a harder Latin quality that underlies their elegant timbre, whetted by the discipline of opera and classical ballet. What at first was in danger of becoming no more than an evocation of the past developed decisively and more felicitously into something more contemporary; colours,

---

* From 'Über *Undine*. Von der "Sicherheit des Schwankenden" ', an article in the *Rheinische Post*, 11 May 1957, written in answer to a review in that paper.

notes, décors and dance steps came together, and *Ondine*, which was still in gestation, acquired more and more clarity in the search for a beauty concealed in our own time.

I hope that the way my music has developed in this score is as far removed as possible from what is 'expected' of me. Since the premiere of *König Hirsch* my 'attitude', my 'position', has become unclear; I am accused of having betrayed the cause of new music, and many feel that by turning away from the serial method of composition I have taken a decisive step towards the abyss. That I have now also incorporated jazz into my vocabulary (in the ballet *Maratona di Danza*) is further proof of my 'disloyalty'.

I have never worried a great deal about this; I have never yet allowed myself to belong to any group or school. I love music very much, but I detest politicking, the struggle for or against something in music; music reaches people of its own accord, when it wants to. It cannot be imposed, can hardly be explained, cannot be propagated; leading articles make it no better and no worse. We Germans with our renowned, incomparable and vigorous musical life often tend to consign music to categories, to theoretical values, instead of applying liberal individual criteria. Many people read about music instead of listening to it; this may be pleasurable, but it is not the same thing, and does not necessarily always further their understanding of music.

I was the first of the German post-war generation to become involved with the dodecaphony; today everybody is using it, often before they have learned to write, so perhaps I can allow myself to be 'disloyal'. I am not 'positionless' because I am bored by the thought of using techniques that I have already used, or those that are in general use by everyone from film composers to students of theory, and have now been used up. Nor do I think that there exists an essential musical language for our time, as one often hears said; a method is not a language, and the use of an old or of a new technique says absolutely nothing about the quality of the work in which it is employed. Every method can at any time be nullified by the will of the artist.*

* 'A necessary impulse, which for the moment I can identify in no other way

## 'Wavering and Positionless'

I 'waver' and am 'positionless' in that when I start a work I never have a plan, a preconceived opinion or a theory to direct me. I do not think so little of music that I fancy I know more than it does. Thus with each new composition everything is difficult and problematical until I have found a way—call it, if you will, a technique—in which I can express myself clearly. But the value of this technique dies out when the composition is finished; some lessons and experiences are perhaps carried forward, but the next work is bound to present problems different from those I expect.

It ought to be unnecessary to make these points, but in view of the current fashion in Germany of using a set of rules to judge the work of musicians, indeed perhaps even to influence it, one is forced to speak up. With my music I would very much like to be in touch with people, but not with those whose criteria permit no divergence from certain fundamentalist norms. My certainty lies in my wavering. My wavering is ambivalence about a world that has populated itself with people whose papers are all in order. Is one meant to congratulate, to applaud them?

---

except as a moral impulse before all morality, has been spoken of, an impetus for a thinking that at the outset is not concerned with direction, a thinking that aims at understanding and aims to reach something with language and through language. Let us provisionally call it "reality".'

Ingeborg Bachmann, *Frankfurter Vorlesungen* I 1959–60

# The Message of Music*

Language and music are two parallel spheres that are often connected; more than half of all existing music consists of settings of words. This relationship has diverse forms; sometimes music seizes violently upon language, and crushes it in its embrace, or sometimes language wants to seize upon music; they both can degrade but also can elevate one another. This is a phenomenon as old as music itself. In recent years more has been said about the division than about the possible connections; doubts have been raised whether any *rapprochement* is still possible unless music, whose purity is damaged by language, obliterates words and robs them of their meaning and origins, so that it can absorb them in this purified form, as sound. There are musicians who in language see only the words, and in musical phrases only the individual notes. In the words and single notes only the sound delights them (just as a few decades ago the noise of motors and hooters was considered by some to have musical potential). They wish to see the components separated from the movement or delivery of a musical or linguistic phrase. But it seems to me that such separation makes language into an intellectually unsatisfying thing: a hybrid that oscillates between disjointed meaninglessness, and a noise inferior to music, the organized art of sound; in every respect inferior to language, the highly formed art of thought.

When we contemplate a montage of disparate objects we end, in practice, by analysing their original provenance. Uncovering the joke temporarily results in paranoid goose-pimples, a short-lived

* 'Die geistige Rede der Musik.' *Essays* (lecture at Brunswick Chamber Music Festival, 1959).

*[84]*

*frisson*, which it is said many are capable of perceiving, but which unfailingly ends in indifference. But even in their isolation, and freed from a context, words retain a meaning that cannot be extinguished, just as the second note that follows the first already conveys a musical meaning. For anyone whose consciousness has been penetrated by sentences and linguistic conceptualizations, something has formed in his subconscious that—over and above the sound of language, the circumstances under which the idea occurred, the echoes of memory—enables even words in isolation to continue to exist as emotional qualities. A focus of infection has formed, a source of wealth in the subconscious, whose nature is immutable.

In her poem 'Rede und Nachrede' Ingeborg Bachmann turns her attention to the word:

| | |
|---|---|
| *Wort, sei von uns,* | Word, be from us |
| *freisinnig, deutlich, schön.* | free in spirit, clear, beautiful. |

And she writes:

We have given up looking for 'poetic content' in music, and for 'word music' in literature (*Dichtung*). It is true that both are temporal arts, but how differently time is measured in them: with incomparably more rigour in music, with incomparably more spontaneity in language; even in the chains of a metre, the length of a syllable is vague, indeterminate. If it is maintained that music does not and does not wish to express anything, and seeks to communicate without demeaning itself, does this suggest that music is afraid of losing its purity in its relations with literature? Furthermore, given that music has already taken instruments to the limits of what can be played; that it attempts to treat their particular qualities in a new way or even to shake them off, wishing to get rid of any obstacles; and that in its quest for renaissance and a new innocence it gazes into the infinite—in view of all this, is it afraid that with a mortgaged language it will have to surrender itself to the human voice? For no amount of progress is going to alter the specific nature of this voice.

It thus appears that language cannot meet the intellectual demands of music, and the voice cannot meet its technical demands. It would seem as though the two arts had reason for the first time to go their separate ways.

Banished from music, the word would be able to come to terms with itself. We who are concerned with language have learned what speechlessness and muteness are—our purest states, as it were!—and have returned from no man's land with language, with which we shall continue as long as life is our continuation.

But must the arts really go their separate ways, at a time when each failure is a missed rescue, when every misunderstanding of the spirit promotes a deathly sadness in a kindred spirit? Our need for song is there. Must the song come to an end?

Although we are inclined, as never before, to surrender, to make adjustments, we hold on to the suspicion that there is a path leading from one art to the other. There is a phrase of Hölderlin's which says that spirit can express itself only rhythmically. Music and literature share, indeed, the same spiritual gait. They have rhythm, in the original sense of conveying form. For this reason they can understand one another. For this reason there is a path from one to the other.

Is there not also new literature at every turning-point of music? Does not a new neighbourhood bring with it new inspiration? Words are no longer searching for the accompaniment that music cannot give them. Not a decorative environment of sound, but unification: that new state in which they sacrifice their self-reliance, and gain a new force of conviction through music. And music is no longer looking for an insignificant text as a pretext, but for a hard currency language, a value against which it can prove its own.

For this reason music clings like a stigma to those works of literature for which it feels love, those of Brecht, Lorca and Mallarmé, Trakl and Pavese, and the earlier writers who are always in the mainstream of today: Baudelaire, Whitman and Hölderlin. (How many one could mention!) These writers continue to exist in themselves, but they have a precious second life in this relationship. For just like the new truths, so the old ones can be awakened, confirmed and wrenched forward by music, and each language that speaks these truths—German, Italian, all languages!—can be assured through music of its participation in a universal language.

Through words, music for its part attains an avowal that it cannot set aside. It becomes answerable, it underwrites the explicit spirit of yes and no, it becomes political, compassionate, sympathetic, and involved with our destiny. It abandons its asceticism, accepts a restriction among those who are restricted, becomes assailable and vulnerable. But it need not feel itself lessened by this. Its weakness is its new worth. Together, and inspired by one another, music and words are a vexation, an uproar, a love, a confession. They keep the dead awake and rouse the living, they precede the desire for freedom and pursue impropriety into sleep. They have the strongest need to be effective. (*Musica Viva*, Munich 1959)

Music possesses something to which it can repeatedly be traced back, a constellation that rotates within and around itself, composed of tensions that are generated within it. (This state of affairs obtains even in music drama: the role of music here, even where the composer has not intended it, is that of an interpreter of sequences of notes and rhythms. The canon of the famous G major quartet in *Fidelio* proceeds independently of the four different emotions that the text expresses; the information lies solely in the music, derives purely from the notes, and coalesces the text.) The basis of the tension, the level of the resolution and the purity of the craft produce a certain effect in the audience; according to talent and degree of preparation this effect is stronger or weaker, nebulous, uplifting or depressing: an effect that many would like to interpret psychologically, whereas with the ideal listener—and it is only of him that we are speaking—it is none other than a reaction to a full grasp of the process that has been presented. The difficulty in which unknown music—conceived with new and unknown methods—repeatedly finds itself is to make itself intelligible. Intelligible: not so as to flatter philistines, not to delight stupid reactionaries, but in the sense that this music, set against centuries of experience, must undergo a trial of strength that only naïvety or ignorance could allow it to underestimate or reject. We do not simply mean that, if demands have not risen, they have not in any event been lowered, but that the clarity and transparency of artistic achievements between the fourteenth century and our own—where certain immutable properties of music were captured, inventoried, particularized and localized—are entitled to demand an equal measure of clarity and transparency from us. We are dealing here not with aesthetic questions (which today are often dismissed as untimely, because they are too uncomfortable and cannot be taken up at the moment—much that is uncomfortable and needs to be driven out of one's consciousness can in this way be shunted on to a siding), but with technical and theoretical requirements that can be discussed soberly.

Musical notation, with its signs and symbols, has throughout centuries of development always been regarded as a plausible method of mediation between author and consumer. The problem of notation, of encoding, has preoccupied musicians at all periods of our music. People have worked and work still to perfect it, to make it correspond exactly with the imagined sound down to the present day, when new problems of notation have arisen, and when the over-emphasis on notation sometimes makes performance nearly impossible. This leads to solutions, dissolutions, liberations, as improvisations are suggested to the performer, and the written text is abandoned; but this raises the question whether you really can speak of liberation, or whether it would be more accurate to say 'simplification', and whether this instead produces a new burden far more difficult to bear than the weight of tradition, which has only recently reached its peak with Webern and certain tendencies deriving from him.

For the writing down of the score, together with the resultant musical practice, does not really represent that lack of freedom, that grim compulsion, that is often complained of; and it is by no means necessary that because of the complex universality of grammars and formulas a composer should feel deprived of the use of his imagination, or that the tyranny of pentagrams should leave no room for unforeseen spontaneous feelings. Admittedly it is more difficult to be subject to the five lines of the stave, to instrumental restrictions and the natural limitations of the human voice than, freed from these constraints, to evade the difficulties in an uncaring fashion. There are moments when music theory identifies itself conceptually with the practice of composition, when it threatens to destroy the practice of writing, or at any rate monstrously to engulf it, when rules destroy the laws of music; but attempts have repeatedly been made to escape this engulfment by sidestepping, outwitting, and even by brutally destroying music theory. Again and again it has proved possible to make a selection from the wealth of available material, which seemed exhausted and no longer productive, and thereby let the notes realize themselves in a new way; whereupon others have then turned this new configuration itself into a mechanism: something that was initially a kind of Noah's Ark, in which one hoped to survive the Flood of theory, became a general purpose tool, a mechanism, a new system, over-growing everything with theory, only to become unusable in its turn.

We believe that even today, when certain works have been taken to the limits of what can be performed, or indeed read, another way out is possible, apart from taking refuge in the silence of notelessness, or in a world of improvisation or mere sound. The only way out for those convinced that music is at an end is to create no more music. The others, who insist on pursuing the new favours of the old beauty—within the European repertoire of symbols and within inherited tradition—will have to build on tradition. A balance must be restored between text and performance. It must all be thought out once again. I believe that the symbols, the signs, the ciphers, embody something that belongs to music as limbs belong to a body; the difficulty of handling them nowadays is not an invitation to relinquish them, but a challenge to take their pulse again, to revalue them, perhaps even to destroy existing laws. But none of this will work simply by manufacturing ornaments; it will not work unless one also conceives of a new intellectual discourse in the new sounds, unless one adds something to the technical construction, unless the new works are brought into relationship with the occidental tradition.

Saying this raises suspicions, of course, on the one hand that we covet success—for what could be more successful today than to be associated with 'culture'?—and on the other hand that we are romantics. This suspicion is so difficult to dispel because the term 'romanticism' is itself swathed in mists, to the accompaniment of Wagner tubas, and hence difficult to specify. As a result we do not know whether the suspicion, were it confirmed, would greatly displease us, especially if it emerged that the romanticism referred to was not some world-wide disease, not those folksy homesteads for *Schwärmer* whose passion for the imprecise knows no bounds, but denoted definite regions that have produced such diverse men and movements as C. D. Friedrich, Verdi and socialism. For the untimely romantic dreamers cannot or will not engage with the intellectual and political realities of the day. Amid shibboleths and technological details they forget what really matters, they avoid confrontation with reality, and in their irrational way come to Buddha, Jesus or the *Zupfgeigenhansl* ('hippies')—by which time there is no further point in discussing musical difficulties.

The notes of the equal-tempered system, irrespective of the order in which they are conceived and the perspective in which they are viewed, offer themselves anew to the present as an unknown, uncharted field. For if Stravinsky or dodecaphony had a different conception of the treatment of notes from their predecessors and successors, how has this exhausted the notes themselves? Why should they have become superannuated because they were fixed for a time in specific systems? They are a resilient raw material that does not change. Only we change, in our attitude towards this raw material. In so far as we realize the extent to which we are burdened by history, the burden disappears. We must be able to separate notes in their determinateness and their intrinsic properties from their history, to recognize their power. Once an awareness of the prehistory of notes, and of their experiences and tragedies during the last five hundred years, enters our subconscious and becomes a part of us, a patrimony that supports us and to which we owe nothing and everything—the human and logical desire for exactness and independence—once we no longer see ourselves oppressed by history but sustained by it, we can make a fresh start with freedom.

The degrees of tension between intervals (physically proven, attested by our experience) are a commensurable factor which can be avoided only by escape into worlds of sound that lack these relationships of tension and, therefore, lie outside our musical thought. Within it, however, the following possibilities have been discovered. Intervals rich in tensions will regain their force in a new way if we take their tension factor into account once again. Timbres, rhythms, chordal and thematic elements must be devised in the light of the goal of the work. Constructions and their rules result from the figures and inventions displayed at the beginning of the work; their development and variation are not subject to any external factors, and are wholly dependent on the requirements of the given work. The rules lose all their validity after the finale has been written. However you try to alter and adapt it, the image of the interval of a 'fifth' or 'seventh' remains unchanged. You can detach it from its historical use, you must view it independently of its traditional formalization; the essence of the interval is in no way prejudiced. At this point no spectre of limitation appears; in this respect music appears in a new light today, its creative possibilities under a new aspect. Art is constantly in danger and must incessantly be re-invented, to ward off the encroachment of mechanical processes. It is striking that the constant use of intervals rich in tensions, which has become systematic and customary during the past centuries, ultimately developed into a kind of linguistic feature that could be described as 'slang'. Here a new fastidious approach is necessary. Just as bombarding language with the unusual has blunted it, so that it now requires new nuances based on elements that were previously fiercely rejected, so too in music a greater variety and suppleness is expected. Whether or not the surfaces of these new figures thereby give an impression of regression will be a secondary question. The answer is to be found in the technical procedure of revision.

A word on forms. Perhaps it is true that forms such as the sonata no longer have any constructive significance. In any event, with the abandonment of functional harmony they are called in question. Despite the disappearance of some of their characteristic features, typical formal factors have remained; tensions continue to exist, and new polarities, which once again approach the beauty of these old forms under new aspects, have been and still can be invented with new means. Means are exhausted more rapidly than forms: the massacre of a form often derives from revolt over the lack of means with which to fill it. Concepts such as passacaglia, fugue, and the infinitely rich and malleable concept of variation—whose fruitfulness has been more attentively considered only in recent decades—could acquire a new authenticity by an imaginative and free use of our means. The ideas behind them contain many unexpected stimuli which impose no limits on the imagination. In our work we are not burdened by the past. Through our work we influence the past to present itself 'to today' differently from 'to yesterday'.

The appearance of the chord with all twelve notes, which stands at the end of a long process undergone by occidental music and its harmonic language, does not signify the end of music as such, but merely a historical moment, the fading of one of many static properties. The end of functional harmony first gave authority to the individual notes of the tempered system; here for the first time, independent of serialism and dodecaphony, they present themselves in their full strength and immanence, alone and indestructible.

The current situation of music points towards a new day beyond the stage labelled the 'dilemma of modern art'. Music preserves itself against security, patterns and routine. We are dealing with late, nervous and disparaged material that must be brought to flow again, pruned, seen anew, reinterpreted. If efforts are concentrated in this direction, if a critical reflection of objects upon themselves begins, then they will prevent the distortion and decline of their intellectual and philosophical significance. Not through reaction, denial or annulment, but by drilling, breaking open, hammering and igniting, something could be produced that would be worthy to enter the light of history.

# Visconti and Opera Production[*]

Lessons learned from Italian music, literature and painting brought contact with their contemporary representatives, new friends different perspectives, new approaches. Especially stimulating theatre performances: nineteenth-century comedies (Altavilla, Scarpetta) in San Ferdinando in Naples; Goldoni, Alfieri, Chekhov in Rome; Donizetti, Bellini and Verdi at La Scala. I was particularly struck by that universal man of the theatre, Visconti.

Deriving from Stanislavskian principles, his productions are marked by a great creative respect for literature and music and by his phenomenal brilliance in expressing the subject-matter of a work in stylistically appropriate scenic forms. This involves the finest and most exact details of décor and costumes, as well as the precise characterization of 'human local colour'. Moods are produced by textual exactness; the production is a reconstructive analysis of the work. Humility such as is expressed in this attitude is something rare, but it is no accident that its results are the more magisterial, serious and weighty.

This humility is in contrast to the widespread, fundamentally more uninhibited procedure of producers who solve their problems by chopping classical texts about, and removing classical works of music from their context so as to reproduce them in modernistic forms, in styles these works have never dreamed of. I am thinking above all of stagings of Rossini operas beyond the Italian frontiers, where the producers evidently start out convinced that the 'Swan of Pesaro' is such a boring old bird that it would be impossible to

* 'Studien in Neapel.' *Essays* 1964.

present him to the spoilt modern public in his original form, and therefore the score must be cut about, the libretto rewritten, and the plot gingered up with all sorts of 'desirable' frolics and pranks. If this were done to a work such as *Così fan tutte* there would no doubt be a public outcry. The oeuvre of Rossini in the original forms of his *opere buffe e serie* should be treated with the same respect for the text as that of Mozart, Verdi or Wagner. The *buffo* elements are not 'humoresques' (Is there really such a thing as 'funny' music?) but rapid tempos, *staccati*, *crescendi*, hard cold marble, frugal elegance; their scenic equivalent should be dry in the manner of Goldoni, stylized, ceremonious; a circumscribed minimum of gesture should suffice, as the scores prescribe, with more precision than words could attain. Thus the spirit of Rossini, steeped in the rich experience of the Italian theatre, would all at once be standing in front of us again, close enough to touch; this would be 'living' theatre.

But even the works of Verdi and his forerunners are vulnerable; they are not taken quite seriously. Some producers believe they are serving the cause of Verdi when they consider the scenic requirements he specified no longer valid and ignore them, and by using décor borrowed from the repertoire of modern painting, lose sight of the original spiritual landscape of the composer and his music.

It is typical of this trend that the producer pays less attention to the visual form of the work that emerges from the music than to the possibilities of conceiving the opposite of what the composer and librettist might have intended. What I suspect is involved here is, at least to some extent, fear of the avant-garde press, and of a restorational public which has just reached the level of 1930s dramatic modernism, and for the time being is not prepared to think again and try to understand that there is only one scenic solution for a theatrical work, namely the one the author had in mind. As operas from other periods can be staged only in their historical and social context, one must accordingly realize the visual imagination of the age in which they were created and to which they belong. If one emphasizes that, say, the music of Verdi is immortal or has not aged, one has to accept that his visual and intellectual world has aged as little as his notes. If Verdi's music is still young, then so is the painting of his time. Verdi, together with all great masters, had an extremely precise vision of theatre, which is sufficiently documented; their taste was excellent, even if it does not happen to be yours. In my eyes any attempt to approach the scenic realization of these works in a more 'metaphysical' way than is necessary for practical reasons, represents a minor falsification, an expedient, but not an artistic and not a creative answer. Producers, especially of opera, who feel the creative urge should first of all apply it to investigating the precise visual and stylistic relationships within the sound image created by contemporary visual and sensual stimuli—and at a stroke music drama would have one fewer dilemma and, in its place, one more fine task.

It may be that certain plays can be staged by *drama* producers freely and in new ways. But as drama has nothing to do with *opera* except in quite peripheral ways (such as the presence of a stage, a curtain and an auditorium), and since in opera the real producer is always the same, namely the musical score, the craft of the opera (unlike that of the drama) producer consists in mediating, in making 'visible' the score, which is the cultural context of the work. There is nothing to be invented or added, things must only be made as luminous and truly beautiful as possible. This alone requires so much *cultura*, inspiration and talent that a lifetime would hardly suffice for an opera producer to master his profession.

Whereas I do not feel it is appropriate to transpose music of other cultures into a form that 'corresponds to our time' (What form would that be?), in the *mise en scène* of contemporary works the entire arsenal of modern art should be enlisted. But here the same kind of inadequacies are encountered as have already been criticized in the production of older works. The internal and external relationships between the two arts are not explored, or only rarely and randomly. This leads to aimlessness, abstract ornamentalism, or to mere quotation of a Modernism that has not merited the title for thirty years or more. Putting the composer's demands to one side is even more damaging here than in the case of older works.

Whereas with older works the ear (thanks to memory) instinctively defends the music against the eye, when the ear experiences a new work for the first time, it (together with the eye) must take at face value everything that is served up. Whenever the new décor does not match the sound world of the new score or express the same things in colour, style and material, the displeasure of the listener (who is also using his eyes) is naturally directed against the music (we are, after all, at the opera) even when it is suspected that the faults lie with the production. The collaboration of set-designer, producer, composer and conductor should therefore be far more intensive; insufficient collaboration, or neglected or ineffective communication (sometimes deliberately so) often enough result in distortions, false conclusions and untruths that serve and give pleasure to no one.

1  Hans Werner Henze with friends at table, Wiesbaden, 1950. Left
to right: Hans Zehden (composer), Irene Strebe (dancer), HWH,
Lucien Mars (dancer)

2  Passport photo, 1945          3  At the piano, Berlin 1958

4   Margot Fonteyn, Frederick Ashton, and HWH at the premiere of
the ballet *Ondine* at Covent Garden, 27 October 1958

5   At home with Italian greyhounds, Coccolo and Dafne, at Castel
Gandolfo, 1963

# Maratona di Danza *

*Maratona di Danza* is not really a ballet in the traditional sense, but rather a spectacle that takes dancing as its theme. The idea came from a particular kind of dance, in which dancing is tragedy itself. It is about Gianni, a boy from the outskirts of Rome, who meets a prosaic and horrible end in one of the dance marathons that were the fashion in Italy after the war.

Visconti had conceived this story for Les Ballets Jean Babilée in Paris, and in the winter of 1955 asked me to supply the music. Through a chain of circumstances, however, the completion of the work was delayed, so that its premiere [at the Berlin Festival, 1957] is only now taking place. In the same way that the world of forms and colours of Veronese or Longhi dominates one of Visconti's productions of classical works, here it is Renzo Vespignani's paintings, steeped in the life of the suburbs of Rome, that set the tone, and nothing seemed more logical than to give him the responsibility for the stage set (which he executed personally in the studio of the Berlin Städtische Oper) and for the costumes. We were joined by the Dutch choreographer, Dick Sanders, who had just done his first work with Babilée. Sanders was entrusted with working out the dance routines in detail, but Visconti 'held the strings'; he built everything up himself, structured it, set climaxes against calm passages, tender ones against coarse, cast a spell over *realismo*, and brought mass and colour into motion. The painter, the choreographer and I were his tools; for his sake we gladly accepted this otherwise undesirable role, and each of us pared down

* '*Maratona di Danza*.' Programme note, Städtische Oper, Berlin, autumn 1957 (part); *Essays* 1964 (part).

his means where asked to do so, and mobilized them where appropriate.

I myself had great difficulties with material that was alien and left me indifferent: jazz. As a part of the proceedings, two jazz bands play alternately on stage, replaced on occasion by a pianist, and even once by a gramophone, and they produce that third-rate dance music that can be heard in suburban dance halls or, as it were, at a dance marathon. To get closer to this material I had to follow up the study of records of professionally played jazz by some acquaintance with the types of music required for *Maratona*. Suburban dance halls, where Sanders and Babilée were carrying out life-studies, and Vespignani was filling sketchbooks, were duly visited to get my ears attuned. What we had accumulated was shown to Visconti, who then in his choices and comments revealed, with constantly dumbfounding precision, his own notions about sounds, colours, tempi and timing. (My difficulties with jazz were only partially resolved at that time; salvation did not come until February 1957, when Hans Rosbaud was going to perform a concert suite from *Maratona* on the West German Radio, and the jazz expert, Harald Banter, helped and made sense of my sketches.)

The jazz played on stage (requiring improvisation at several points) is meant to be realistic, like the events on stage, whereas the music played by the orchestra impels and comments on the action, in the manner of old-style ballets, and thus adopts a position between dramatic description and poetic commentary. So the listener can sometimes detect references to classical theatre music, or rather to its idiom, as if the music wanted to recall the Marathon of antiquity, to call to mind happiness, heroism, the olympic spirit that is in such crude contrast with what the 'dance marathon' imported from America signifies in our time, in its prosaic horror; its grimace stands out even more against a classical background— just as skyscrapers disfigure classical landscapes, or modern dance distorts classical bodies.

It was fascinating to observe Visconti day by day during the rehearsals for *Maratona*. Without fuss, without raising his voice, often giving the impression that he was not willing to intervene in what was still predominantly confusion, when no one seemed to know how things should continue or how they went at all, but occasionally, softly, amusedly, as if as an afterthought, giving his assistants little jobs, pieces of advice, calling somebody over and whispering something in his ear—in this completely composed and unobtrusive way Visconti took control of the entire project. His production took shape just as a spider's web is formed; an apparently improvised mobility became an ever more intricately dovetailed kaleidoscope—something ever more exact that, in the end, turned out to be a most strange, sinister, and for many a repellent image, that was intended to provoke and did so.

Before the team went their separate ways again, each going back to his own four walls, leaving only traces and memories behind, there had been time to talk about new operatic projects, about subjects and forms. Visconti suggested that I should consider Kleist's *Der Prinz von Homburg*. A year later I completed the first sketches.

# Der Prinz von Homburg*

The Prince of Homburg, our cousin, the 'Hamlet' of Brandenburg, is the hero of my new opera. Some people may find it impossible to separate this play from the Prussian milieu in which it takes place. Others consider that setting great classic texts to music and transferring dramatic poems to the stage is a treasonable enterprise. This objection deserves discussion. It would be really tedious if, in the course of time, the whole of dramatic literature was turned into operas. But tell me, who could have written a better libretto for me than my friend, Heinrich von Kleist? When I was trying to find a language that would make fresh demands on my music, a language that my music was looking for, I came across the Prince. Ingeborg Bachmann adapted the text for me; she reduced it to libretto form, fashioning vehicles for recitatives, arias and ensembles. It is evident that it is possible to abstract from Prussianism the world Kleist created in this work. But it seems to me that the work is *ab initio* already abstracted from Prussianism. It is only by chance, because of the freely adapted historical background, that the conflict is set in Brandenburg. The tension between the existence of the individual and 'reasons of state', questions of disregard of law and order, a human being trembling before the might of the ruling power, the courage to resist it—all these could have occurred today or two thousand years ago, in Sparta or in Athens. Such conflicts are not restricted to Brandenburg or to Prussianism. I like to see all this in the context of Greece; I would like to imagine Kleist's Brandenburg as an ancient royal dynasty (perhaps because, although he destroys

* '*Prinz von Homburg.*' *Blätter und Bilder*, vol 8 nos 58–60, Würzburg 1960 (part); *Essays* 1964 (part); *Melos*, vol 27 no 5, 1960 (part).

classicism, its spirit still lingers); playful elements in the black shadow of high bright Olympus, a dangerous play with unexpected outbursts, bloodthirsty and dithyrambic emotions.

But there is another aspect that emerges from Kleist's text. Everything that happens, how it happens and how it is expressed, is related to the world of Italian opera in its flowering at the beginning of the nineteenth century and its triumphant dominance of the whole subsequent epoch; echoes of this were felt in Kleist's Berlin (see Heine's letters too). My interest in this art form had recently grown, and my need to attempt it afresh was extremely intense when I took Visconti's advice to set *Der Prinz von Homburg*. The angelic melancholy of Bellini, the sparkling brio of Rossini, the passionate intensity of Donizetti, combined and drawn together by Verdi's robust rhythms, his hard orchestral colours and unforgettable melodic lines—these had preoccupied me for years, and after having produced a first echo in *Ondine*, were now to appear as pure *melodrama* (in the original sense).

Greece and the lyric theatre of the Ottocento were the stimulus, starting-points, and points of reference for this opera. As they are only indirectly connected with the concept of German Romanticism—and as the subject of Kleist's play is more a pathological case than a romantic hero—it is perhaps rather easier for me this time to escape the unwelcome criticisms of those who accuse me of 'romanticism' (whatever they mean by that term) as of some kind of sin, or impute it to me with a shrug. (If you really want to know, the moon in *König Hirsch* was not a romantic moon but a lantern devised by circus clowns; the moon in *Ondine* was a piece of cardboard illuminated by gaslight; the moon in *Der Prinz von Homburg* is a beam of light beneath which the sleepwalker wanders, loses his way, tussles with life.)

A large chamber orchestra has been chosen, capable of a wide expressive and dynamic range. The basic mood is that of chamber music. Each scene has a particular instrumental grouping, a particular form, partly transformations of old techniques (such as passacaglia, fugue, rondo) into today's possibilities. The music is contrapuntally worked out; my preference in recent years for harmonic development is here pushed into the background. What I was trying to do was to free my musical techniques from the burden of Expressionism which they constantly recalled. In the process they were naturally subject to substantial changes of function and value, so that the question has even to be asked, how far they are really still the same thing.* The main task, as in my immediately preceding works (*Kammermusik 1958*, *Drei Dithyramben*, *Sonata per Archi*, *Des Kaisers Nachtigall*, Piano Sonata), was to study the degree of tension within each horizontal incident, and the related counterpoint of the lines themselves. This led to the discovery of other means, and made possible the representation of grace and hardness; cold and fire; the invention of formulas for the euphorias of the princely *sonnambulo*; the capturing of his language of silk and steel, and its transposition to singing voices and instruments; and their transformation into curves and accents. It illuminated the relationship between us and the times of the poet, who took his own life; it linked his hymn-like iambic rhythms to our sounds of today.

'His Majesty the King has ordered that the play performed yesterday, "Prinz Friedrich von Hessen-Homburg", shall never be performed again.' The order of 1 August 1828, delivered by *Kabinettsrat* Albrecht to Graf Brühl, was an additional ban on Kleist, and with the jeers of the Viennese first-night audience, Goethe's rejection, and an unending chain of disappointment and humiliation, constituted the reaction of a world that had no place for his genius; his love for his own country was not reciprocated. It is only today that we have learned better to appreciate what Kleist gave to the German language and the German theatre.

*Der Prinz von Homburg* is about the glorification of a dreamer, the destruction of the notion of the classical hero; it sets itself against the blind unimaginative application of laws, in favour of the exaltation of human kindness, an understanding of which reaches into deeper and more complex realms than would be 'normal' and which seeks to find a place for a man in this world even though he is a *Schwärmer* and a dreamer, or perhaps because of that. The cry

* Cf. De la Motte, *Der Prinz von Homburg, ein Versuch über die Komposition und den Komponisten*, Mainz 1960.

## Der Prinz von Homburg

'Down with all enemies of Brandenburg!' that at the end of the play
rings out for this idealized land where, according to Kleist, love,
understanding, forgiveness and grace played so powerful a role, is
equally directed against the rigidity and indolence of 'reasons of
state', and forms a frightening discord to the ban on Kleist's play
pronounced by one of the rulers of this promised land of
Brandenburg. No words are needed to underline this glaring irony.
It can still be found, threateningly enough, in our own time.

The vigorous iambics, further heightened in long rhythmic
phrases, demand a comparable rhythmic quality in the score. Here
the music can strengthen, guide and transcend the process of
intensification. I had already attempted something similar in my
Hölderlin setting, *Kammermusik 1958*; although the rhythmic
patterns of the poetry were quite different from Kleist's, the
problems are closely related when one sets out to transfigure words
with music, and to interpret and 'see into' the intellectual and
dramatic content of poetry, to raise it to a level where it begins to
resound.

Several tendencies in my works of the past few years seem to have
reached a new point in this drama: namely a new polyphony, and
the freely chosen constraints associated with it, as can be detected
for instance in *Sonata per Archi*, and the new piano sonata, which
was composed between the second and third acts of the *Prinz*. But
this polyphony here acquires a particular quality, under the
constant stimulus of Kleist's compressed language, which seems to
drive the singing voice upward through the tension within the
interaction of silk and steel, through the shrill loneliness between a
dream world and a real world—all things that can leave no musician
unmoved. Ingeborg Bachmann's adaptation enables these tensions
to emerge clearly; it is a genuine libretto, yet one which does no
violence to the original. It is conceived in operatic forms, with
opportunities for arias and ensembles and linking recitatives. More
strongly and unmistakably than before, I have here been able to
make the construction and shape of the 'opera itself' my own.

This has made possible an opera that is a manifestation,
supported on every side by the music and the words, that there is a

striving for unity in which my thoughts on theatre and music, music and language, our relationship to history, and our current situation with its problems, questions and counter-questions, all find a place and form a whole.

Over and above this concept, I wanted to get to a point with this work that is some distance from my previous pieces for the theatre. *König Hirsch* and the ballets that followed it, *Maratona* and *Ondine*, contain the clearest examples of where my language has been extended into territory hitherto alien, and to which I was primarily drawn by the desire to get to the root of certain formal, linguistic and timbre phenomena. The results of this research became somewhat clearer from piece to piece over the years, and are now brought together for the first time in *Prinz*. I have striven for greater freedom, or at least what I understand by it: certainly not improvisation, but independence, and a preparedness for decisions outside established categories. Music is not musicology, and the logic of a work rests on a unique constellation of incident, encounter, experience, agreement; it transcends inherited rules, construction, calculation. It seems that the vegetative element of music surpasses its other, lesser, musicological dimension, and that, as in the life of the Prince of Homburg, illuminations and discoveries take place in dreams, not in the laboratory. Not, however, in a state of haziness, but in the wakefulness of sleepwalkers, where facts are perceived with abnormal clarity.

# Elegy for Young Lovers
## (1) Birth of the Opera<sup>*</sup>

Naples, summer 1960. The old houses of Pizzofalcone, surrounding mine, are being torn down. Cranes appear and reach out across the scene; to the roar of bulldozers concrete palaces tower up, obscuring the view from my terrace: Posilipo, the fishing village of Mergellina, the peninsula of Sorrento, Capri and Vesuvius. Work on *Elegy for Young Lovers*, which had just been started, had to be abandoned. Looking for a suitable place where it could be continued without distractions, I hit upon Berlin.

Autumn and winter, cool clear air, quiet in the Grunewald, willing friends help me with my work. While the Munich Opera had long since begun production of the first act, and sections of the second arrived bit by bit, like part-work magazines, the third act was still far from completion. Nevertheless the first performance did take place in Schwetzingen at the end of May 1961.

Weighed down with the experiences of three previous productions (in Schwetzingen, Zurich and Glyndebourne), *Elegy* now appears (at the Cuvilliés Theatre in Munich) on the stage where it was first rehearsed. In the meantime the pendulum of its reception has swung to opposite extremes; strongly contradictory judgements have been aired. Critics had once complained that this opera did not get to people's hearts but on their nerves, and so much so that it

---

* 'Über *Elegie für junge Liebende*.' *Essays* 1964 (part); *Blätter der Bayerischen Staatsoper*, Munich 1961.

could make you ill, if not insane; or that the applause bestowed on the piece was merely a symptom of the decline of the theatre and its audience; or that the madhouse had been the source of inspiration, with anything that was mentally healthy (whatever that may mean) considered suspect. But it has also now been said that a libretto has here been elevated to a work of art, and yet again that the work is the triumph of a distinctive musical language, the final breakthrough. Lastly, to compensate for the accusation of having once more not proceeded according to the recipe book, and having left open the question 'Quo vadis?' that evidently so preoccupies the music-lover, friendly French critics have maintained that *Elegy* represents an exception to the rule that dramas about 'Alpine suicides' rarely produce good literature, and even more rarely good music.

W. H. Auden, one of the librettists of *Elegy for Young Lovers*, is a man who deciphers truth, in Stravinsky's words 'a genius who plays with the art of poetry', and is not going to set down on paper without good cause banalities such as here and there seem to punctuate *Elegy*. The laughter that is produced by irony, absurdity, wickedness, and a by-no-means cosy humour, has a dramatic function. In fact it always occurs where least expected, where a gentler mood would mask the seriousness of the piece and distort its form. Soft emotion is not tolerated, but crudely countered or turned bitter by a joke. That is technique, discipline. On the other hand a situation is here never as transparent as it seems, and the evident is certainly also ambivalent; much is unstated, but you can pick up where the text leaves off, and for instance move directly from the 'tomorrows' of the second act to Macbeth's soliloquy that begins with the same words, and weave associations with the poor player and the tale told by an idiot, full of sound and fury. . . .

During composition I was spurred on by the skilfully constructed libretto. Almost all the essentials of the plot are unfolded in the first act, so as to allow the second to be taken up with ensembles, and the catastrophes that issue from it to run their course only in the third. But from other less qualified quarters the libretto has been criticized as artistically suspect. As if every decent libretto did not contain a good portion of artifice, as if it were not indeed the essence of opera that the improbable is transformed into the probable, fiction into higher truth, artificiality into nature. Opera is an artificial form, no less than a string quartet or a piano sonata, and the stage is the opened eyes of the score.

Chester Kallman, more than just a collaborator, has a significant share in the work; as in *The Rake's Progress*, part of the ideas and large sections of the text (whole scenes) stem from him. He is the superior practitioner and connoisseur of opera, and probably first aroused Auden's interest in it. Auden now believes that only vanity could prevent a writer from opting for the subordinate role of librettist, and prefers opera to any verse drama, even one written by himself: '. . . the writer must be convinced that opera offers possibilities that are excluded from drama, and that these very possibilities are worth more than everything of which drama is capable'.

Despite the love for the nineteenth-century Italian opera that inspired our collaboration, expressed in set numbers and the style of the ensembles, including imitation of the metres of Felice Romani (Hilda Mack's visions are modelled on the stanzas of the mad scene in *Lucia di Lammermoor*), several new musical elements are introduced. There are the clock-chimes, divisions of time, which symbolize the protagonist's obsession with time, and the ends or beginnings of scenes. At some points the clock-chimes are replaced by other realistic sounds, and always when disorder threatens: for instance the whistle of the train that marks the entrance of the fateful Toni Reischmann; in the second act the cow-bell that accompanies the tipsy Hilda Mack, relieving the tension at the most extreme point of dramatic conflict; in the third act the metallic clatter of a heavy object that falls to the ground at the very moment that Mittenhofer tells his murderous lie. The clock stops here too, and is started again only some time later by Carolina, who herself has turned into a clockwork doll.

The instrumentation, too, grew out of these chinoiseries, with the idea of linking the mechanical notion of time symbolized by the clock, and the eternity symbolized by the glacier, that crystalline mass which follows its own time-scale, and dominates not only the landscape but also the souls of the people who live in its shadow. Obbligato solo instruments are allotted to them which, so to speak, portray on another level the mental states depicted in the vocal lines. The remainder of the orchestra, in particular the percussion, functions as *concerto grosso*; it is intended to create the atmosphere, the background for the instrumental cardiograms.

To mistrust the implied greatness of Mittenhofer is to be like the spoilsport who regards Leporello's list as a scandalous exaggeration, or who judges Don Giovanni's skills as a seducer only by the manifestations of his libertinism visible on stage. In fact, on top of references in the dialogue, *Elegy* contains several unmistakable indications of the real power of Mittenhofer's personality (and of his renown). For instance, he manages to win back his love merely by talking about himself, and when he wants to hand her over to the younger man—if only to provide a good way out for himself—all he has to do is talk about the work he is engaged on at the moment to get everybody into his power again and become master of the situation. And nothing could bring Gräfin Kirchstetten to rescue the young lovers from death on the mountain if, to do so, she would have to prove the master to be a liar and contradict him. But this is not what the work is about. It is the portrayal of the *eroico furore*, the evil St Vitus' dance, the unending conflict between the creative individual and his environment set against the background of a culture of guilt that permeates Christian and modern European thought. If no monologue tells us anything about the Master's true feelings, and the only picture of his work as a poet (albeit behind the stage) is malicious and grotesque, this is less a lack than a concealment. At the end, then, the music stands alone, wordless, the only art that, as Auden says, is not in a position to condemn or to judge, and can therefore pour forgiveness over people like pure wine.

# Elegy for Young Lovers
## (2) The Artist as Bourgeois Hero*

The introduction to the first volume of *Blätter für die Kunst*, founded by Stefan George in 1892, reads:

The name of this publication itself says something about what it is trying to achieve: to serve art, in particular poetry and letters, to the exclusion of everything political and social.

It aims at SPIRITUAL ART on the basis of a new sensibility and craftsmanship—an art for art—and is therefore in opposition to that worn-out and inferior school that grew out of a false conception of reality. It also cannot concern itself with projects to improve the world and dreams of universal happiness, in which today one sees the seeds of all that is new, which may indeed be extremely fine but belong to a different realm from poetry.

The 'pious timidity' with which the writer refuses to contemplate the origin of his ideas and feelings can be understood when their root is revealed, and his concern that he might no longer be able to write if he 'knows too much' is not wholly unjustified, for when you no longer believe in them yourself, it is far more difficult to make lies credible. The argument, as you can read in every newspaper, is that the artist ideally creates from his subconscious. Now it may well be that, when the artist of our time switches off his intellect, or restricts it to purely mechanical functions, he may indeed babble

* 'Der Künstler als bürgerlicher Held.' Introduction to *Elegy for Young Lovers* when the work was given as a guest performance by Scottish Opera at Stuttgart 1975. *Musik und Politik* 1976.

one or two truths in the process—and this might even cast a beam of light on to his intellect. But it is not exactly a good sign for a society that only the inarticulate and the inebriated speak the truth, or are prepared to speak it. The trouble is that the artist usually manages to draw only errors and lies from his subconscious. He in fact draws from it only what has been put into it, and if the drawing out is unconscious, the putting in was usually very much conscious.

Auden and Kallman supplied the central figure in the libretto of *Elegy for Young Lovers*—the accused writer, Mittenhofer; real figures underlay this creation: George, Rilke, Yeats, Wagner and others. The problem of the elitist existence of the artist is shown in our opera in the form of a parable. The authors themselves have made the following comment:

This is a genuine myth because the lack of identity between Goodness and Beauty, between the character of man and the character of his creations, is a permanent aspect of the human condition. The Theme of *Elegy for Young Lovers* is summed up in two lines by Yeats:

*The intellect of man is forced to choose*
*Perfection of the life or of the work.*

Aesthetically speaking, the personal existence of the artist is accidental; the essential thing is his production. The artist-genius, as the nineteenth century conceived him, made this aesthetic presupposition an ethical absolute; that is to say, he claimed to represent the highest, most authentic, mode of human existence.

Accept this claim, and it follows that the artist-genius is morally bound by a sacred duty to exploit others whenever such exploitation will benefit his work, and to sacrifice them whenever their existence is a hindrance to his production.

As composer I would like to quote what I wrote on the occasion of my 1971 Edinburgh production, for it reveals how the work has become more and more clear for me since its first performance ten years ago, and easier to grasp and more concentrated, with the passing of time:

In earlier productions of this opera, including my own, the artificiality of its form has not been adequately brought out; only when this is made apparent, however, can the frictions between farce, tragedy, *opera buffa* and psychodrama be understood and savoured. This production attempts to make clear that what is being shown is essentially the birth of a poem, the poem that comes into being during the three acts, and whose genesis we follow from the initial idea to the final public reading. The grotesque, ridiculous, vulgar, malevolent and base events that surround this birth serve to call in question the figure of the artist as hero, that concept of the hero's life created by the nineteenth century, and not yet completely abandoned by the twentieth. An ingredient of this concept is the catastrophic notion that the artist has to live in isolation for the sake of his creativity, and that he has to be an outcast, an outsider, or someone who places himself in a state of suspension, to whom different rules apply from those for normal people. The closing scene of the opera reveals the horrifying aspect of such notions. From this point we can look back over the whole work as if it were conceived as a didactic piece.

In what sense is the bourgeois conception of art mirrored in the music, and how and with what literary and musical methods is it depicted, criticized, denounced? The methods in both libretto and score are parody, sarcasm and 'overlaps'—mixtures of these; but also simple clear portrayal where the feelings are simple and human.

The most direct reflection of bourgeois conceptions of art is to be found in the figures who, loving, hating, serving, surround the writer Mittenhofer. From their behaviour, outbursts, reactions, one can gauge what art means in such a world, such an environment, and to what extent people are prepared to devote themselves to it and its producers. Delusion and madness play a major role here, as well as the Jugendstil stirrings and whisperings of an alienated Nature.

These are people whose faces wear handsome masks with deceitful eyes, their malicious smiles preserved for all time in the waxen glass sculptures of Despret and Décorchement. They are the cold Alberts, and the Albertines as pale as gardenias; actors of our pain, frivolous messengers of games and rituals that would one day be taken to their brutalized conclusion under fascism; incapable of thinking beyond the boundaries of their class.

The settings are an Austrian Alpine inn at the beginning of the century, a snowstorm on the mountain, and at the close a Viennese theatre. The piece begins with a prologue by an insane woman of sixty, Frau Hilda Mack. Her fate is tragic, and no doubt not without its comic aspects: this lady has been waiting in vain for forty years for the return of her husband, who set off on their wedding-night to bring her back an edelweiss from the Hammerhorn mountain, as a token of his love. It is her visions—poetic and somewhat vague hallucinations—that make Mittenhofer, the writer, go up into the mountains each spring. He records Hilda's visions, and transforms them into his own products. The title of the poem that the Master starts work on in the first act of the opera (after Hilda has had a long-awaited vision) is also the title of our opera. 'The young lovers' are Elisabeth Zimmer, the Master's companion, and Toni Reischmann, his godson. They are sacrificed by the Master for two reasons: personal revenge; and to supply a good title for his new poem, so that when it is read in the capital on the occasion of his sixtieth birthday it can be called an 'elegy'.

Hilda's music is kept in the idiom of the 1950s, not only in instrumentation (obbligato flute, accompanied by harp, celesta and tuned percussion) but also in its flow: wide leaps between intervals, coloraturas, a preponderance of sevenths and ninths—that precious and artificial genre is familiar. But here it becomes a climate, that very 'mountain air garnished with lyricism' that strikes Hilda as so unbearable, when in the third act she returns to the city cured, to begin a normal life at long last. Even after the corpse of her spouse has been brought back from the glacier and after she is cured, this kind of music still clings to her. It accompanies her during her gradual transformation, disillusionment and humanization, except that it no longer sounds precious, but awkward and clumsy. This produces the impression that tones of warmth and humanity are circumstantial or even impossible in this kind of music. It has been taken off its pedestal, and has to produce rhythms, intervals and chords for which it was not designed, which do not suit it, which it cannot 'manage'.

However, much of the visionary madwoman's musical material has gone into the thematic structures of the hero, Mittenhofer, and even into those of the young lovers. Not only does Hilda's great vision, which occurs at the very moment that Elisabeth and Toni confront one another for the first time, provide material for the poem, of which we catch a glimpse in the last twenty-eight bars of the opera (but which is otherwise withheld from us and our judgements), but life, plot, action, develop precisely as foretold in the vision's fragments of thought. It is because the plot unfolds analogously to the elegy (about whose progress we are from time to time given hints) that the old idea that reality is an illusion and the truth is to be found in art alone is unmasked. Cheated of their lives, victims of the murderous tendencies of a representative of this theory, the two young people nevertheless manage to make the moment of their death their moment of truth. This is the only note of reconciliation in the whole work, apart from the cure of Hilda, who also ends up purged of her illusions. The librettists describe the love affair between Toni and Elisabeth as 'illusory but rhymable'; nothing credible can be derived from it, only rhyme.

Thus a whole universe of bourgeois notions is supported by artificial music, by the 'crystalline sound' of the mad woman at the edge of the glacier. Just as in *The Bassarids* the music of Dionysus keeps expanding until by the close it has stifled the rational music of Pentheus (like the vine-leaves that, according to the libretto, enclose the entire stage), so here the music of Hilda encroaches into the emergent poem on the one hand, and into the music of the remaining characters on the other. Everything that occurs between those under the spell of the poet-titan is depicted and characterized by illusion and artificiality. Towards the end of the second act, when Mittenhofer is speaking of the development of his poem, which is not yet called 'Elegy' but only 'The Young Lovers', the obbligato instruments allotted to the characters are silent, just like their own wills. The only accompaniment to this scene is the mad woman's harp, which here becomes a parody of Apollo's lyre. While the writer is speaking, those present break in, one after another, each of them elaborating one of the thoughts of the poem as a monologue. Peace descends, a silence, like the silence of the beasts tamed by Apollo. This is in fact the moment of the drama when the hero subjugates everything, thanks to the suggestive power of his work. He irons out all contradictions and pushes any resistance out of the way—*his* way, naturally. This is the quietest moment in the opera, but also the one nearest to being crucial.

Only one person has remained silent, ominously attending this scene, and now saying tonelessly: 'They forget the soil, who forget the hour. Where nothing can root, nothing will flower.' This is Countess Carolina von Kirchstetten. (Kirchstetten is a village in Lower Austria where Auden lived from 1960 until his death.) She is one of those people who adoringly devote themselves to artists, sacrificing their own existence, their independence, their money. The history of art is full of such figures. In our parable her fate is operatically magnified. In the third act this intellectual and aristocratic lady becomes, at a moment of emotional hesitation, partly responsible for the death of the young lovers, an accomplice. Under the spell of artist and art she too prefers falsehood to truth; moving in the opposite direction from Hilda, she slips from an absence of illusions into madness, while the murderous snow is falling and the world is growing dark, and the fire of the tiled stove within conjures up a private miniature *Götterdämmerung*. The music makes the reference unmistakable, while the writer is saying:

> *Everything must be paid for*
> *Eventually*
> *In time or in the service*
> *Of eternity:*
> *I do not ask the price for*
> *They shall pay for me.*

The cor anglais has accompanied the Countess as an obbligato instrument throughout the opera, through sad, comic and lonely situations, and it has also sometimes enabled us to hear her unspoken thoughts; it becomes silent, while she becomes an automaton, totally without feeling, a living clock, a secretary in the literal sense. The crystal ball of Hilda Mack's vision leads here into the expressionless ticking and whirring of a monstrous clock mechanism, as the accompaniment to a new madness.

The sound-realm of madness and of the mountain clothes a different form of illusion in the last scene of the first act, which Auden and Kallman headed 'two follies cross'. Hilda has just come to the painful realization that her husband has been brought back from the glacier after forty years, still young and handsome, having been preserved in the ice. She remains alone to reflect upon what has happened. This period is taken up with Toni's thoughts of his mother, who died when he was young: a song in three verses, amid which the sounds of the glacier can unmistakably be heard, atmospheric, like a threat and a warning. Then on the split-stage the 'crossing of follies': Toni leaves reality behind, by giving himself up to the feelings of love that he now transfers from his mother to Elisabeth, and Hilda thanks her dead husband for his return, as this allows her to leave her madness and enter the world of today. The sound of the mountain and glacier music is now like the sound of cracking ice; also, so far as Toni is concerned, like the breaking of the shell of boyhood from which the youth emerges. In the epilogue one can hear the trumpet, associated with Mittenhofer, aggressive and threatening: the poet has just lost both his muses, Elisabeth to Toni, and Hilda to reality.

The idea of attaching obbligato instruments to the characters and carrying it through as a dramatic principle, by hook or by crook, leads to combinations of sounds that are full of frictions, and apparent discontinuities which can be understood only in the context of the dramatic relationships and situations. The music is thus compelled (with some violence) to take part in the action, to experience it, to act it out. This is particularly clear in the relatively unimportant role of Toni's father, Dr Reischmann, Mittenhofer's doctor and friend from his youth. He is depicted as a *bon vivant*, whose joviality testifies to a bad conscience and cowardice. To underline this he has been allotted a bassoon, whose jollity has something artificial, something involuntary about it, and for the occasional outbursts of explicit sentimentality a saxophone in addition. You can imagine how unpleasant the howling tone of this instrument is, compared to that of his son Toni, who despises him, and whose last days and hours are accompanied by a softly romantic and discontented viola. Despite the apparent irreconcilability of these two instruments, there is a family resemblance, thanks to a certain affinity of tone. It should also be pointed out that each obbligato instrument corresponds to the register of the character. Hilda, the mad widow, is a coloratura soprano, and therefore has the flute. Elisabeth, loved first by the Master, then by Toni, is a soprano; she is accompanied by the violin. Carolina, with the cor anglais, is an alto. Toni, with the viola, is a tenor, and his father, with the bassoon, is a bass.

The Master, the powerful one, Dracula, has the three brass instruments of the *Elegy* orchestra at his disposal: horn, trumpet and trombone, in which his unshakable self-image is manifested in three basic attitudes. First the gentle contemplative, with an affinity to the forest, to Nature; that is the sound of the horn. Then there is the proclaimer and ranter and hysteric; that is the trumpet. Finally the hallowed man of wisdom and wild boar; that is the trombone. The artistic challenge lay in coping with the relative immobility of these instruments, which were supposed to elucidate the most complex and diverse emotions and to rule out any doubts about the literary significance of Mittenhofer, especially as the events on stage constantly and deliberately provoke these very doubts, and as no direct insight into his art can be provided, because literature (in the theatre) cannot be portrayed by literature.

I wanted the musical structures and forms to be metaphors for the characters, and to undergo transformation with them. For instance, the first entrance of the Master is announced by dull gong beats, to which piano and harp arpeggios are added. The first sound on the brass is a chord of the fifth, E flat to B flat, followed by the horn playing two intervals of a fourth, E flat to A flat and then back again to E flat. The principal musical characteristics of the poet consist of the ascending and descending fourth, and the intervals of a sixth, minor second, major second, major sixth, and minor second. A whimpering flexatone is also added to his first entry, which plays nine notes of the complete twelve-tone row and creates a horror-film atmosphere. The flexatone returns only once during the second act, at the moment when the writer is planning his crime, half consciously and half unconsciously—the music is already incriminating him—and once again in the third act, when the crime is actually committed. The writer's main motif recurs several times in a slightly changed form, for instance at tea in the second act or, in a minor colouring, when Elisabeth is on the point of telling Frau Mack the truth about her husband's death, freeing her of her illusion and thereby robbing Mittenhofer of his medium. In his great self-portrait at the centre of the second act and the zenith of the work, where he manages to make Elisabeth doubt her love for Toni, the three brass instruments take over the task of accompanying his eloquence, in ever new variants. Alto flute, cor anglais, saxophone and bassoon are also used in this scene.

The music of the lovers represents a world opposed to that of Mittenhofer. From the beginning of Act 2 the intervals become more and more simple, cantabile, and tonal, seeming as though they would naturally end in folk song. In fact a 'folk song' sung by the lovers is heard at the beginning of the third act, when the two of them leave the hotel to set off for the mountain. This song is permeated by a mood of parting, grief, solitude, senselessness. It is a symbolic moment in the drama and in the music. The singing grows more and more distant. The music that remains in the house withers, dries up, crumbles away, ends in silence.

In the third act the clock no longer strikes, for things are out of joint: nothing can remain ordered in this world of petty feelings, where the social context has decayed, where love cannot exist, where people sponge and steal, and where indolence has become the chief occupation, in a tonal spectrum of pink, pale green, cyclamen, gentian, sky-blue and prussian blue. The predominant colour scale is that of Jugendstil, the only art form invented by the bourgeoisie. It is the style in which, as Walter Benjamin says, 'the old bourgeoisie disguises the presentiment of its own weakness by cosmicly swarming into every sphere and, intoxicated with the future, misuses "youth" as an incantation. . . . Its formal language expresses the desire to avoid what is imminent, and the misgivings that rear in front of it; furthermore that "spiritual movement", which strove to renew human existence without considering the public dimension, amounted to a reversion of the contradictions of society to those hopeless, tragic convulsions and tensions that characterize the life of small sects.'

The music drama *Elegy for Young Lovers* is about precisely these hopeless convulsions and tensions, these frontier and terminal situations.

# Castelli Romani*

Summer 1961: a new environment, known as Castelli Romani, where medieval castles give their names to rock-coloured little towns around them that blend in with ihe landscape. Vineyards, knolls of cypresses, the blue and slate-coloured Abruzzi mountains in the distance; the sea in the west, bluish-silver by day, a reddish-gold strip at sunset, sends its seaweed scent in this direction.

Rome, which can be reached along the Appian Way, is tangibly near. Coldness, hardness, the city, princes, city lights, layabouts, marble, *palazzi*, granite; a rapidly growing town, breaking through the walls, it has already reached the Campagna, rampant, a deluge; *le belli arti*, obelisks, fountains, hordes of cars, noise, silence at night, moon, aqueducts, wind, the night's delicate bouquet of cornflowers.†

1962: Fifth Symphony. As Goethe says:

Let me be brief! The human spirit is in a marvellous state when it reveres, when it worships, when it lifts up an object and is uplifted by it; but it cannot long remain in this state, the generic character left it cold, the ideal lifted it up above itself; now, however, it would like to return to itself, it would like to enjoy again that earlier

---

* 'Castelli Romani.' *Essays* 1964.
    † 'Quelle folie! diront bien des gens. Oui, mais quel bonheur! Les gens raisonnables ne savent pas à quel degré d'intensité peut atteindre ainsi le sentiment de l'existence; le coeur se dilate, l'imagination prend une envergure immense, on vit avec fureur; le corps même, participant de cette suréxitation de l'esprit, semble devenir de fer. Je faisais alors mille imprudences qui peut-être aujourd'hui me coûteraient la vie . . ..'

Hector Berlioz, Mémoires XXXVII, L'Italie sauvage

inclination towards individuality which it has felt, without returning to that state of limitation, nor does it want to relinquish what is significant, what lifts up the spirit. What would become of it in this state, if beauty were not to come along and happily solve this riddle? It is beauty that gives life and warmth to the scholarly, and by tempering what is significant and lofty, and pouring heavenly charm over it, brings it closer to us. A beautiful work of art has come full circle, it is now again a kind of individual, which we embrace with affection, which we can claim as our own.*

Manhattan *mon amour*: 'O Falada, da du hangest.' Cooing of doves, seagulls that screech around the growth of smooth, Abruzzi-coloured metals on the walls of skyscrapers, asphalt rain. Fairy tales, all the nightmares of childhood, all avenues end in the sea, old Europe floats mythically in. Salt air, seaweed, vice, police raids, minorities, clavichords, Edwardian Rooms, sevenfold song of death. Garish nylon, gangs, god, neon, jeans, bangs, hot dogs, cops. W.H. and dear C. in the Village. The left-handed Timon of Assens in the grey stairwells by night, his heart trying to burst out of his body. Silks, gold, ebony, subway shafts, black velvet, *maraviglioso fior del vostro mare*. Everything is going to darken: crystal chandeliers, the whites of eyes, the sand of the sea, the sun itself.

1963: cantata *Being Beauteous* (Rimbaud) for soprano, harp and four cellos; *Ariosi* (Torquato Tasso) for soprano, violin and orchestra; *Lucy Escott Variations* for harpsichord; *Adagio* for eight instruments; *Los Caprichos* for orchestra; cantata *Tu sei la fiaba estrema* (Elsa Morante) for soprano and chamber orchestra. Goethe again:

Who can feel intensely without having the wish to express what he has felt? And what do we in fact express that we do not create? And not just once and for all, that it be there, but so that it moves, ever grows, and becomes again and brings forth again. This is precisely

---

* J. W. von Goethe, *Der Sammler und die Seinigen*, Sechster Brief, in *Propyläen*, Zweiten Bandes zweites Stück 1799.

the divine power of love, of which one does not cease to sing and to say that, at every moment, it brings forth the marvellous qualities of the loved object anew, develops them in their smallest details, embraces them as a whole, rests not by day, reposes not by night, takes delight in its own work, is astonished by its own nimble activity, always finds the familiar new, because at every moment, in this sweetest of all trades, it is produced anew.*

* Ibid.

# Music as a Means of Resistance[*]

Only with the aid of suppositions and comparisons can we ascertain and evaluate the relationship between contemporary art and the past and the future. What we can see ten years behind or in front of us is still too close; we lack the distance that would make clear perception and cool observation possible. What has just been is oppressively close, almost tangible, as yet without a name. (Later it will be the past, perhaps belong to history, less and less touched by the advance of life, less and less susceptible to the fickleness of taste, to blindness and over-exposure.) We impel ourselves forward, towards the unknown that arouses our curiosity. How good to know that what steps further into the background with the passage of time, provides through its crystallization a foothold; firm ground, where experience has accumulated and solidified. Looking back to past ages offers strength, stimulus, connection; here parallels and similarities to the present can be found, and the manifest presence of something crystal-like, in inner repose, which radiates a phosphorescent power—a power that reaches down to the present.[†]

* 'Musik als Resistenzverhalten.' First part of a lecture at the Technische Universität, Berlin, 28 January 1963. *Essays* 1964.

† 'We tend to dwell with satisfaction upon the poet's difference from his predecessors; we endeavour to find something that can be isolated in order to be enjoyed. Whereas if we approach a poet without this prejudice we shall often find that not only the best, but the most individual parts of his work may be those in which the dead poets, his ancestors, assert their immortality most vigorously. And I do not mean the impressionable period of adolescence, but the period of full maturity.'

T. S. Eliot, 'Tradition and the Individual Talent', in *The Sacred Wood*

[*122*]

## Music as a Means of Resistance

In our world, which leans towards self-destruction, a tendency seems to grow up within music to deny its own time, to work from within against its manifestations and objectives, and to adopt a posture of rejection. Music in our time is granted little opportunity for glorification and flooding people with illumination. The flames of Hiroshima have gone beyond all that. The constant threats to life and individual freedom have forced artistic and creative tendencies on to the defensive. In the sixteenth and seventeenth centuries music could realize and glorify itself, and its own time, because it was supported by it. Later, increasingly detached from society, it became more and more an individualistic pursuit; today music that truly wishes to speak, to be open, virtually resembles an esoteric cult: under attack, sometimes even persecuted, in flight from the dangers of mass society and standardization under dictatorships, and elsewhere from the platitudes of aesthetic slogans.

For as long as I can remember, I too have been accustomed to regard free music, the music of freedom, as something mysterious, hostile to authority, as something that needs to be protected against outside dangers. During the last years of the war, when I started composing, the free (and hence forbidden) music that could be heard only on forbidden wavelengths and secret transmitters still seemed a symbol of isolation: an idiom that in any circumstances was and would continue to be exposed to incomprehension and trivialization, even though the fragility of its material lay not within itself, but in the onslaughts of destructive misinterpretation and profanation.

The end of Nazi rule signalled the beginning of a new age, in which the innocent, the pure, and those purified through remorse, would be permitted access to what was free and remote—the potential for *noblesse* that slumbered unrecognized in people, that was obviously untimely, and furthest removed from brutality. This was a situation filled with a sense of new beginning and expectancy, which disappointments, temptations and insults could scarcely impair. It was sustained for years, until it seemed necessary to close oneself off again, against phenomena that one had indeed thought were dead, and that now—in remarkable variants of fascism—

opposed the new picture of the world one had constructed. To see in my country how only a few years after dictatorship, impulses have been reawakened that indicate that the spirit of intolerance has not died—this provokes a disappointment that not only lasts, but grows and allies itself with anger and shame. It makes me in my work swim even more consciously against the stream than hitherto, and with, in and through my work plead the cause of a life in which brutality, neglect of charity, and the withholding of intellectual and social freedom are unknown.

This tension between my desire to live and work actively and positively in our age, and the fact that it is impossible to find in it much cause for affirmation, probably results in a stance of resistance that embodies and brings with it contradictions. There is no harm in this. But it is the foolish response to the nineteenth century, aesthetic puritanism, which characterizes so much of our musical life, and makes it seem so petty bourgeois by comparison with past ages, since it aims by mechanization and depersonalization to restrict the impact of music on provincial 'consumers'. The naïve respectability of the progressives, according to whom music will once again be rescued by technical innovation, leads me to assume that I will continue my journey unaccompanied.

I cannot tell you, at any rate not yet, how I visualize the role of music in our time. My own music keeps its distance, and will continue to do so, as long as it is still possible for people with authorized murderous intentions or an unpunished murderous past to listen to it, talk about it and judge it.

I have definite ideas, indispensable to my existence or the existence of my music, about what music can achieve, what its purpose in the world could be, what it consists of, what it contains. But for the moment I will restrict myself to talking about fictions, uncertain arrangements and suppositions. What I know, have lived through and experienced, what I am, think and do, has clearly opposed me to the decrees of popes and the rules of monks. Only curiosity has ever made me take any interest in the newly devised decrees and theories amid which the initiates jubilantly embraced the technological age; and it seemed to me that hardly had a thesis been set up and the first notes deduced from it, than the end was always clearly predictable, long before its validity had run out of steam in the course of the season, for the end was already contained in the beginning of the thesis.

Proclamations and agendas swept through the provinces; every musical sensation, every workshop secret that should not be divulged (that is, that concerns only the composer himself), and every new discovery that affects only the discoverer, was made public. Jurors stood on the sidelines and got on with their business of commenting, taking note of things, wanting to instruct, advise and write further manifestoes. They exercised a form of control: backslapping, providing safeguards on every side, always eager not to miss the boat, always ready to disclaim last year's idea in the service of a new one; they unconsciously produced self-analyses in their writings, where they spoke of failure and lack of ability, laid down demands, allowed this to stand and rejected that, advising against the possible, yet spurring one on towards the impossible: cavilling, bourgeois-reactionary fans.

In its urgency to become sound, in its haste to come into the world, to make itself manifest, music by its nature tends to make manifestoes superfluous. The path it takes is never expected, required, prescribed. Music ignores theoretical correctives, and dissolves dogma whenever it wishes. Its realms are neither reification nor chaos; it spreads itself between these two poles, knowing about both of them, but existing only in the tension between them, by which it is energized. An awareness of urgent harmonized forms, formal ciphers and idioms is needed to master chaos, a chaos that would be as boring and just as ugly as a completely reified work. Infinitude, boundlessness, explosions and chaotic images are needed to resist oppression by the mathematical, which is just as much a part of the static raw material of music as the disordered and chaotic. All the misfortunes, doubts and age-old torments of music-making are embodied in the knowledge of this polarity. *Le compositeur s'arrange donc entre les deux*, to enable himself to write at all. His writing is a matter of haste and urgency—each day could be the last. He will find his way, settle down, seal himself off from the noise of social routine, to make his ears all the more sensitive to the still unknown sounds that await him. Only that which remains open, has not yet become analysable, and has not yet been written down, is capable of engaging him.

Wherever music has attempted mechanically to absorb by-products of physics (as though music were not a mathematical business in any case, as long as it remains in its state of lethargy) and has thus moved closer to a terminal state, a new freedom which breaks with previous rules and customs has managed to infuse new life: a life that once again transforms it into something opposed to nature, something that belongs to the realm of the intellect and imagination. The same thing has been happening in the past few years. After so much reification through technology, the demand is heard for a more vigorous body of thematic materials that will make new forms possible. The question is again being asked, where do the forces lie with which music can be kept alive, where is the enchantment? And thus the circle is closed, which began with the demand for the wholescale demolition of the metaphors of which music is made up. People are calling for a new start, now that everything has clearly been exhausted, and yet all this time the calm, intimate pulse-beat, that almost ineffable yet greatest quality of music, did not cease for an instant, no matter what attacks and outrages it was subjected to. As a matter of fact, even during the last ten years of upheaval, disintegration, annulment and standardization, important works have been produced here and there. The result of these efforts, both successful and unsuccessful, has now become fodder for a whole host of imitators throughout the world, while the works themselves, which have already grown independent of their momentary fate, stand before us isolated, unprepared to serve as models, pure music, polyvalent, already far removed from their creators.

What crops up in academies and studios as a learnable modernism is a colloquial language which is no longer capable even of conveying anything serviceable as foreground *Gebrauchsmusik* (utilitarian music), and in which not one single word can still be uttered. In this context any corrective in the form of a recourse to older worlds of sound seems more invigorating and promising. Could it be predicted, was it intended, that a musical language which at the beginning of this century, in the hands of a few people, was capable of expressing the highest and deepest things, and was something utterly exceptional, should now become anybody's simple trade? So much so, that the demand for something new is understandable, even though it comes principally from those who have industriously participated in producing this dilemma? I do not know the answer. One thing is certain: that the different and the new that are demanded in the music press will have a quite different *musical* shape from what those making these demands would like to see.

We must get used to the fact that, even if music is approached with the greatest amount of technical knowledge and ability, and larded with refined and progressive-sounding words, it breathes the same air as sustained it in previous centuries and cannot manage without those old essentials: ideas, imagination, excitement. In this respect it is no different from the music of earlier periods, which aimed to portray, represent, communicate. The insights and conclusions of modern modes of thought—whatever is understood by that—cannot be worked in directly; changes of direction are required, perhaps a childlike belief in realities and ties, and a sense of culture that consciously relates itself to the histories and adventures of music.

Each new piece is the first you have ever written. The whole realm of feeling has been emptied and made ready for messages from your own subconscious. Composition is a process of selection, of decision: what, out of the universe of immanent possibilities, will I make the work's own? I can master only a small section. What I retain is only a fragment of the whole; what I create is limited by time. What should this extract, this construct, be like? What should be made clear? What must remain imprecise, so that what is to be precisely understood stands out? What I am composing is, at root, a single work, which was started fifteen years ago, and which one day will end; the beginnings and endings of individual pieces are only apparent. Or perhaps I should say, with somewhat more modesty, that the beginning lies five or six hundred years in the past. Between one piece and the next there are stretches of time that can be described as gaps only in so far as no music is written down during them. The pleasure of transforming traditional models, or the attempt to acquiesce in their conventions and see them in a new light, appears in different forms, perhaps as an exchange of masks, but also as a corrective that shapes and uncovers relationships. Since the self-confrontation that composition consists of signifies something that might be described as communication, message, expression, which in its strongest moments also achieves the strongest degree of self-revelation and sacrifice (what should be kept secret can no longer remain silent), you must produce especially simple forms, which counteract the thematic confusion, and an especial clarity of gesture. Where the intention is to afford insight into difficult processes, you must make use of images, and have a 'key'. I consider it inadequate merely to produce hermetic music, like a puzzle without a solution. The essence that resides within things lies behind their external manifestations; it strives to be recognized, and its custodian, once convinced by the strength of this striving, will do everything to hand over the 'key'.

I have never been sure that the things I was concerned with could be made visible only in the way I had chosen, but I have always tended to give the most difficult musical process the simplest formulation I could find. Despite its use of pre-existing forms and figures, my music is not susceptible of literary interpretation; it is direct. Only with difficulty could you find things to be read between the lines. It has just as much to offer the naïve listener as the connoisseur who can investigate and evaluate the symbols. And yet, where my music seems easily accessible and within reach, it is in fact distant, saying nothing to the average secondary-school ear, and is acceptable only in such guise; whereas where it seems closer to fashion (giving it a proximity to the everyday language of the contemporary festival) it in fact contains relatively simple things, pastorals and bucolics. Thus all my works, not only the instrumental ones but also those for the theatre, contain interim

[*128*]

6   With soloists at the premiere of the cantata *Novae de Infinito Laudes*, April 1963, Venice. Left to right in the front row: Peter Pears, Dietrich Fischer-Dieskau, Kerstin Meyer, HWH, Elisabeth Söderström, Karl Amadeus Hartmann

7   With Ingeborg Bachmann, librettist of *Der junge Lord*, during rehearsals for the premiere, Berlin, 1965

8 The British premiere of *The Bassarids*, English National Opera at the London Coliseum, 10 October 1974. Left to right: Autonoe (Josephine Barstow), Tiresias (Kenneth Woollam), Pentheus (Norman Welsby), Dionysus (Gregory Dempsey), Agave (Katherine Pring). Designed by Timothy O'Brien and Tazeena Firth, produced and conducted by HWH

9 At rehearsal in Berlin for the 1966 Salzburg premiere of *The Bassarids*. Left to right: the producer G. R. Sellner, librettists Chester Kallman and W. H. Auden, HWH

stages (*Zwischenstadien*), states of fluctuation (*Schwebezustände*), things that are fleeting, serious, transient, still to come, or which have to do with recollection, anticipation, and dialectical drama.

The work of every composer, however discontinuous it may seem on superficial investigation or when sustained study is impossible, contains a continuous development, a growth which is enriched and transformed by ever new influences from outside and ever new discoveries from within.

# Instrumental Composition*

The significance of chamber music is that in dealing with the intimate it can attain to the ineffable. Chamber music conceives itself as a world of sound that has external boundaries but no internal ones. It is music to reflect upon and develop with one's own thoughts, to a far greater extent than that heard in large concert halls and opera houses, which must aim at more direct effects than music that is in fact addressed only to the players, and demands much practice and patient rehearsal. Since the time that chamber music has been written for distinguished virtuosi instead of distinguished dilettantes, it has generally been hard to play, often reaching the limits of what can be performed. This suggests that difficult intellectual conceptions are also difficult to play. But it does not mean that one should permanently and without hesitation set extreme problems for instrumental technique. On the contrary, one should not overlook that for instance in Mozart's instrumental music, or in Verdi's treatment of the singing voice, today there are still problems of interpretation that make prodigious demands on the performer, and in some cases cannot be solved and overcome. One must beware of thinking that performers, spurred on by the composer's demands, can constantly reach new levels of technical achievement. There are limits to feats of skill, beyond which lie the realms of nonsense. Everything is quite difficult enough as it is, and what is simple actually comes hardest.

Throughout my instrumental compositions there are alternations between counterpoint, and *cantabilità* supported by chords.

---

* 'Über Instrumentalkomposition.' Second part of a lecture at the Technische Universität, Berlin, 28 January 1963. *Essays* 1964.

## Instrumental Composition

Certain characteristics, first found in *Apollo et Hyazinthus*, have been developed from one piece to the next; in the chamber works the counterpoint is naturally more complex, but such orchestral works as *Sinfonische Etüden* and *Antifone* are also full of it. In other places, for instance in *Fünf neapolitanische Lieder* and *Nachtstücke und Arien*, the cantabile element dominates and counterpoint is avoided, but without the 'thematic work' (the development of the piece out of motivic nuclei) coming to an end for that reason. The constant alternation between contrapuntal and cantabile pieces (a polyphonic North German temperament in the *arioso* South) could be interpreted as indecisiveness, but also as an artistic means of clarifying tension and resolution, rigour and effortlessness, brightness and darkness; as something theatrical, perhaps even as the intention to interweave things that are irreconcilable. There is no attempt at synthesis. The resulting frictions produce a dramatic effect which differs from work to work.

Everything tends towards theatre, and returns again from it. The proximity is visible in my orchestral pieces, although the characteristics of certain symphonic traditions are not lost sight of. With the development of personal means of expression, formulations become more concise, and the transmutation of the conventional is more easily achieved. Hitherto my orchestral pieces have always been planned as symphonies or embryonic symphonies. Works such as *Quattro Poemi*, *Antifone*, *Nachtstücke und Arien* and *Ode an den Westwind* each incorporate different formal experiments in the greatest Central European form of instrumental music, the sonata. My first venture in this direction, the First Symphony (1947), was a complete failure. I have now made a new version, rearranging the material and attempting to reconstruct what I wanted at the time, like a teacher helpfully correcting his pupil. The Second and the Third Symphony, both in three movements and written in 1948 and 1949, have more in common with the sinfonia of pre-classicism than with the nineteenth century; they contain chaconnes, *ostinati*, *ariosi*. The Second is serious and dark; the Third brighter, more dance-like, hectic. In the Fourth Symphony, written in 1955, the involvement with traditional form can be detected clearly. It contains five movements in one: an overture, in which the material for the whole work is prepared, followed by a sonata, variations, a scherzo-like movement in A-B-A form, and a rondo finale. It was originally conceived as an end to the second act of *König Hirsch*, but I later extracted it, and incorporated the vocal parts, as Alban Berg did in his Symphonic Suite from *Lulu*. In the Fifth Symphony (1962) the first movement is a further essay in sonata form; the second is a kind of song with variations; the finale (*moto perpetuo*) could be regarded as a rondo, but is really a set of thirty-two variations on the *arioso* of the second movement.

These five orchestral pieces that have been termed symphonies are essays in those great forms which our tradition has taught us to regard as vessels for the supreme achievements of absolute music. Now, as we know (and yet do not wish to know how gladly people insist on this statement), these vessels are broken. The expansive power of late Romanticism burst them open. For fifty years and more the symphony, as understood by the nineteenth century, has no longer existed. Between Stravinsky and Webern everything that still passes itself off as a symphony seems either a replica, an obituary, or an echo. It is as if today's musical language were no longer master of the old forms, or as if the old forms no longer possessed mastery over the new language. However this may be, I have not allowed myself to be pessimistic. Mahler's *adieux* were to his own lyre, not to the symphony as such. We may develop the line of thought of his music, for above and beyond its incontestable necrological qualities, it contains many new starting-points, challenges and stimuli.

It is the nature of every artist to create his own picture of things, to contrive his own world, without regard to the facts, *mores* and fashions outside that world. It is only by ignoring or by transforming such circumstances into images that reach his imagination, by reversing, reinterpreting and renaming, that it becomes possible for him to respond to his environment. His world is filled with freely invented categories.

In my world the old forms are striving to regain significance, even where the music's new sounds scarcely, or no longer, permit them to come to the surface. If it is true that strength of emotion, the only thing that can master these forms, is not sufficiently present in modern man, and even if it has been shown that the constructive capacity and tonal quality of contemporary music will produce only mirages of these forms, nevertheless they enable me—in the light of such impoverishment—to portray things that make up my world. In my world Mercury and Jupiter, Virgil, fauns, harlequins, tritons, Leonce, Touchstone, Hamlet and Gloucester raise their voices and wish to become visible. Old forms seem to me, as it were, like classical ideals of beauty, no longer attainable but still visible in the far distance, stirring memory like dreams; but the path towards them is filled with the age's greatest darkness and is the most difficult and the most impossible. To me it seems the only folly worth living for.

# Der junge Lord
## (1) The Making of an *Opera Buffa*<sup></sup>*

There's as much to be said about an *opera buffa* as about an *opera seria*, and finding opera subjects is easy, though finding libretti that can be set to music is much harder. When I felt like writing a comic opera, I in fact wanted to set Shakespeare's *Love's Labour's Lost*, and had asked Ingeborg Bachmann to adapt the text for me. It was only gradually—months afterwards—that I managed to get it out of her that she was not exactly thrilled by the idea of this Shakespeare adaptation, and so I saw all my hopes for realizing my dream disappear. We spent a not particularly cheerful evening together, with abandoned projects all around us. The right note had been struck for the composition of an elegy. Yet the next morning she suggested an original theme to me—after a parable by Wilhelm Hauff—'Der junge Engländer' himself, and I accepted the subject straight away and with the greatest joy. My joy was dimmed only by the fact that I suspected I should have to wait a couple of years at least for Bachmann's promised libretto.

The only solution was brute force: I took her with me to my house in Castelgandolfo, locked her in a room, took away the key, and released the prisoner (and allowed her to eat) only when she had fulfilled her quota for the day. Escape attempts to Roman couturiers were foiled; I even saw an attack of toothache as merely a

---

* 'Der Einzelgänger' (The Loner). From an interview with Klaus Geitel on the occasion of the premiere of *Der junge Lord*, 7 April 1965, at the Deutsche Oper, Berlin, first published in *Die Welt*, 2 April 1965.

'flight into illness', and though I did take the prisoner to the dentist, I supervised the treatment, which on my instruction had to be started and completed at once. The door immediately closed again behind my poetess—and six weeks later the libretto was ready. There were only a few minor changes and embellishments later.

There comes a time in life when the existence of comedy can no longer be denied. After *Elegy for Young Lovers* I wrote the (fairly optimistic) Giordano Bruno cantata *Laudes*, followed, however, by the hard and gloomy Fifth Symphony, and a series of rather mournful pieces: the *Ariosi*, the *Lucy Escott Variations*, and the cantatas *Being Beauteous* and *Fiaba Estrema*. They became ever more slender, filamental in texture. Pedal notes were more and more rigorously excluded. The music was becoming increasingly transparent. The path toward *opera buffa* was clear.

Operatic models I had in mind while working on *Der junge Lord* included the first finale of *The Barber of Seville* and the end of the second act of *Figaro*, but above all Mozart's *Così fan tutte*. As luck would have it, the day before I started composing I went to the West Berlin opera and heard *Die Entführung aus dem Serail* conducted by Karl Böhm. I had already worked out in my head the instrumentation for my new opera, but now, as I bent forward and looked down into the pit, I saw the extraordinary economy of orchestration that had sufficed Mozart: pairs of woodwind, horns and trumpets, and a little Turkish janissary percussion.

I was so delighted to have all this before my eyes again—for of course I know *Entführung* quite well—that I immediately denied myself any extravagances. I wanted to manage without the bass clarinet, alto flute, double bassoon, and modern percussion. The 'classical' instrumentation that I chose in the end is an indication of the type of discipline to which my new opera is subjected.

In the music of the Vienna School there is nothing truly lighthearted. This in the first place is probably the result of these composers' sense of mission, of the post-Wagnerian High Romantic Spiritual World in which gaiety—to say nothing of humour—was regarded as quite out of place. It is true that there are moments of heavy comedy and persiflage in Berg's *Lulu*, but not gaiety.

Stravinsky almost alone, it seems to me, managed to bring out some humour in twentieth-century music.

It would take a doctoral dissertation to investigate whether the decline of comic opera can be traced back to the turning away from traditional tonality. In my view this turning away conjures up a feeling of *angoisse*, in all its imaginable variants; an indeterminate anxiety, which is the opposite of gaiety. This kind of composing permits one to achieve an extraordinary feeling of musical levitation; a certain beauty is also peculiar to it, but robustly human appeal, on which the impact of humour rests, is denied it. If it *is* used in humorous context, its sphere is that of travesty and parody, at best.

In my works for the theatre I have therefore never completely left tonality, not even in the earliest ones. My music is nourished by just this state of tension: the abandonment of traditional tonality and the return to it. Rather like tensing a bow, it is here a kind of 'tensing the ear'. This is why I also think that one would be bidding a final farewell to music if one were completely to sacrifice tonality, with which just as much can still be expressed as in the past: that is to say, everything.

The gaiety of *Der junge Lord* does not lie in the parody of old forms but in the ciphers of the music, which resists the temptation to play on quotations from Rossini, Mozart, or the cheerful minor masters of the nineteenth century. It is music without nudges or winks. It does not play the coquette with connoisseurs. Indeed, had I not worked my way through the pieces that I had written since *Elegy for Young Lovers*, I might perhaps have ended up with a parody of a nineteenth-century *opera buffa*, and used at second hand the obvious, conventional comic techniques. But now the musical material flowed as if of its own accord towards the sound world of comic opera.

The greatest amusement of *opera buffa* is always to be found in the ensembles. That is why this opera has only one aria, for soprano, and only one duet; all the other numbers are allegros for more than two voices. *Der junge Lord* is thus a genuine ensemble opera, a piece for singing ensembles.

## Der junge Lord: (1) The Making of an Opera Buffa

My first comic opera fits in with its serious predecessors because there are always 'loners' at the centre of my operas, and this is true of *Der junge Lord*. The simpleton Armand was swept into the hurly-burly of *Boulevard Solitude*; 'König Hirsch' went back into the forest; the Prince of Homburg and Mittenhofer in *Elegy* created their own worlds too. *Der junge Lord* has two central figures: old Sir Edgar, the mute 'ringmaster'; and young Luise, for whom there is no happy ending even at the close of this comic opera.

I am not worried that the opera's chosen Biedermeier theme may be criticized as reactionary. Such criticism would strike me as superficial. After all, an opera is a musical form of expression, as the symphony or a piece of chamber music is. The stage is only the opened eye of the score. Besides, a strongly critical and satirical trait can of course be found in the story of *Der junge Lord*. Here, in Biedermeier Hülsdorf-Gotha, English eccentricity is cheered and imitated just as the Beatles are today, or to turn to another field, the artistic gimmicks with which the cultural scene now likes to intoxicate itself. A lack of individuality always aims at extremes. To direct one's attacks at such extremism, in whatever guise it appears, is perhaps a fruitful and timely task—above all in an *opera buffa*.

# Der junge Lord
## (2) The Spectre of Mendacity*

It becomes less and less possible for me to use language to describe and explain my work or express thoughts and feelings, as music becomes more and more my very life, determining it and permeating it; music says everything better than the words I can find, and when another person's language comes into play and makes its contribution, as in the case of opera, and the stage makes everything stand out more clearly, I become really confused when I ponder what useful commentaries I could add, because they are basically all things that a third party, an outsider with a clear mind and more or less impartial, can ascertain, determine and point out. For instance, why the Vienna and Post-Expressionist School—to be more precise the one that works with the emancipated twelve semitones—has no way of expressing gaiety (except involuntarily); or to what extent parody is not to be confused with gaiety, being alien, indeed hostile, to the essence of *opera buffa*; or whether there really is sad music and, in contrast, cheerful music; or what it is that makes people cry and what makes them cheerful and lighthearted. Asking finally whether in this specific case the *allegria* of *Der junge Lord* has a more serious and sad quality than the melancholies of earlier operas, or which the *espressioni* are that this score tries to convey, and how much darkness and fear is necessary in life to stop one from joking and in consequence make an attempt on *opera*

* 'Über *Der junge Lord*' (1965, 1972). Programme note to the Frankfurt production, 1972.

[*138*]

*buffa*; and what this work is trying to accomplish (since private motives can be ignored), or whether with it or through it, and in a spirit of conciliation, I have been able to conjure up a characteristically German landscape in the manner of Heine's 'Heimkehr':

| | |
|---|---|
| *Am alten grauen Turme* | By the old grey tower |
| *Ein Schilderhäuschen steht;* | There stands a sentry-box; |
| *Ein rotgeröckter Bursche* | A fellow in a red tunic |
| *Dort auf und nieder geht.* | Marches up and down. |
| *Er spielt mit seiner Flinte,* | He plays with his musket, |
| *Die funkelt im Sonnenrot,* | Which gleams in the red sunset, |
| *Er präsentiert und* | He presents and shoulders |
|   *schultert—* |   arms— |
| *Ich wollte, er schöss mich tot.* | I wish he would shoot me dead. |

Collages, mixtures, alienation. The lovers embrace for the first time to the cry of pain of a tortured animal which later will destroy their lives. The melismata and chords that symbolize torture are subsequently associated with quotations from Goethe. Luise sings her confession of infidelity (in the fifth scene) on these very melismata. At the end of the work these notes, when they return for the last time (from the mouth of the alleged Lord Barrat as he departs), appear like hurricane lamps that perhaps bring comfort, or irreconciliation, from the other side of the swamp. Things can be found that are hostile, uncanny, and date from childhood experiences, from my generation's youthful memories: the adults, thin and angular, upright and fat, inspiring fear with their punishments, irrational principles, persecution. A world of canes. The wasteland of piano lessons, which were supposed to implant a petty-bourgeois consciousness, and whose clichés have eaten into every counterpoint, causing mildew and rust.

There is so much that is deathly in this *Gemütlichkeit* (cosiness). I quote Mahler, appeal to him. To define my characters I call to mind the music that was in fashion in their day. It comes out German. Further reminiscences, mostly sad things that sound cheerful. The racist children's rhyme in the fourth scene was heard and noted down by Karl Kraus in Vienna. Sometimes tonality is established directly and 'unbroken'—in the love-duet of the fourth scene and the passacaglia at the beginning of the sixth—but again not entirely: love is a mistake, is already betrayed, and in the sixth scene deception and error are beyond cure. The whole thing develops as though controlled by strings, a puppet play, but not entirely. We no longer feel at home or know our way around; we get lost. Guilt and *Polizeiangst* (fear of the police) are written into the score. The memories I love are also to be found in this *marché aux puces*: I am making fun, but not entirely.

In this staging (the first time that I have produced this opera) I am trying to make visible what was intended by this type of composing. What I had visualized while writing the music should be clearly shown, at least at some points, and perhaps even which motives, feelings and memories had an influence on it.

The essential subject of this work is: mendacity. It is born of unsatisfied curiosity, frustrated material hopes, provincial pretentiousness and wounded vanity. It spreads as rumours do (in the *entr'acte* between the second and third scene) and perverts and lays bare to an increasing extent the characters and their musical material. This is the source of the reactions of the opposed milieu (the world of the Englishman) which, by means of a 'scientific' experiment, sets itself against lying and the aggression that comes in its wake. The musical ambiance of the Englishman develops in parallel, gains ground (from the fifth scene on) and opposes that of Hülsdorf-Gotha, ultimately to destroy it. At the close, as soon as the foreigners have left the scene, the whole work falls back into that conventionality and pedantry with which the opera had begun. Nothing has been learned, so it seems; nothing has changed. It was only an incident. There was, as Lenz would have said 'kein geistiger Mutwille' (no spiritual mischief), there were only 'körperliche Zufälle' (physical accidents). But perhaps not entirely.

## *Der junge Lord*
## (3) Hints on Staging<sup>*</sup>

Rome, 22 February 1973

Dear Professor Pscherer,

Some days ago I received a letter from your chief dramatic adviser. In connection with it I should like to take this opportunity of writing you a few lines about *Der junge Lord*. I am extremely pleased that the work is at last being put on in Munich, almost ten years after its premiere, and I am looking forward to the first night. So I would simply like to say one or two things, which in fact concern the conductor rather than the producer.

The citizens of Hülsdorf-Gotha should not be seen as wealthy provincials. The people are thin, somewhat shivering, poorish (impoverished or not yet wealthy, as the case may be). They have a certain amount of bodily hunger, for instance for change, and a great deal of spiritual hunger, also for change, but in addition for something that is not clear to them; it is almost the romantic yearning of that era, and is revealed to them in the extravagant milieu of Sir Edgar. They think that this is beauty, the object of their ardent yearning. So for them the fifth scene is fulfilment, to say nothing of the sixth scene, where everything becomes German and evil beyond measure. It should also be clear to the audience that Sir Edgar's world, where so much friendliness, composure, *serenità*, equality and sophistication prevail (in other words self-evident elegance, fine materials, good food, good manners and eccentricity),

* '*Der junge Lord* 1973—Brief an Kurt Pscherer.' (Pscherer was intendant of the Theater am Gärtnerplatz in Munich.) First published in *Musik und Politik* 1976.

must seem the 'ultimate' to the citizens of Hülsdorf-Gotha, because it has everything that Hülsdorf-Gotha has not; and the audience, too, should see Sir Edgar, his entourage, the things he travels with, and later his rooms and even the circus, as something wonderful. It is only then that the fuse of the drama can be lit.

The contrast can and must emerge clearly in the music too. The scenes in Hülsdorf-Gotha must be played in a coarse and rustic fashion—very much so—and those with Sir Edgar elegantly and silkily. (A third element, the music for Luise and Wilhelm in the first scene, and the duet of the fourth scene, must sound tragic and painful.) It is essential that the music should not be played as *buffa*, nor should it be staged in that way, but rather as *opéra comique* (and thus *not* like Lortzing), and indeed in a demonic, aggressive or evil manner. The music owes a great deal to Mahler (and quotes his 'Fourth' several times for this reason), and mostly comprises moods of malaise—uncanny, bitter, as in its model. The virtuoso and bravura elements of the instrumentation should not mislead the conductor about what underlies them. (Please tell him that the big chaconne at the beginning of the sixth scene must not drag, and that the tempo should fluctuate according to the emotion. The whole very agitated, the vocal line flexible.)

Everything sharp, straightforward, not droll. This Biedermeier is hungry, has fleas, TB; even the Baroness can offer only a dry biscuit and half a cup of weak tea. People are careful with firewood. Their coats are thin. The mayor may have a fur collar, but it is badly moth-eaten. *Vous comprenez?* It is thus that the prosperity and sophistication and festive nature of Sir Edgar and his milieu come to seem socially inhumane, and that the piece acquires its dramatic pungency.

Good luck with the production, and best wishes.

# The Bassarids
## (1) Tradition and Cultural Heritage*

During the 1962 Glyndebourne rehearsals for the British premiere of *Elegy for Young Lovers*, W. H. Auden and Chester Kallman spoke to me for the first time about *The Bacchae* of Euripides. But unfortunately they pronounced the Greek title in such a peculiar way that I did not understand it—and I was too embarrassed to ask them to repeat the word. When I was back in Rome again (almost a year had passed), I eventually flicked through an edition of the tragedies of Euripides and was immediately taken by the dramatic power of the work.

I was not bothered by the fact that *The Bacchae* had already twice been set as an opera, nor had I been bothered, while writing *Boulevard Solitude*, that the Manon Lescaut theme had already been treated by Massenet and by Puccini. In fact I knew neither Egon Wellesz's *Bacchantinnen* (1931) nor Federico Ghedini's *Le Bacchanti* (1948). An obstacle might perhaps have been Richard Strauss's *Elektra*, which stands like a road-block in the way of all composers who approach Greek tragedy.

Auden and Kallman agreed to write the libretto for me on one harsh condition. Auden forced me to listen to *Götterdämmerung*, sent me to the Vienna State Opera for this purpose, and sent Kallman along too, to make sure I really sat through it right to the end. Just as Auden, that experienced old pedagogue, had led

---

* 'Tradition und Kulturerbe.' From an interview with Klaus Geitel on the occasion of the premiere of *Die Bassariden*, 6 August 1966, Salzburg, first published in *Die Welt*, 13 July 1966.

Stravinsky to the peak of classicism with the libretto for *The Rake's Progress*, so too he wanted to squeeze things out of me that he had already detected in other pieces of mine, for instance my Fifth Symphony, such as the way the music 'forgets itself' at certain moments, the stripping away of all stylistic apparel, the crude shamelessness of the musical statement. To make sure I got the point, Auden insisted I listened to *Götterdämmerung*.

I had always avoided Wagner's work out of a certain antipathy. Auden found this quite unnecessary. Of course I am well aware what Wagner signifies, wherein his greatness lies; *Tristan*, which I have never seen, although I have studied the score in detail, has subsequently become a kind of bible for me. But now Auden wanted me to overcome my dislike for Wagner, and just as a pupil passively bends to the will of his mentor I yielded to him and sat through *Götterdämmerung*—quite joylessly. After this, in May 1963, we had a second meeting about *The Bassarids*. At the end of August, completely unexpectedly, I received the finished libretto. I read it with the highest admiration for Auden's and Kallman's work—and then laid it aside, even though *Der junge Lord* was not even planned then.

I was prevented from starting work on *The Bassarids* straight away by the feeling that I still had to grow into it. Reading the libretto came at a time when I was beginning to discover the great forms of nineteenth-century symphonic music (and *Götterdämmerung*, of course, had made its impact, too). I was also gathering valuable new experiences as a conductor. Conducting helped me on. It was, as it were, a matter of physically gauging the proportions, just as one measures out a terrain, one's own territory, with one's feet. I conducted various performances of Schubert's Great C Major Symphony, Brahms's Second Piano Concerto (with Claudio Arrau), and Mahler's First Symphony. This physical experience of the orchestra, through sound, was valuable. To put it crudely, it was a question of physically kneading the material, to make it pliable for my own work. It was a time during which my admiration for the work of Mahler was translated into concrete action.

# The Bassarids: (1) Tradition and Cultural Heritage

If there are signs of this admiration in the score of *The Bassarids*, then in the sense that I have already suggested, it is that with Mahler too there occurs a self-forgetting; there too conformity to a sham civilization is cast aside. In my eyes this is such a significant achievement that I really don't understand why even some of his admirers feel the need to defend these eruptions into an immense new freedom, almost as if they were defending the acts of a musical rapist. I believe that the road from Wagner's *Tristan* to Mahler and Schoenberg is far from finished, and with *The Bassarids* I have tried to go further along it. I am not prepared to relinquish what the centuries have passed on to us. On the contrary; 'One must also know how to inherit; inheriting, that, ultimately, is culture.' That was Thomas Mann's view, and I willingly subscribe to it.

One of the most important things for which I should like my music to be known is the vulnerability of its sounds—a fact too frequently forgotten. Also, an awareness of the symbolic quality of music that has passed into history. Anybody who consciously wants to free himself from it falls into an absurd nothingness where there are no precedents. He is committing an intellectual *lapsus*, and music takes its revenge by summoning up undesired associations. Music makes fun, as it were, of the musician. It passes him by.

With *The Bassarids* I am now pushing forward to a through-composed large-scale form of opera. But this form, too, follows old rules: those of the four-movement symphony, which structure the single act of *The Bassarids*. A sonata movement is followed by a scherzo—a series of bacchanalian dances with a calm vocal ensemble as trio. The third movement is an adagio with fugue, interrupted by an intermezzo—the satyr play, an opera within the opera; the fourth, with its Ash Wednesday mood, is a passacaglia.

It may be unfashionable to continue musical traditions in this way, but with Goethe under my pillow, I'm not going to lose any sleep about the possibility of being accused of eclecticism. Goethe's definition ran: 'An eclectic . . . is anyone who, from that which surrounds him, from that which occurs around him, takes what corresponds to his nature.' If you wanted to do so, you could count Bach, Mozart, Verdi, Wagner, Mahler and Stravinsky as eclectics, and then I would be happy to be considered an eclectic, too. But Goethe goes on: 'Of a different order is that spiritlessness that, from lack of all inner determination, like a jackdaw, brings back to its nest anything that happens to be offered from whatever side, and thereby, as something originally dead, cuts itself off completely from a living whole.' Well—in the light of that, everyone can examine himself to see whether or not he qualifies as an ugly eclectic. But that is not something that concerns me. I prefer composing.

# The Bassarids
## (2) Psychology in Music*

*The Bacchae*, the tragedy by Euripides on which Auden and Kallman based their libretto, treats the mother-son theme against the background of a religious power-struggle. My sympathies could lie neither only with Pentheus, nor only with Dionysus. For me the experiential pivot lay in the years of preparation of two musical worlds, that of Pentheus and that of Dionysus, which are let loose on one another and finally become one. In each person there is a Pentheus and a Dionysus. In Erich Neumann's *The Origins and History of Consciousness*, one of the most important modern studies of myth, intimately related to psychology, we read:

Pentheus belongs (similarly) to those who resist, but are not yet capable of a liberatory heroic deed. It is Bacchus Dionysus whom he resists, but as his fate and his sin show, here too the real enemy is the terrible figure of the Great Mother. It is well known that Dionysus belongs to the orgiastic realm of the Great Mother and her son-lover Osiris, Adonis, Tamuz. The problems and reinterpretations of the figure of Semele, the mother of Dionysus, need not concern us here. Bachofen associates Dionysus with the Great Mother, and modern scholarship supports him.

At Delphi Dionysus is worshipped as an infant or a *putto* in the

* 'Tiefenpsychologie in der Musik.' From an interview with Horst Georges on the occasion of the German premiere of *Die Bassariden*, 28 September 1966, Berlin, first published in *Opern-Journal der Deutschen Oper Berlin*, September 1966.

corn-hopper. It is an earth cult, with the moon goddess Semele as earth mother. Since he originates from Thrace and settles in Asia Minor, fusing with the Magna Mater cult there, he probably perpetuates a universal early cult of the original pre-Greek religion.

The heroic King Pentheus, proud of his reason, and with his mother the closest relative of Dionysus, advances towards the orgies and is overwhelmed by the orgiastic power of Dionysus. Pentheus suffers the fate of all victims of the Great Mother; he goes mad, and comes to the orgies in women's clothing, where he is torn to pieces by his own mother, who in a fit of madness takes him for a lion. The fact that she triumphantly carries his head home with her is a residue of the castration that originally occurred, in addition to the dismemberment of the body. Contrary to her own consciousness, the mother thereby becomes the figure of the Great Mother; the son, despite the resistance of his ego, becomes her son-lover. Madness, women's clothing, transformation into animals, dismemberment and castration, the archetypal fate, are fulfilled in them.

I do not think that one can speak of the archetypal figures being 'alienated' by Auden and Kallman in the Brechtian sense, only because they are allotted to various periods between antiquity and the *belle époque*; one should rather speak of clarification, explanation. What has occurred is an interpretation—resting moreover on a Christian world view—of Euripides' play, by laying bare the primal mythical motifs it contains. Of course, in the process all elements come to the integument of contemporary problems: the discoveries of Freud, Adler and especially Jung play a part, not only in the diversely elaborated mother-son theme, but also in tension between Dionysus and Pentheus themselves. The timelessness of the themes requires no alienation but, at most, to be brought up to date. Finally, this is the first time that psychology plays such a conscious and decisive part in a music drama of mine. And yet everything in this opera is the way it is, the way one sees it and hears it. Let those who have eyes, see; those who have ears, hear.

In the introduction to the Italian edition of Auden's works Aurora Ciliberti says: 'Culture is for Auden not scholasticism, but a real knowledge of the facts; its core is faith; it is not something one wears like a piece of jewelry, but what makes a human being.' Every sort of Papageno likes complaining about 'prodigal richness of material' when his mental powers are not sufficient to cope with it, and to understand it. Furthermore, the stage communicates to every person what he deserves, what he is entitled to. Goethe:

*Wer nicht von dreitausend Jahren*
*Sich weiss Rechenschaft zu geben,*
*Bleib im Dunkeln unerfahren,*
*Mag von Tag zu Tage leben.*

(Whoever is not able to settle his acccount with three thousand years of history, let him stay without experience in the dark, may he live from day to day.)

It has struck me that many people are still clinging to the ideal of the kind of modern theatre they knew in their youth, for which they perhaps fought doggedly and respectably. But please let us not forget that in the meantime half a century has gone by, and that the 'modern theatre' (whatever that may mean; who in fact defines it, ordains it, gives it its name?) looks different today from forty years ago, and from twenty years ago. That applies also to many kinds of music which in some quarters are still taken to be modern, although generations have passed them by. The charm and the fascination of the theatre lie precisely in the multitude of possibilities with which it can reflect life in ever new shapes and forms. That neither motor cars nor aeroplanes appear in this opera may strike some people as unmodern, but an attentive reader will perhaps be compensated by the insights of modern scholarship contained in the libretto. This work is a tragedy, a funeral symphony, a requiem (ending with a gloria). Its goal is truth, and truth is serious, difficult and cruel— not culinary.

Neither 'irony' (against which there is nothing to be said) nor 'alienation' are the object of my musical interest. The piece contains neither visual nor musical alienation effects, nor anything ironic or parodistic. Everything is meant to be taken as it is.

A detailed study of the score would make the motivic work and the interweaving of themes clear to anyone interested, but a knowledge of such details is not an absolute prerequisite for understanding the opera. As a matter of fact I think that the architecture of the music fulfils its function directly, more so than the listener is conscious of, even at those points where the full sum of its expressions, directions and modes does come over all at once. For instance, even at a first hearing, the listener will surely perceive the opposition between the Pentheus and Dionysus themes, and the gradual dominance of the latter, until the end, when it has eliminated everything else. As everybody knows, listening to music only once is in any case insufficient evidence on which to base a comprehensive verdict. A valuable theatre and concert-goer is the person who takes the trouble (as good breeding once demanded) to absorb a new work slowly by reading the libretto beforehand and by hearing it several times.

Fundamental human and existential problems give rise to music. For me, theatre music has to be just as concentrated and 'demanding' as absolute music, and the events on stage must derive from the music and gain their weight and their expression through the music; indeed the music must predetermine the colour scale of the décor and the movements of the production. In this respect I am in accord with the theatrical conceptions of Mozart and Verdi, and in opposition to those where music has been allotted a decorative, culinary function as accompaniment. Each inner impulse, all atmosphere, every circumstance, even every physical movement is prefigured in the orchestra; the music 'knows' what is going on in the visual and scenic dimension, for the scenic is its visual aspect.

It was not without consternation that I noticed that my technique, which aimed at occasionally steering the listener towards the desired direction and mode of expression, by means of quotations that he would recognize (especially at moments of dramatic and emotional significance), has been taken by certain aesthetes to be 'ironic' in intent. As this is an elementary misunderstanding, I would like to clear it up: in *The Bassarids* there are four quotations from works by Johann Sebastian Bach, each consisting of a few notes or chords.

## The Bassarids: (2) Psychology in Music

At the points where they occur, the music attempts to establish landmarks: associations with the parallels between Dionysus and Christ, Pentheus and Adonis, and with the mythical martyrdom that all four have in common. This technique of quotation can be found to a high degree in Mahler's works; it also occurs in the classical masters, albeit not to the same conscious and psychologizing extent as with Mahler, from whose Fifth Symphony—as if to invoke him—I have paraphrased two figures at the central point of my opera, the duet between Pentheus and Dionysus. Out of 150 minutes of music in *The Bassarids*, 15 seconds are taken up by these quotations.

# The Bassarids
## (3) Symphony in One Act<sup></sup>*

I have on occasion said that music drama interests me because for me music is a language that people have not yet mastered, and about which they do not yet know enough. Today there is a terrible danger, as people are bombarded with music everywhere they go, that this situation will harden into a kind of paralysis of the ear and the organs of sound perception. So instead of the human psyche and intellect being developed to understand music as language—as a part of the sign-system of our civilization—there is a total idiotization, an impoverishment of the possibilities of perceiving the true meaning of musical signs. A major part of my efforts is concerned with communicating the language of music as such, and as a language that comes from the history of our civilization, that has an origin, a present and a past, and will have a future for which we, the composers, are responsible. This sense of responsibility is one of the reasons why from time to time I give up composing for over six weeks, and change my way of life, living in a strange town and doing nothing except work as a producer in theatres with singers, trying to help audiences understand music properly, with the help of gesture, mime, familiar words (those of everyday speech). That is why I am so dismayed when I see opera staged by drama producers who cannot read a score, where the music is either ignored or regarded as a distraction, where the aim appears to be not

* 'Komponist als Interpret—Gegen die "Materialdisziplin".' From an interview with Klaus Schultz on the occasion of the Frankfurt production of *The Bassarids*, published in *Frankfurter Opernhefte*, 10 May 1975.

to interpret music in scenic terms, but to produce theatrical effects with musical accompaniment—the opposite of what *I* am engaged in.

Quotations play a definite role in my music, but they don't appear in quotation marks as the music quoted and remembered is assimilated into my own musical language. Let me begin with the quotation from the *St Matthew Passion* in *The Bassarids*. This is one that Auden had asked me to make. It appears at the end of the intermezzo, when the fun is over, and one is suddenly made to realize the fact that Adonis is being torn to pieces by Mars on Mount Lebanon has links with Pentheus' similar fate, so the same Bach sounds come again towards the end of the opera when Pentheus' body is brought on. Thus Auden presumably wanted to do what I have also often done in my instrumental music: to employ quotations at certain points as signposts, as guides for thought, which make the listener hear and think in the right direction. Quotation is a factor in the strategy of my work; my point of departure is that music is a language. Literature has a tradition in which ideas, sentences, words of past writers are translated to the present, where they rise up again in a new light and acquire new connotations. This kind of continuity, this kind of historical thinking, which is taken for granted in literature, has been bitterly opposed in music during the last thirty years. It is very close to my thinking. It preoccupies me, and is the reason why music seems to me still a young means of communication, pregnant with possibilities. I think that musicians can and must learn from poets. The composer cannot spend all his time destroying language instead of developing it dialectically.

It is no accident that my *Tristan* contains a quotation from Brahms's First Symphony; it is no accident that it is built on a world of sound that came into existence in Wagner's prelude to *Tristan*, and about which the last word has by no means yet been said. The entry of Brahms's C minor has a brutal impact here; it frightens and injures the ear and the psyche as if with terrifying dissonances. My relationship to quotation derives from Mahler and Berg, two composers who also have quite a lot to say to one another. Berg saw himself as a Mahlerian, as continuing Mahler's tradition. Berg is the only affinity I have to the Vienna School, to dodecaphony and twelve-note technique. I can understand dodecaphony in Berg's sense, in other words as a language, and never quite in the sense of Webern or Schoenberg, where for me it remains theory, grammar, esotericism perhaps; a bourgeois self-affirmation.

Webern's conception of music and his taste are elements of a home-spun musical thinking, in contrast with that of such men as Mahler and Berg, which opened different doors and linked music more inwardly with life, not least because they looked on their age with their senses open and therefore reflected its intellectual and political tendencies with sensitivity and awareness. This is specifically expressed in the fact that with Mahler and Berg music becomes critical, self-critical; it calls music in question, and questions itself, whereas with Webern it is uncritically affirmative. Music in a state of decomposition is brought back as a state of purity there as if nothing had happened; as if there were no class struggle, no imperialism, no wars, as if society were in order; as though everything were as untouched as blades of grass high in the Alps.

We know from history that it happens only rarely that the artist is an exemplary person apart from his work. According to the orthodox bourgeois conception, madness, disease, extravagance and political stupidity seem to be indispensable aids in the creation of art. I envisage as my utopia, and it is also that of my friends, that one day this ideological war memorial will have disappeared from the streets and squares, and that music, humanity and society will come together in a moral unity, in which subjective reactions to the world around us can be a positive response, and no longer an escape into monologues, enigmas and 'pure' form.

There are young composers who say to me that their music is not going to be played, that they will always have failures and never success. But, they say, it's the material that forces them to write these failures; the material demands it. That is a sad and grotesque situation. The artist must have his material freely at his disposal. The alternative is enslavement, fetishization. There is no such thing as the discipline of material. One of the reasons why I haven't been to Darmstadt since 1955 is that I have known Boulez to reject scores by young composers because they were not written *à la manière de* Webern. And I have seen young Viennese, who otherwise composed in the style of Orff, travel to Darmstadt, following the contemporary trend, and writing twelve-note pieces on the train—the ink still wet when they arrived in Darmstadt—which were then received favourably and with interest by Boulez.

Questions of form are not exclusively questions of style. The forms of music have grown up with society and are connected with our culture, in other words with something that goes beyond problems of style. They are archetypes of our civilization—especially in literature. One can explain why fugues exist, and also why they can no longer be written today. (Because the tonal system, from which a fugue derives its tensions, no longer works. There are also twelve-note fugues, which are truly formalistic; an old form is reproduced, without the tension of the material that once made such a fugue dramatically effective and alive.)

In literature certain forms, modes and metres have existed for centuries; sonnets are still written today. Forms in art are in fact also forms of behaviour as between people—modes of communication. They are connected not so much with style as with possibilities of making yourself understood. I believe that you have to realize this, to understand that discussion about forms is unproductive when conducted abstractly and not dictated by the necessity constantly to reinterpret art as a mode of communication. How often has it been said that the novel is *passé*! In the last few years we have seen an enormous renaissance of the novel, just at the moment when people were saying that literature was dead. I do not believe that it is possible to decree when a form begins or when it ends. At any moment social reality, and the demands of that reality, can show up the pointlessness of talking about forms. You can diminish or enrich the effectiveness of a form, that is all, unless we want to behave like romantic clowns, walking the tightrope of sensations, or like puppets, year after year mechanically supplying new styles, new products, new answers to the demands of the market and of fashion. But this sort of thing has nothing to do with the possibilities of creative artists who seek their truth beyond questions of style and form, and who at least surmise that in their work they must increasingly be prepared to defend culture. A period of rethinking is beginning. Art is living and essential only where it is involved with people's needs and problems. Art, in all its spiritual richness, must be conveyed from its present threatened state to a new reality.

The basic conflict in *The Bassarids* is between social repression and sexual liberation: the liberation of the individual. It shows people as individuals breaking out of a social context, as a road to freedom, as the intoxicating liberation of people who suddenly discover themselves, who release the Dionysus within themselves. On the other hand, the person who suppresses this freedom movement, officially and within himself, is the King of Thebes, a well-meaning young man, brought up by the modern philosophers of Greece, who becomes the victim of his repressed sexuality. The whole piece is simply Euripides re-read 2,400 years later, re-interpreted, with the addition of two of the most important achievements of mankind in the intervening period: Christianity, which plays a major role in this libretto and constantly emerges as a corrective to the archaic Euripides; and psychoanalysis, whose procedure is anticipated by Euripides, remarkably enough, in the dialogue between Cadmus and Agave. Then Auden and Kallman produced an ending for the work—the finale is not in the original. Euripides ends with Dionysus exiling the Theban royal family. With Auden there is the apotheosis of Dionysus, who asks Persephone to hand over his mother Semele and, his request granted, rises up with her into the sky, from where he will henceforth rule the world with her. A clear and unmistakable analogy with Christ.

# Gustav Mahler[*]

The music of Gustav Mahler already played a part in my early years as a composer: not a patriarchal or threatening role, but fraternal, corroborating. It influenced my writing to an increasing extent. Today its realism is more indispensable than ever. I believe that the essential artistic and moral decisions about the music of our century have to be made in the light of this art. Mahler's music speaks as with the voices of a thousand people; it contains the most simple formulations for the most difficult things. The conflict between Man and Nature is experienced in a new way, as it has never been portrayed and expressed before.

With the increasing distance of time, Mahler's music has lost what a quarter of a century ago still prevented many from approaching it, namely its semantic affinities with Jugendstil. With hindsight its greatness can be recognized, and two things become visible: first, that we have here a continuation of the great German symphonic tradition; and second, that music is here radically called into question. For the first time in musical history, music is interrogating itself about the reasons for its existence and about its nature. The demands it makes on itself are on a level with the age from which it originates; it is a knowing music, with the same tragic consciousness as Freud, Kafka, Musil. Its provocation lies in its love of truth and in its consequent lack of extenuation. Like all great music, it too comes from the singing and dancing of the people; but that in no sense makes it simple, no, it makes everything real, and

* 'Gustav Mahler.' Programme note for a concert at the Stuttgart Staatsoper, 26 November 1975, when the author conducted Mahler's Second Symphony.

really difficult. It contains much grief for things that have been lost, but messages for the future of mankind should also be discerned: one of them is hope; another, directed at the very essence of music itself, love. Mahler's music looks forward to a new generation of musicians and to concepts of music shaped by his own example.

# Second Piano Concerto*

In 1967, two years after *The Bassarids*, I wrote my Second Piano Concerto. Whereas the First Concerto of 1949 is compressed into a work of short duration, as if the music had no time to spare and had to express itself as quickly as possible (the score of *Boulevard Solitude* was produced shortly afterwards), in the Second Piano Concerto my musical language and its grammar are pushed towards harmonic consolidation and deepening. It is a work in which the antagonism between strict form and formlessness, compulsion and freedom, moderation and excess, is resolved in various frames of reference. One could say that it was the continuation of the *lamenti* of the finale of *The Bassarids*, transferred to instrumental music: a depiction of the destroyed city of Thebes after the triumph of the vengeful Dionysus. It also contains something of the attempts at liberation that grew up in those years, of new motives and new and different dreams. It forms a bridge from the bacchants and maenads of *The Bassarids* to the dying soldiers and workers of *The Raft of the Medusa*. The 'fantasia' of the third movement, where every traditional conception of form is abandoned, consists of a meditation on Shakespeare's sonnet, 'The expense of spirit in a waste of shame', a condemnation of the bacchanalian anti-apollonian world.

The work's three movements run without a break. The first consists of a cantabile three-part piano movement, in which the (three-fold) invention form (with cancrizan inversion) is maintained throughout the orchestral prelude, interlude and epilogue. At the very beginning certain semitone intervals can be heard that

* *Musik und Politik* 1976.

crop up again throughout the work in constantly varying colouring; they establish a relationship to the sound of Japanese Gagaku music, that stuck in my mind from when I first heard it in Tokyo in 1966. You can consider the composition as emerging from this sound, from its harsh and magical alienness and remoteness, so as to move through large circles and keep returning to its spell. The second movement has been forced into a scherzo form, consisting of a wild, violent dance. To my mind it has an evil, wicked quality, in which the smile of the Bassarids hardens into a threatening glance that promises no good. In the extended closing movement, as a result, the thoughts are constantly expressed in new shapes, in the manner of a monologue or recitative; tenderness becomes terror, misfortune, helplessness. The piano cantilena from the beginning reappears; with it the epilogue (the coda) begins, develops further, and brings the music to its provisional close.

# The Raft of the Medusa*

This is a documentary oratorio in two parts, in which the German writer, Ernst Schnabel, gives an account of the frigate Medusa, which was shipwrecked on the coast of Senegal in 1816. The text is based on a diary kept by one of the few survivors; this document was published in Paris a few months after his rescue, and was then immediately banned by the authorities, because it clearly showed that the captain, officers, government officials and priests had escaped in long-boats, leaving three hundred sailors, soldiers, women and children to their fate on an improvised raft. During this long ordeal almost all of them died.

The event gave rise to considerable outrage in France and Europe as a whole, and was one of the factors that helped to prepare the climate for the revolutions of 1848. The closing scene of the oratorio, the moment when the raft is found by a rescue ship, has also been captured in Géricault's painting of the same title. This monumental canvas, filled with pathos, may be regarded as the inspiration for the style and colour of the score.

The concert platform is divided into three sections. On one side is the choir of the 'living', and the wind instruments; their spokesman is the sailor Jean-Charles (baritone), one of the survivors. On the opposite side are the string instrumentalists, with the 'dead', whose numbers grow in the course of the performance, while those of the 'living' decrease. The 'dead' sing stanzas from the *Divina commedia*. In front of them stands Death (soprano). In the

---

* 'Das Floss der Medusa.' Introduction to the oratorio, on the occasion of the Maggio Musicale, Florence 1975. *Musik und Politik* 1976.

centre of the platform is the percussion; in front of it Charon, who serves as narrator.

This music was written in 1967–8, and is to be regarded as a requiem for Ernesto Guevara, who was killed in action in Bolivia in October 1967. Various archetypes of the liturgy may in fact be detected in the structure of the music, though they are nowhere directly quoted. The oratorio should also be seen as an allegory: it sings of the heroic struggle against death, against the temptation to give up, against the comfortable surrender to despair. Names of freedom fighters of the Third World have been incorporated in the text; almost all of them are unknown, but none the less important for that.

This score marks a major step forward in my work, because my means of expression have been deepened in it. Everything is dictated by the emotions I have felt over the events of those years, and my involvement in them.

# Experiments and the Avant-Garde*

As you might remember, I steered my own experimentation as quickly as possible (after about 1950) in the direction of consolidation, in order to have a vocabulary that could meet the demands of my artistic aims. I consider the experiments of the young avant-garde—so long as it is young—not only necessary, but natural. When one is young, one experiments with everything in life, one sets oneself against the *status quo*, attacking obstacles that can later be seen to be non-existent, or can be understood and dealt with. I would rather not comment on the experimentation of older ladies and gentlemen.

On the one hand I feel alone; but that is what I wanted, almost as if the goal of all my striving was one day to reach this aloneness. I have provoked people and made mistakes; I have often been uncertain, and my provocation has been directed against something that I could only feel, and scarcely define. Now, when I can define it, I hesitate to do so; it no longer seems necessary. Perhaps one day I will speak and write about it, if music leaves me the time. On the other hand, I am glad when I come across affinities. I know several young composers—young enough to be my sons—whose aims are radically different from those of the antiquated post-Webern tendency and of electronic music. I have the impression, which I share with Boulez, that electronic sound material cannot develop. To some concert-goers, its murmurings seem like the intoxication of a 'Good Friday Music' or a 'Ride of the Valkyries' brought up to

* 'Experiment und Avantgarde.' From an interview with Wolf-Eberhard von Lewinski, *Melos* vol 34 no 11, 1967.

date, but not everyone can sustain this misunderstanding for long. Unlike Boulez, I have never yet worked with electronic means. My experiments are all directed towards the creation of clear 'signs' that rest on experiences with history.

Discoveries and inventions result less from experiments and research than from aiming at unknown musical objects when composing. The research is directed inwards, towards the composer's self, not outwards; it takes on, outwardly, the shape of the inward idea.

Today one is inclined to see and to discuss the externals, almost exclusively. While science is making advances towards the most hidden centres of the human psyche, music generally operates on the outermost periphery of its own material, as if in the course of running away from itself it had already arrived at its own denial, in conformity with the emotional status of the declining, but still ruling, class.

You ask whether my 'latent penchant for musical and literary romanticism has turned me away from making bold experiments'. But where have I shown an inclination towards literary romanticism? Is Kleist a romantic? Bachmann? Kafka? Bruno? Morante? Tasso? Hildesheimer? Cramer? Auden? Rimbaud? It would be truer to say that I have circumvented literary romanticism. As you know, it is difficult to define what musical romanticism is. Some people think that unhistorical adventurism and speculation and experimentation—in other words the very opposite of what I am doing—are typical of a romantic posture. I am neither interested in romanticism nor its opposite, but in a certain clarity, and also truth; in the precise registering of emotion, spiritual states, atmosphere. With these things I have more work than I can cope with in my lifetime. I am not in a position to say whether that is romanticism or not. All my music is a striving for form, for order. Even the dramatic failure of a form is a statement, its composition is evidence of a need to say something. I believe that the sonata/fugue problem will keep coming back to us, again and again, and will demand to be answered.

Do I think that the search for new forms of music theatre as undertaken by Nono and Ligeti will be significant for the future of opera? The only work of Ligeti's that seems to have anything to do with theatre is *Aventures & Nouvelles Aventures*, and in all innocence he says something about it that is quite alien to me: 'When aspects of "society" are ironized by being assembled in a new way, indeed caricatured and demonized, this takes place without any political slant. It is precisely a dread of deep significance and ideology that makes any kind of engaged art out of the question for me.' I think that if his dread continues to prevail, we have little hope of drama from him. On the other hand Nono has hitherto undertaken only one experiment that embodies a strong tendency towards 'engaged' drama, without one's being able to speak of a new form of music drama. It is therefore difficult to answer this question. But every striving, even for the future of opera, has a meaning if it is accompanied by humanistic motives, and adopts an unmistakable libertarian anti-fascist stance.

You wonder whether the signs of synthesis that many people claim to detect in my works are evidence of an intention to unite the styles of Stravinsky and Schoenberg. Stravinsky and Schoenberg, I think, continue to be opposites: a chasm separates them. Neither my music nor I know anything of tendencies towards synthesis. I have learned from Stravinsky and from the Viennese School what I had to learn, just as I have learned from much earlier masters, going back to Bach. I am still learning, and I hope this process of learning never comes to an end.

In contrast to some of my colleagues, whose comments on Stravinsky consist of shrill whistles or rude mutterings, I find it superfluous to deprecate his late work. I wrote *Der Prinz von Homburg*—whose plot and music are about the 'great question' of inspiration versus compulsion, intuition versus materialism, form versus dissolution, with many ramifications and interweavings—in honour of him (and quoted from his sublime *Perséphone*), and that was long after *Agon*.

Soon the 'clusters', the serial recitatives and the 'happenings' will have exhausted themselves, and the young composer will look around in vain in this wasteland for something to nourish his hungry soul. I believe, in contrast to Boulez for whom the neo-classical Stravinsky is 'very weak' (there they go, forty years of musical history, brushed aside in a couple of words!), that in the next few years he will be seen properly for the first time, and understood in all his greatness and significance. The history of music knows plenty of examples where a reorientation has been necessary. This will be the case in the near future too.

# Does Music Have to be Political?<sup>*</sup>

I came to the Left just like anybody else, I imagine. People of my generation, after all, are bound to have a very clear recollection of fascism. To have seen that Hitlerism lived on after the fall of Hitler, that fascism had put on a different mask, has left many people, including myself, with a fascism-trauma. To have seen that fascism lived on in people's mentalities was an enormous shock, especially as one could do virtually nothing against it after 1945. If one did react, one was usually not understood; anti-fascism was *passé*. So all that was left to the majority of German artists and writers of my generation such as Enzensberger and others was to emigrate. Our impotence has lasted for a long time. During this period, from 1953 to the present [1969], I have been in Italy, where I have worked with and learned from Italian intellectuals, every one of whom is left-wing.

Turning-points were the National Liberation Front war of liberation in Vietnam, and the liberation struggle of the blacks in the USA, which I have experienced personally and intensively, and still do so today. You ask me about the scandal over the premiere of *Das Floss der Medusa* in Hamburg (9 December 1968). This has always been misinterpreted by the press, with the exception of the *Frankfurter Rundschau*. Perhaps there is some point in setting the record straight, once and for all. At the start of the concert in the Hamburg Radio there was a 'go-in' with slogans against consumer culture; the audience was bombarded with thousands of leaflets. All

* 'Musik ist nolens volens politisch.' From an interview with J. A. Makowsky, first published in *züricher student*, June 1969.

*[167]*

this was organized by three different groups: the Berlin SDS (Sozialistischer Deutscher Studentenbund) 'Culture and Revolution' team, members of the Hamburg College of Music, and of the Hamburg SDS. Then there was the poster of Che Guevara which had been attached to the podium, and which the programme director of the radio tore up out of hand. Thus the real protagonist was this enraged radio station boss who, although he knew that the work had been written in honour of Che, was unable to tolerate his picture hanging there.

Students had put the poster up. I had done nothing at all, and hadn't planned anything of the sort; all I wanted to do was to conduct. But that's how it turned out. Then other comrades put up a red flag instead of the Che poster. I was now called upon by the Radio's legal adviser to have the flag removed, or else be responsible for the consequences. Thereupon I said I couldn't care less about the consequences, because I was not prepared to submit to such blackmail. The rest was as reported in the press—part of the choir refused to sing in the presence of a red flag (!) and walked off. While negotiations were still going on, heavily armed riot police came in and began to beat up and arrest students as well as Ernst Schnabel the librettist of *Medusa* (once head of the Hamburg Radio), making the concert physically and morally impossible.

The ending of the work is structured in a way that leads directly from music into reality. Musicians and audiences can carry on from there and continue the evening singing, discussing, taking action. Of course this was a utopian and much too optimistic idea, and as such it will remain as a little monument of that terrible evening. The contradictions emerged more dramatically than ever before.

If a committed artist wishes to articulate his commitment—for instance if he is a composer who writes orchestral music—he has to rely on the modern symphony orchestra if he wants to use the resources of a large ensemble. He has to rely on record companies or radio stations, and to depend for everything on what the system has to offer. He undoubtedly finds himself in a dilemma.

One shouldn't try to fool oneself; the artist is dependent, no matter what, even if only on the dole. If one bears in mind that the revolutionary struggle in Europe is going to last a very long time—unless there are unforeseen and surprising events—I think that simply to hand everything over to the system and opt out borders on counter-revolutionary behaviour, if it does not actually constitute it. Nothing is achieved by that; on the contrary, one should take advantage of every available opportunity for communication. This also connects with the 'long march through the institutions' spoken of by Rudi Dutschke, and it has something to do with social responsibility. Here are positions that one simply must not give up. This seems to me to be a better strategy than the opposite alternative. Opting out has absolutely no effect on the system.

The development towards socialism, which is also a development of a new consciousness and is now taking place throughout the world, is especially difficult here in Europe, because it is so contradictory. I could imagine every artist participating in his own way, as best he can, in this growing consciousness, by taking part in the general development through his own work, as a witness. This means that in his behaviour as an artist he should react, like a seismograph, to what is taking place. He himself should repeatedly attest to the way in which this development towards socialism is reflected in his work, whether it is music or painting or something else. For this reason one should conceive of a committed musician as quietly (or preferably disquietingly) continuing to write his works as he thinks fit, on the one hand, but at the same time placing a part of his labour-power at the disposal of another kind of music. For instance he should test how far music is suited to agitation; he could write school music; he should come into contact with as many people as possible, so as to be able to recognize and gauge in their emotional needs his own artistic obligations.

Practical work also includes, in my opinion, studying the possibilities for music to move towards street theatre, so as to enrich it. But that also means composing quite simple songs. Paul Dessau is a good example: three times a week he teaches music in a school; he writes pieces for the children and gets them to compose for themselves, which I consider particularly important.

In the course of the development of music I can even see, or rather sense, possibilities that complex orchestral or symphonic music will move in a direction where it will all of a sudden come upon pop music. It could come about one day that the difference will disappear between *musique savante* and the music that young people enjoy so much.

I recently read in an interview with a representative of the National Liberation Front in Vietnam (she was a schoolteacher) that when soldiers of the NLF are withdrawn from the front and have a few days of rest, they listen to music. What they find most beautiful, what most encourages them and gives them strength, is Beethoven! That did not surprise me, but it did move me a great deal. It gives one food for thought about this anti-historicism of an Artaud or Cage, for instance. Completely to eliminate historical thinking and action strikes me as unmarxist and undialectical. For one who is fighting, all music that has accompanied those who have fought before him—and that has preceded him in history—has subversive significance. One can find subversion in Mozart, in Beethoven; in both one can find a utopian conception of freedom. Mozart makes me think of the utopia intimated in Kleist's essay 'On the Marionette Theatre'. Such ideas are also relevant to the artistic behaviour of people of our time. But to maintain that one can write music today that is not fractured, that does not reflect the state of devastation to which people are subjected, means writing music with blinkers, to put it mildly. On the other hand I welcome any attempt to further the development of music despite everything, because it must go on.

I think that the most important composer of this century is not Webern, but Mahler! It is true that he made little contribution to freeing music from its grammatical impasse, and did little to invent new systems; yet he was a witness to his time. His portrayal of frustration and suffering, in an unmistakable and direct musical language, seems to me more interesting and more important than the achievements of the Viennese School. I find Mahler un-aristocratic, whereas all three Viennese placed a great deal of emphasis on the aristocratic element of their artistic practice. This 'laying oneself open to every humiliation', in the words of Franz

Werfel, can be found only in Mahler. One might think that the difference lies in the techniques employed, but I would maintain the difference lies in the effect which the composer wanted to make. Beethoven regarded his whole enterprise as a contribution to human progress. As with Marxism, his goal is not God but Man, whereas there are other artists who have never given a thought to the moral function of their work; for instance Richard Strauss, who is for me—perhaps I'm going too far—something like a court composer to Kaiser Wilhelm II.

I can conceive of utopian possibilities only in socialism. Utopia is defined by the absence of capitalism, the absence of the dominance of men over men, the liberation of art from its commercialization. I visualize the disappearance of the musical elite and of globe-trotting virtuosi; the overcoming of all this ideology of stardom in music, which I regard as a relic from the previous century and as a *maladie de notre temps*. It would mean that the composer is no longer a star, as today, but an *uomo sociale*, someone who learns and teaches. He would be someone who shows other people how to compose; I could envisage composing becoming something that all people can do, simply by taking away their inhibitions. I think there is no such thing as an unmusical person.

Music would then be something that belongs to all, that is not alien but a part of people's lives. People will no longer be alienated, but will be able to develop; they will be able to open themselves to all the beauties of life. That is one of the things that so moved me in Cuba, this lack of hang-ups about art, this unlimited curiosity about art, and the natural way in which art is approached.

One idea prevalent in the West is altogether wrong. There are those people who say that all previous music has been bourgeois music, and must therefore be done away with. It is not just that it seems odd that, under capitalism, some people want to do away with something that is humanistically essential—while others are trying to do away with capitalism by means of a humanistically essential revolution—but that wanting to do away with art is completely inhuman, unmarxist and monstrous.

# El Cimarrón<sup>*</sup>

My interest in *El Cimarrón* began during a conversation with Hans
Magnus Enzensberger in about 1968, when we were discussing the
difficulties of writing political songs which could go beyond or
circumvent the achievements of Eisler, Weill and Dessau. At that
time the most likely solution to the problem seemed to me to be a
cyclic form, from the rich possibilities of which perhaps something
new would emerge. On this occasion Enzensberger told me about
the Cuban publication of the autobiography of an old black,
Esteban Montejo, who was living in Havana and had recalled his
youth as a slave. Enzensberger suggested this subject for my
experiment.

*El Cimarrón*, however, did not turn into a song-cycle, nor was it
conceived as such; it was, rather, a trial run for a new type of
concert. I wrote the music in Havana in the winter of 1969–70. It
was originally conceived for a singer, a flautist (equipped with a
variety of flutes), and a percussionist. For the part of the singer I
had in mind William Pearson, whose work with Kagel and Ligeti I
had followed with interest. For the flute music I found Karlheinz
Zöller; besides the flutes, he was also allotted some percussion
instruments and the jew's harp, together with occasional singing,
whistling, speaking and shouting. As percussionist I chose Tsut-
omu Yamash'ta, about whose technical abilities I knew little when I
wrote the music. In early 1969 I heard Leo Brouwer play the guitar
for the first time—until then I had only known some of his music,
which I liked—and decided to add a guitar part to the *Cimarrón*

---

* '*El Cimarrón*—Ein Werkbericht.' First published in a book of the same title,
edited by Claus H. Henneberg, Mainz 1971.

ensemble. As a result the sound would be extended and harmonically enriched; in the original conception, a harmonic dimension had existed only by means of the double and triple stops on the flute. Leo helped with the composition by coming along with new ideas about extending the sound of the guitar. His part was supplemented also by bongos, marimba, wood blocks, shell-shaped and cow bells, with the aid of which he too could intervene in the improvisations that were planned, and produce some of the many quotations of Cuban rhythms.

This, then, is a piece for instrumentalists, working under unusual conditions, far removed from the conventional practice of, say, the modern orchestra. It is a piece that an ensemble must work up slowly. It cannot be done in a few days of rehearsal. The players must invent many things in the score for themselves; there are points where only a 'graphic' serves as clue, stimulus or signpost. Often only the notes are given: volume, phrasing and rhythm are left to the players themselves, who are thus actively involved in the process of composition. The same applies to the singer, who finds passages where he can determine the pitch at will, and invent rhythms for himself. It was interesting to see how a musical unity emerged, after weeks of rehearsal: a product of the 'style' suggested by the composer and, at least to an equal extent, of the interpretative and creative material produced by the four performers (each of whom had a different cultural background).

Each of the four has an aural centre: the singer his bass-baritone range; the flautist his flute; the guitarist his classical fingerings; the percussionist his drumheads. Throughout the piece each circles around these centres, bypasses them, avoids them, and lingers in extreme registers that are strained and unfamiliar, as if the specific qualities of the instruments were to be forgotten, as if for long periods the performers forgot what beautiful sounds were—namely those for which the instruments were built (or which are 'most natural' for the voice)—and yet a relation to the instruments' centres, and thus to their history, is implicitly sustained. So it is not a matter of transcendence or destruction but of appreciation of the results of extending the instruments' scope.

# El Cimarrón

The preparations included making the personal acquaintance of Esteban Montejo, the *Cimarrón* himself. Miguel Barnet introduced me to him. I had never seen such an old man. He was then 107 years old, tall as a tree, walked slowly and upright, his eyes were lively, he radiated dignity and seemed well aware that he was a historical personage. I could barely understand his Creole; Barnet interpreted. He told stories of the *cimarronería*, and of his sexual life, which must have been unusually promiscuous. His speaking voice had that melodious quality that seems constantly about to break into song. Our visit lasted about two hours, during which time Esteban smoked one cigar after another. Then the dinner-bell sounded and the veterans [of the Cuban war of independence] gathered in the dining-room, while a single table was laid on the terrace for Esteban, who had not learned to eat in company. (I recognized some of the old men from the ICAIC film reconstruction of the battle of Mal Tiempo.)

The composition begins with sounds of indeterminate pitch: with a violin bow (more manageable than the double-bass bow I originally had in mind) the flautist produces a buzzing noise from the edge of a suspended cymbal; on occasion, and with a certain amount of luck, this can even produce a high whining note. The guitarist holds his instrument on his knees like a viol and plays the strings with a bow, while the percussionist sets large temple bells vibrating by rotating a leather clapper until a howling sound is produced, rich in overtones. To this is added the vowel *u* produced by the singer. Thus begins the description of the landscape of Cuba, its climate and its natural catastrophes, like a bridge to the tale of the origins of slavery. An extended piece for the guitar on its own, like fragments of an old song, represents the transfer of African culture to the Caribbean. This is softly accompanied by a Yoruba rhythm. (Yoruba is one of the African religions that have survived in Cuba, but whose rites were prohibited under the Batista dictatorship; the ban was lifted by Castro, and today Yoruba enjoys much popularity, not only among the blacks.) The rhythm is beaten out at the front of the stage and on a level with the singer, on a conga; then the player moves the instrument over to his percussion kit.

From this point on, the rhythms are all derived from this Yoruba motif.

Parody crops up at several points. In the second piece there is a *habanera*, sickly and sentimental, when the gastronomic delights of the rich whites are mentioned. Later, in the second part, during the 'Bad Victory', where Spanish-American dance music breaks in, there are scraps of Yankee tunes on the mouth-organ. I tried to write a *son* (national dance dating from the early nineteenth century, still to be regarded today as the characteristic music of Cuba) for the first piece of the second part, 'Women'; this turned out to be quite difficult to put on paper. Grasping its rules— rhythmic peculiarities and the 'lifted' third beat of the bar, its syncopation—was one thing, reproducing its 'mood' and translating it into a personal idiom quite another. An earlier *son*, 'The Forest', where Esteban laments the lack of women, went wrong and couldn't be incorporated.

Other theatrical moments include the 'Ave Maria' in the third piece, 'Slavery'. It is a cry of hatred, and the sound of bells is none other than the rattle of chains. Torture is described by the wailing of a flute, with 'overblowing' effects and microtones. The escape-plan, hatched during sleepless nights, is represented by a nervous drumming of the fingers on flute keys, the body of the guitar, and wooden drums, rising and falling.

Esteban's self-liberation: he holds a chain in his hands. He sticks his fingers in his mouth and whistles. (The overseer turns; according to Esteban: 'Then I took a stone and threw it right in the middle of his gob.') He drops the chain on to a stone slab (in the score, a metal sheet). Then you hear the jew's harp (played by the flautist in front of a microphone), which represents the stars in comic strips that, on such occasions, dance in front of the eyes of the injured party, and Esteban says: 'I hit the target. I know I did, because he screamed. . . .' There follows the 'Seize him!' from the other side of the stage, shouted into a megaphone by the guitarist, and this (while Esteban is running) unleashes an ensemble of sounds: whistles, heckling, panting, the sound of nimble feet; the singer takes a microphone as though he were in a music-hall and improvises cheerfully in jazz fashion, then dances to the percussion music, which is becoming more and more exuberant. All this is left to the imagination of the performers, with the exception of a piece for the piccolo, which limits the duration of this 'escape'.

The following episode, 'The Forest', contains several aleatory episodes where singer and players unfold a multitude of pianissimo 'natural sounds', and a section (accompanying the text 'I spent many years out there in the forest', whose melody is made up of free variations of Afro-Cuban tunes) where the three players quote a *toque* (a rhythmic theme) from the music of another religion, Lukumi. This *toque* is played during the adjurations to Babalú Ayé, the goddess who protects you from diseases. This (literal) quotation I put there in order to ensure that Esteban may survive the many years in the forest without illnesses and that he is not captured again.

Later, when he is back among people, you hear in 'The False Freedom' a false *allegria* on flute and vibraphone. The former slaves' fears for their survival, and their anger when after the official abolition of slavery they find little has changed and their working conditions are no better, are portrayed by *ostinato* instrumental strokes which, hollow, strident, hard and expressionless, interrupt Esteban's words.

In the second part, during the section on machines, I have attempted to portray factory work, the glitter of modernization, the sound-world of a sugar refinery, mechanization; I had in mind the conveyor belt scene in Chaplin's *Modern Times*. The percussion is arranged in such a way that the body of the performer seems to become a machine while he plays, and the singer's words are constantly interrupted by a mechanical arm-movement caused by his playing a guiro, giving the impression that his head and his body are subordinated to two different systems.

The priests are depicted in No. 10 with their own sounds; bored litanies, mawkish babbling, the howling of an out-of-tune harmonium, empty baroque phrases. From time to time African drum music acts as a reminder of another, more powerful reality.

In 'The Battle of Mal Tiempo' instruments of torture and

machines are turned into weapons. At the very end, sounds from the beginning return. The pre-revolutionary situation is reinstated, looking backwards is ruled out, everything is now directed forward towards a new identity.

# Art and the Revolution[*]

I take it for granted that no one is capable of thinking, saying or doing anything that is not based on the experiences of his own senses. The process whereby I gained my first political consciousness was not initiated by theoretical reflection, but inseparably linked with the circumstances of my life. I grew up under fascism, and was compelled by my father to take part in the Hitler Youth. My hatred of my father became entwined with my hatred of fascism, and was transferred to the nation of soldiers, which seemed to me like a nation of fathers. So my early anti-fascism, which was then reinforced by the experiences in military service during the last two years of the war, was psychologically rather than politically motivated.

When I was at last able after the war to begin my work as a musician, I came across the legacy of fascist rule in every nook and cranny. I saw a new state growing up out of this legacy, with the same old wretched figures. I reacted as did many others—Enzensberger, Peter Weiss, Andersch, Hildesheimer, Ingeborg Bachmann: I left Germany as soon as I could. But that again was not an exclusively political gesture.

I would like to draw a distinction between what is generally understood by the 'Italian experience' of Central European musicians, painters and writers (of which there is a great tradition), and my own case. What mattered to me were not so much the pines,

* 'Die Krise des bürgerlichen Künstlers—Politisierung—Nutzbarmachung der Kunst für die Revolution.' From an interview with Hansjörg Pauli, first published in *Für wen komponieren Sie eigentlich?*, edited by Hansjörg Pauli, Frankfurt 1971.

the sea, the ancient buildings; I simply wanted to live at last, to lead my own life, free from fear, and undisturbed by scandals. So in Italy I built up a world of my own, around myself and my work, out of my ideas, my wishes and dreams. I did not notice that I was obviously isolating myself, that my music was becoming more and more private, that its motivations were private ones, that it contained private communications, that it addressed itself to individuals, to private beings. Doubts I dismissed, even when voiced by people who were close to me; I acquiesced in flattery and praise. The crisis, towards which I was heading without suspecting anything, broke out while I was writing *The Bassarids*. All at once I felt that I did not understand anything any more, that I had nothing, that I was cut off; I realized that I was living in a desert where one stops thinking, and concerns oneself only with feelings, with cultivating feelings. In the past everything had revolved around my work; now work itself revolved around the question of eliminating unhappiness. But I continued to nourish the illusion that this situation could be overcome without changing my habits, my life.

Eventually I became ill. That was something I could not get round, could no longer deny, and that was perhaps the beginning of the development of a new consciousness, or for the need of one. In autumn 1967 I went to Berlin to meet Rudi Dutschke, the leading spokesman of the new German Left.

Perhaps I was already prepared to meet him inasmuch as such people as Renzo Vespignani, Luca Pavolini and Luigi Nono had belonged to my circle of Italian friends since the late 1950s. All of them were Marxists, with whom I could talk for hours, but without feeling the need to deepen and radicalize things in the way *they* had done; I thought that applied only to Italy, that it concerned me no further; I thought that my generalized anti-fascism was commitment enough. Of course I had followed events in the Federal Republic, with increasing rage; I had also on occasion made my views public: in 1963 in a lecture at the Technical University in Berlin, and in 1965 as a speaker during Willy Brandt's election campaign—but with a feeling of impotence and uselessness. From

Rudi Dutschke and his comrades, with whom I gradually came into contact, I now learned to see contexts, and to see myself within those contexts.

Today I can rationalize and analyse my problems; as a result they become unimportant, because they are no longer a threat. I have learned to understand myself as a consequence, not to say a victim, of the structures of this society. To have understood that once, means to be able to develop resistance, and to be able to activate that resistance, to translate it into practice. My solidarity with the oppressed is thus not a solidarity that comes via the intellect—say as a result of reading Fanon—it is rooted in the awareness that you and I, my brother here and my comrade there, are products of social structures.

So I was able to dismantle a whole series of mechanisms to which I had hitherto been helplessly exposed. I no longer know the feeling of jealousy; I am no longer personally ambitious, I no longer write music to please myself and a few friends but to help socialism, and if I am currently so involved in my work, it is because I see how it is increasingly freeing itself from my person and my past, and how I can myself transform my own experiences, make them into something new, something usable. Above all I learned to read, to study theory. The process was lengthy and difficult. It is not yet complete today.

I have taken the decision that in my work I will embody all the difficulties and all the problems of contemporary bourgeois music, and that I will, however, try to transform these into something usable, into something that the masses can understand. Now that does not mean that I want to operate on the level of commercial music and 'hits'. But neither do I think, on the other hand, that there is any place for worry about losing elite notions of value.

I believe that if it had been possible for me to break with my past by means of an act of will, this would have called into question not only what I have done in the past, but also what I am attempting to do today. Just as the process whereby I attained political consciousness is linked with my earlier life, just as this has been and still is something continuous, so the music that I write today derives from my previous music. The new content changes the external sound-forms only gradually. But I think the tendencies are already clearly recognizable. For instance in *Das Floss der Medusa*, in its more precise psychological delineation. I abandoned my previous vocal style, and used the singing voices in a more expressive, more *telling* way.

In the Second Piano Concerto (1967), in a new viola work *Compases para preguntas ensimismadas* (Questions asked of one's soul), and in the *Sinfonia* No. 6, I have overcome the division between soloists as individualists and orchestral players as an undifferentiated mass, not only in the structure but also in practice: the orchestral apparatus is dissolved into an ensemble of individuals; orchestral players and soloists work together with equal responsibility on the same material. In *Versuch über Schweine* (1969), written shortly after the *Medusa* scandal, I took further what I had started in the latter work: I made use of new possibilities of vocal production, and thereby opened up areas of expression into which I had never before entered, because they had nothing to do with my life. They seemed to lie outside my possibilities and my needs, so I suppressed them. Today my work is freely exposed to all the contradictions of this age. In one case I did in fact try to free myself violently from my musical past. That was in the Symphony No. 6. In that work I wanted to use my experiences, the experiences of a bourgeois who had been supplying music to the ruling class for twenty years, to compose music against the bourgeoisie. Instead of nostalgia and scepticism I wanted affirmation, direct avowal of revolution. Writing the piece down was laborious; but I had the feeling that I would manage it. Since then I have conducted the work several times, and I know that I did not manage it. For me the one thing that is new about this symphony is the fact that the problems of musical language are consciously articulated, that the failures are admitted, and that the difficulty of writing symphonies today is not concealed. But affirmation did not come to pass. It was a record of difficulties, nothing more.

Although it is far more problematic than in vocal music, I have indeed a notion of instrumental music as the place where a specific number of 'signs' about whose meaning there is agreement, a convention, is transcended. And I believe that it should be possible to do something new with these signs, whose strength rests on the fact that they have deeply impressed themselves on human consciousness: to place them in new contexts and arrange them in such a way that one arrives at unequivocal results; perhaps less effective and direct than with the help of texts, but nevertheless. . . . Of the many tasks I have set myself, whose realization is so difficult and demands so much time, this is one—on a branch line; it is not in the foreground. But whenever I think of instrumental music, it is from that standpoint. I can see that it may look as though in this symphony I had returned to the territory of the avant-garde, at least so far as its formal problems are concerned. And—apart from the fact that no one seems to know any more where and how 'avant-garde' takes place—there could be a danger that my new music would be listened to only on account of its modernity. But I would not overestimate this danger. For I would indeed employ contemporary techniques but would attempt to transform them and give them a political utility, which for me means to make them impure. Impure in the sense of Pablo Neruda, who with reference to committed poetry speaks of *poesía impura*. I would like to do this in as clear and unequivocal a way as possible.

Sophistication is not a quality in itself, and it is perfectly possible to express sophisticated things in a clear and unequivocal way. Since Brecht we know that the problem of making oneself understood can be solved, though I do not want to imply that Brecht's solution can be generalized and transferred to music. The proletariat is, fortunately, far less crippled than we are. It is deliberately kept ill-informed, certainly, and bombarded with miserable mass-produced products of the mass media. But in Italy, for example, the workers react in a lively and inquisitive fashion when one takes the trouble to show them things to which they otherwise have no access. They have a great deal of unused receptivity; Luigi Nono would confirm that. We must not fall into the trap of seeing our path towards solidarity with the working class as an act of self-mutilation. It is not that. There is a fine phrase of

*[182]*

Osvaldo Dórticos, the Cuban President: 'Al pueblo, no se de-sciende, se asciende' (One does not go down to the people, one climbs up to them).

By joining workers' groups we can protect ourselves to a certain extent from the failure of our attempts at solidarity, and in constant conversations and discussions we can hear from our brothers what they need and what they expect from music.

Today I consider it more important that music should take up and mirror the contradictions that a musician encounters in his society. But the problem of how such a dialectical musical thinking can be socially mediated is a class problem which cannot be resolved outside the revolutionary process. The view that one can, so to speak, with a single stroke cut the Gordian knot, is profoundly bourgeois.

# Natascha Ungeheuer[*]

In contrast to *Tristan*, which was written years later and whose existence had begun with the creation of *musique concrète* tapes, the entire score of *Der langwierige Weg in die Wohnung der Natascha Ungeheuer* (The Tedious Way to Natascha Ungeheuer's Flat) was ready when the tapes were to be produced. The score specifies *bruitage*, and requires the electronic treatment of crowd voices, dark and bright street noises, beat music, military music, of a chord from my Symphony No. 6, a flexatone, motor horns, and a fourteen-part cluster.

During January 1971 some friends helped me to record street sounds near the Zoo Station in Berlin, and they also provided the material from which a many-voiced crowd of people was later constructed: they read newspaper extracts on to tape at various levels of pitch and at various tempi. We worked in the rather poorly equipped studio of the Technical University, with the help of the technician, Rüdiger Rüfer. The inadequacy of our results did not worry us too much; the finished product was to have a touch of *arte povera*, among other things.

The subject of the piece is described as follows by its author, the Chilean poet Gastón Salvatore (who was an oustanding figure in the 1968 student rebellion):

Natascha Ungeheuer is the siren of a false utopia. She promises the bourgeois leftist a new kind of security which is meant to enable him to retain his 'good' revolutionary conscience without taking active

---

[*] *'Natascha Ungeheuer—Ein Versuch über den Realismus.'* (1971) *Musik und Politik* 1976.

part in the class struggle. This false utopia is to be viewed as an immobility that negates everything; as a kind of cowardice that enables one to fancy one is identified with the 'revolution' and to think that the mere identification can be equated with the realization of the 'revolution'.

This existentialist, unhistorical mode of political self-reflection puts the bourgeois leftist in the position of merely using the proletarian struggle as a kind of moralizing balm. He oscillates between the temptation to abandon his awareness and return to the old class, or choose one of the two possible forms of perplexity: that of the lonely avant-gardist in his own four walls, or that of social democracy.

Natascha Ungeheuer promises both possibilities. The bourgeois leftist sets off for her flat, plagued by all the fears and weaknesses that characterize his social situation and afflict him in every political crisis. Natascha knows these fears and weaknesses. She torments him, challenges him, and at the same time entices him into her flat where he would find the promised peace, without being confronted with his betrayal of socialism. The bourgeois leftist who is the subject of this work refuses to go to the end of the road, to Natascha Ungeheuer's flat. He has not yet found his way to the revolution. He knows that he has to retrace his steps and start again from the beginning.*

But I think that there is something else there too, and that is the problem of being a stranger on foreign soil, which Salvatore knows and names. The 'grey city by the sea' is to him an alien landscape. He walks around it, consumed by a peculiar homesickness, by a longing to be absorbed and lost in these bars, dives, homes, just like the others, people who belong there. He would truly and without reservation like to succumb to the style of a central committee meeting and therefore no longer have to grasp contexts and connections. He sacrifices himself for his goal, he exaggerates,

---

* Sleeve note from the recording of *Der langwierige Weg in die Wohnung der Natascha Ungeheuer*, DGG 25 30212.

endangers himself! And again falls out of step, lags behind, loses ground and the hope of integration.

This state of mind underlies the picture of Berlin that he draws: a portrait coloured by a mood of disquiet and disorientation. This is the city as experienced by the stranger: a harsh and terrifying sea of stones, hideous, implacable, brutal, which seems to offer no refuge, which has nothing for the stranger except prostitutes, Aschinger's soups, a pass to the university canteen or a season-ticket for the theatre, and the terrible certainty that everything will remain thus. Hence hopelessness, hence the danger of suffocation.

The course of this 'tedious way' is unfolded in eleven sections, in a complicated language that has something outlandish about it and also reveals something of the university ambience, the technical vocabulary of the academic Left buzzing around our hero:

1.   'Planimetry': he plans his odyssey. With the names of streets that he quotes, history springs up out of the morass: the empire, battles, wars. In his student bed-sitter he sets about organizing his journey to the utopia of Kreuzberg in the manner of guerrilla strategy. He is playing at war in a reality which he knows is controlled and manipulated; there is little that he can do with it, or it with him. He will come to measure the narrowness of this reality.

2.   Ballad about the events of the late 1960s (while the subway rattles past, beneath his window). The conflicts of the young comrades; their euphoric militancy; their rigour; the struggle with the 'real warriors', the heavily armed police serving the interests of industrial and technological power. The absence of tenderness and even of togetherness; the impossibility of loving. Achilles, still hidden among the women, soon will no longer have any chance of rejecting the victor's demands.

3.   There is an element of misuse and sacrilege in displaying a lyrical frenzy whenever the theatres of the international class war are mentioned. Achilles must strip himself naked for war, as if for prostitution. Awareness of the ambivalent relationship to war and death, which presents itself as reason, creeps in like despair.

4.   'The joyless watcher': Salvatore, howling with pain, would like to sacrifice to utopia all that he has. It is not much that he can

offer, practically nothing at all. Natascha sarcastically demands his male member or, as substitute, 'at least a finger'. He tries to escape, and contemplates writing that something 'about trees' which Brecht had said could scarcely be done without committing a crime:

| | |
|---|---|
| *Was sind das für Zeiten* | What are these times |
| *In denen ein Gespräch über* | In which to talk about |
| *Bäume* | trees |
| *Fast schon ein Verbrechen ist,* | Is almost a crime, |
| *Weil es ein Schweigen* | Because it means passing over |
| *Über so viele Untaten einschliesst.* | So many misdeeds. |

But for Salvatore to write about trees would be a retrogressive development, would mean suicide, and no better than accepting the idea of war. So he throws in his lot with the aggressors (turning rice-fields yellow in Vietnam), continuing to get off with the girls and to act the role of Achilles; nothing happens, while reality, like the landscape during a bus journey, rushes past outside.

5. and 6. 'Introduction to the difficult bourgeoisie, and attempts to return': an outbreak of despair. Salvatore takes part in activities of the student Left, acquiescing in everything that enables him to anaesthetize his feelings of guilt, his 'bad conscience' (a constantly recurring theme); soon, however, he castigates himself for these self-deceptions, and identifies his political indecision with sexual frustration and *vice versa*.

7. New sequences of images that pungently outline his separation from reality: on one hand, the fashionable hippy-like side of a certain section of the Left, with its literary pretentiousness; on the other, Vietnam's dead children and Latin America's active revolutionaries. Attempts to escape this impasse by means of tricks *à la manière de* Münchhausen.

8. 'German Song': Natascha's voice can be heard again. Utopia reveals itself as armchair theory, monotony, hibernation. German Song. Salvatore passes through communes in empty factories filled with clouds of hashish, now as quiet as a graveyard. All contradictions have apparently become silent, and so too has he.

9.  'Surveying': Natascha asks him, 'Why are you silent?' With his reply comes the realization that his journey to Kreuzberg was a wrong turning. He sees there is nothing to be found here except an escape into peaceful repose, into a theology full of self-deception and chimeras. This recognition of the truth brings Salvatore to the end of his journey.

10.  'Speech exercises': it becomes clear that none of the available big words and gestures is capable of doing justice to reality, or even of approaching it; they are tautology, which repels reality and awareness and keeps them at a distance.

11.  A reactionary attempt at colonization is concealed in Natascha's utopia. At length Salvatore recognizes himself as the petty slave of his own class, the bourgeoisie, even though he may have turned away from it and exists at its periphery. He has traversed the arc of his researches, degradations and self-mutilations, and has reached the zero point, whence alone reorientation is possible.

I too know a Berlin of despair and hopelessness; another Berlin, and yet the same: I too experienced dangers there in the chaos and despair of winter during the late 1940s; I know the endless bus journeys between grey towering walls, snow beneath, black sky above; I know the piercing cold, and that quite special kind of cosy *Gemütlichkeit*, which has such a feel for dissolute forgetfulness, which is indulgent and Polish and good, and which also has a simple metropolitan grandiosity that can still be found only in New York and London. Perhaps these are remnants from the Weimar years and the catacombs of anti-fascism. Most of it takes place beneath the surface, which is smooth, self-satisfied and stupid. The surface, so it seemed to me, was what had remained of good society, a conglomeration of those who had been denazified, starlets, and cold warriors. Of course with the years this all turns more and more sour, and counts less and less. Grass grows on the Kurfürstendamm, as on the dance floor of Bill's Ballroom in Bilbao. Fascinating. In the late 1950s and early 1960s many were drawn to West Berlin, myself included, not least because of the fine orchestras and the audience, which can look back on a tradition of intelligent and critical reception of music.

What I know of Germany I know from West Berlin; my perspective is lop-sided. But I have seen and heard a great deal there, and several times in my life when things were going badly for me I sought out old friends in Berlin. What I saw of the city, besides auditoriums and rehearsal rooms was, in fact, again and again the landscape described in *Natascha Ungeheuer*. I know the S-Bahn, the dead rail-tracks, dead dolls, the narrow-minded old queens and scholars, but also those who have glimpsed a new vision, beautiful with their sparkling hungry eyes, who all have something of our German poets as we know them from our school books, out after freedom—a courageous and lucid avant-garde. I know the tenements of Kreuzberg, the bars and canals; I know where Rosa and Liebknecht were murdered and where Rudi was shot at, where Kleist killed himself. I know the detention cells, water-cannon, rubber truncheons, claustrophobia. I have a love for the old streets (with slender streetlamps like those in the *Caligari* film), for the Berlin dialect, its idioms. I am no out-and-out stranger, no foreigner; I have my *amores*, feel warmth and receive forgiveness, and also slowly learn to see reality. I have learned much in Berlin, especially in the years between 1967 and 1970; practical experience came to the aid of my need for clarity.

How right the reaction of the first-night audience was, in the Deutsche Oper in autumn 1971, when it several times tried to interrupt the performance of *Natascha Ungeheuer*, and during and after it showered invective on Salvatore and myself. I found it was right that way; moreover in front of the curtain the noise sounded just like the thunderous applause at the premiere of *Der junge Lord* six years before: no difference for the ears and the nerves. I found it understandable that our portrait of Berlin caused displeasure. It displeases us too, but it is true, and therefore not decorative nor wholesome, alas.

The music is as cold as a November day in Berlin. It has a Berlin dryness and the harshness of the Berlin slang. It tries to express itself with the lapidary precision of a Berlin taxi-driver or building worker. Rapid associations are demanded of the listener, for instance to recognize the significance of the quotations. An example is the first section, where you suddenly hear a Hammond organ playing two and a half bars of the triumphal march from *Aida*. In the context of the text, which speaks of the Schlachtensee and Kaiserdamm, the quotation produces associations with related themes such as colonization (the first performance of *Aida* took place in a specially built opera house in Cairo, to mark the opening of the Suez Canal), Kaiser Wilhelm and the German Empire, racialism, the Third World, and the architecture of the *Gründer-jahre* (the 1870s), which still today—in a rudimentary fashion—constitute the street setting in which the protagonist undertakes his odyssey. This quotation is interrupted by the improvisation of two groups: the brass ensemble and the 'free jazz' group. The first stops after ten seconds' chattering, the jazz goes on: it sounds as if the door to a rock club has opened (you see the colours, there is a smell of fresh 'grass'), and immediately the *Pierrot Lunaire* instruments (of which more anon) intrude until they gain the upper hand, at the very moment that the first preparations for the journey to utopia are mentioned.

The treatment of the music is cinematic: the sound quality, the tempo, the dissolving light, the editing, the narrative change of sets. In this score you could speak of camerawork. Again and again there is the contrast of scenes which at first sight (or on first hearing) seem incompatible. The rhythm of these scenes derives its logic less from the text than from the underlying colours and forms of the setting that shimmer through it, this cast-iron world of railings, subway shafts, booths, steps, markets, building sites. (The visual appearance of the score has itself something of the graphic quality of maps, building-plans, punched cards, electrocardiograms, escape routes.) The zoo is omnipresent. On his journey the protagonist takes on the form of a furry animal, a beaver, which scurries through the shafts and halls, glides up escalators, dives into canals and sewers and climbs up water-towers.

The music of the brass ensemble (five players) is like an old soldiers' reunion. They are in shirtsleeves and helmets, sit on watch-towers, and are the home guard, factory police, caretakers and commissionaires. Tired old jokes are exchanged concertante style, and military argot and catchphrases. *Neue Sachlichkeit, alte Sachlichkeit.* Sentimentally Imperial and bewhiskered military, but it has all become aggressive and offensive.

The players of the other quintet (whose instruments are the same as those in *Pierrot Lunaire*) look like sick doctors who can no longer do anything for themselves—you see a leg in splints, an eye with a patch over it, a blood-stained head bandage, wheelchairs and other paraphernalia—but they wear make-up and fragments of pierrot costumes. The significance of the two types of costume points, however, to one thing: sickness, the sickness of the bourgeoisie, its music, its morality, the suffering of a class that has made itself sick. What they have to say has its origins in Schoenberg's construct, but has departed from it and broken with it, beyond the point of parody towards a new kind of denunciatory analytical music-exercise. All three groups, brass, pierrots and jazz, perform in addition the role of a Greek chorus. So does the percussionist; he is wearing overalls and has a wrecked car in front of him: his instrument. Out of it he manages to tease tinny, rubbery, metallic and wooden sounds, which are bare and lack resonance. This is the utopia of unalienated labour, or rather the lyricism of a misunderstood conception. The percussionist is on his own, and his work (of the utmost virtuosity) appears to be quite independent of what the singer says and does. A mute Sancho Panza. He is ceaselessly occupied; even his pauses are filled with activity. At the word 'Spätheimkehrer' [used of an ex-prisoner of war returning home after many years in Siberia or elsewhere] ('He's late home') he plays some feeble and lonely notes on the mouth-organ. Then, like Wolfgang Neuss, the Berlin cabaret actor, he beats the drum, as if to mask a colon in a text (though he never seems to be listening); he chews gum, and at the mention of 'secret talks' puts on a pair of dark glasses. After a while he joins in the jazz as a drummer, still chewing and wearing dark glasses. He sets the scene for the protagonist's attempts to return to the bourgeoisie, by lighting joss-sticks. He is clearly anxious to incorporate the rituals of the hippy world into the staging, so as to elucidate, localize, and place in a context which would not otherwise be clear, certain things said by the protagonist.

At times this goes so far that he stands in for the protagonist, for instance in a 'modern dance' fantasy, in the 'attempts at return', which he himself executes, in the manner of a silent film, with a rapture that does not appear to be motivated, let alone justified. Towards the end, in 'Metapenthes', he joins the howling choruses of the other groups, as if subjugated, and is absorbed into the collective.

The Hammond organ several times plays quotations, or simply patterns with which our perceptual apparatus associates fixed ideas. It follows the sentence 'Like a broad long act of will, reason waits for desperation' with a foxtrot, banal and flat, which becomes mixed up with a waltz on the brass; our associations conjure up circus animal-trainers and clowns, while the Hammond organ stops and the brass drives coldly on towards the 'joyless watcher'; a 'concerto' for kettledrums, with pedal and flexatone glissandi, in which the howling and wailing of the protagonist is embedded. In 'Speech Exercises' the Hammond organ comes into play with a Bach adagio, as if to recall the Protestant elements of the mental scenery of Berlin: the bleak churches of the Ku'damm, in a gentle glow of Brecht's Jakob Apfelböck, with demonstrations, corruption, prostitution and violence raging around them. In this section the music comes to a complete halt, as if everything had to be abandoned for the sake of a new vocabulary for the protagonist. He must, so it seems, first learn to speak again; as at the beginning of the piece, here too he does not get beyond the consonant 'd'. The instrumentalists, beginning with the doctors, help to articulate the syllables, and with the militia suggesting breathing and lip-movements by blowing on their mouthpieces, the word *Hass* (hatred) is forced out of the protagonist by two loud handclaps. The jazz group imitates him, as if it wanted to keep his stammering going like the sound of a faulty motor. To prompt the word *geheim* (secret) they hum with closed mouths. One of the jazz players now shouts the words *der Krieg* (war) to him through the megaphone. The *étude* nature of this process is further clarified by Alberti basses and Czernyesque

10   *Elegy for Young Lovers* in the Scottish Opera production, Edinburgh 1970, designed by Ralph Koltai, produced by HWH, conducted by Alexander Gibson, with Jill Gomez as Elisabeth Zimmer and David Hillman as Toni Reischmann

11   Paul Sacher and Brenton Langbein with HWH at the first performance of the Second Violin Concerto, Basel, 2 November 1972

12 HWH with Benjamin Britten in Berlin, about 1950

13 With Paul Dessau in Leipzig, 1965

piano-runs. More and more words are teased out of him, as he is roughly pushed further along his train of thought. The whole thing has an element of interrogation, inquisition; the Bach A minor adagio, which can be heard meanwhile, also has its direct traditional connection with this. Ocarina and mouth-organ join the organ's laments, with notes circling around A.

Previously, at the end of No. 9, 'Surveying', after the singer's 'Look, I'm nearly at the end', the organist has borrowed an opera-hat from the tuba player (who has earlier occasionally exchanged it during sad passages for his usual headgear, the helmet), and has put a record on an old gramophone, while a final variant of the fourteen-part cluster emerges with wide vibratos from the loudspeakers of the *bruitage*, and rises up into the air like exhaust fumes. The funeral march from Mahler's 'Fifth' echoes from the horn of the gramophone, the organist stands at attention and doffs his top-hat. I cannot bring myself to elucidate in further detail the layers of parody, anger, laughter and seriousness, and the frictions between them, that are to be found here. The montage technique according to which the entire piece is constructed, makes itself apparent at this point as it were without the composer's intervention. Here too the frontiers of music have fallen, and this results in points of contact with new forms of the visual arts and theatre.

# Second Violin Concerto *

In 1971 I wrote a second violin concerto, twenty-two years after my first. It has several movements (which merge into one another) and a soloist's part, so the name can be justified, and it will be seen that it is not a makeshift solution. But the whole is nevertheless somewhat different from a conventional concerto. It is a drama: almost, but not entirely. The poem by Enzensberger is represented scenically, and can also be heard. The poem has determined the form of the music. There are also traces of attempts at my style of 'action music', variants of *Cimarrón* and *Natascha Ungeheuer*. The virtuoso appears in the light in which Romanticism viewed him, as a magician, a sorcerer with a tragic aura—here at any rate in the guise of a Baron Münchhausen entangled in dialectic who, up to the end of the composition, tries in vain to drag himself out of the swamp by his own forelock, or to carry on fiddling with undying optimism.

From time to time counterpoints to his playing are to be heard from other violins, whose passages are 'alienated' through synthesizers. Fragments of Elizabethan and Romantic music bob up and founder; they can be taken as aural signposts, but they could also be aural traps and lead to misunderstandings. The polyvalency of closed forms, aleatory technique, overlapping of concert aria, concerto and drama, is conceived in such a way that at first glance, on first hearing, it will give pleasure and come over in the playful way that Enzensberger's poem seems to. However, the listener is not meant to stop there.

* 'Zweites Violinkonzert.' (1971) *Musik und Politik* 1976.

## Second Violin Concerto

The lines of the poem, the mathematician Gödel's theorem,* are, ideally, to be recited by the soloist. It runs (in Enzensberger's version):

*In jedem genügend reichhaltigen System*
*lassen sich Sätze formulieren,*
*die innerhalb des Systems*
*weder beweis- noch widerlegbar sind,*
*es sei denn das System*
*wäre selber inkonsistent.*

In every sufficiently complex system
sentences can be formulated,
which are neither verifiable nor refutable
within the system,
unless the system itself
is inconsistent.

* Kurt Gödel, *b* 1906, published his theorem in the article 'Über formal unentschiedbare Sätze der Principia Mathematica und verwandter Systeme', in *Monatshefte für Mathematik und Physik*, vol 38, 1931.

# The Task of Revolutionary Music[*]

In the second half of the 1960s, when I saw the political developments that were going on in Germany, I sometimes spontaneously felt I could not go on composing, and ought to do quite different things. I would like to try to explain this feeling with the help of Adorno, who wrote in the early 1960s: 'If one takes composing with deadly seriousness, one ultimately has to ask whether, today, it is not becoming totally ideological. Therefore, without the consolation that it can't go on like this, one must unmetaphorically come face to face with the possibility of falling silent.' In this quotation we find a puristic standpoint, but not the concept of ideology in the Marxist sense; instead, a rather vague concept of morality, which in a melancholy and unhistorical way yearns for bygone days, when music was allegedly uncontaminated by ideology. What period could he have had in mind?

Only from a class standpoint can I grasp the danger of ideology, which threatens music (and all other art-forms and branches of knowledge). If the arts and the sciences serve the ruling class, they become ideology. One must be aware of this danger. Naturally, in the age of late capitalism—with its mass media, its manipulated and violated music—the artist's work is made exceedingly difficult, but that is by no means a reason to abandon attempts to help the oppressed in their struggle. I will therefore continue to write, to base myself on my experiences, to try to extract my work from the bourgeois context of exclusiveness (where of course—to use

* 'Aufgaben und Möglichkeiten revolutionärer Musik.' From an interview with Hartmut Lück, first published in *Neue Musikzeitung*, vol 20 no 1, February/March 1971.

another phrase of Adorno's—*rien ne va plus*), and to make them usable and harnessed to a goal.

The theory that for music to become new it would be sufficient to develop new forms, is a formalist notion. I am concerned with the struggle of the working class, and with the struggle of the many who want to leave their class. I try to recognize their problems, and come to the conclusion that they are mine. I try to bring about a dialectical contact. That was not the case in my music before. My content has thus become different. New content requires new forms. In the process of deepening this new content, and through contact with my new listener, new structures will also become visible. A worker, an apprentice, a student, will not come to listen to *El Cimarrón* (or another piece of that kind) because of the music but because of the content I am trying to communicate. The musical material remains a problem. Eisler has written songs in a sort of fractured, alienated tonality, Luigi Nono is working in an electronic studio in order to make the latest technological means available for his revolutionary work. For me the problem is slightly different. I have as yet no experience of working with electronic music. Perhaps the more recent manifestations of pop music are preparing the ground for the reception of even complicated electronic compositions. Serving up the songs of the 1920s again would be workers' kitsch; that's out of the question.

I myself, though I do not yet have a great deal to show, am trying out new forms of music drama (inspired by street theatre) to convey situations from the class struggle, with modest means. The individual's problems, desires, fears and utopian elements, which theory is not yet capable of formulating, are also part of such research and presentation.

Every human being is in search of beauty, of a healthy world, a utopia where there are no more chains, where people can develop themselves freely. That world is unthinkable under capitalism, but communism is fighting for it.

I by no means renounce what I said in a lecture at the Berlin Technical University in 1963,* where the expression 'classical ideal

* See 'Some Instrumental Compositions', page 182.

of beauty' occurs in the following context: 'Old forms seem to me
. . . like classical ideals of beauty, no longer attainable but still
visible in the far distance, stirring memory like dreams; but the path
towards them is filled with the age's greatest darkness, and is the
most difficult and the most impossible.' At any rate I know today
how to understand the concept of the ideal of beauty historically,
and no longer as a dream of security and renunciation (and silence).
Music can be something for leisure, for play, imagination,
edification, festivity; it can contain information about social
conditions, and convey a message through the medium of art. One
can even subjugate people through music; waltzes and tangos
themselves carry information about social conditions.

My Second Piano Concerto (1967) is the work of somebody who
expresses his discontent, his powerlessness, his desires within the
accepted conventions, even within the terms and parameters of
such norms; who observes all prohibitions and taboos, and thereby
lays bare the degree of impoverishment and unfreedom for the first
time. This piece does not contain a way out, which is why the form
is in accord with the content. It is a document of unfreedom, and
thereby embodies a moment of awareness.

At the centre of *Muses of Sicily* (1965) there is a love-letter. In
addition this work is an attempt at 'pop'; about unburdening, about
beauty. And it is *Gebrauchsmusik* (utilitarian music): amateur choirs
can learn it easily and have fun with it.

*El Cimarrón* (1969) is my most recent piece; at the moment I
know most about it, especially as in my next piece things will be
continued that have played a role in it. Each of the four players
involved in this work has material with which he can work
creatively. This means that, when preparing a performance, each of
these four people is invited to act creatively, so that a creative
attitude simultaneously makes the adoption of a political position
necessary, as the text suggests. It demands of the performer that he
respond musically to what is happening on the plane of ideas. This
kind of political ballad which can here be done only by virtuosos, by
extremely capable, highly specialized people (two of the current
*Cimarrón* group are also composers themselves), could conceivably

be performed in a similar way, on a more simple basis, in kindergartens or (the next stage) in socialist schools, etc. It could thus become a kind of model.

In *El Cimarrón* there is a great deal of fun, there are *sones* (see p. 175), rumbas, habaneras, improvisations, parodies. The protagonist is a slave who liberates himself, and who regards his struggle not just as suffering but as a simultaneous conquest of happiness. He is utopia become human. Esteban Montejo, the *Cimarrón*, is an exemplar. What can be seen more clearly in *El Cimarrón* than in earlier pieces (and it is dependent on insights into the process of communication acquired in the meantime) is the tendency not to bewilder the spectator, not to engulf him with fog, or hypnotize him. On the contrary, the music itself explains to the listener how it is made, and not only through the demonstrative aspects of the theatrical elements. It constantly says 'Look here, that's quite simple, that's done like this.' It strives to involve the listener, to make him imagine that he could do it too. And so he understands, sees relationships, and is no longer alienated and a stranger.

I do not believe that new musical forms can be snatched out of the air, nor that such forms have the power to change society. For instance my *Sinfonia* No. 6, which I wrote for Cuba and which received its first performance there, is not merely called 'symphony' but tries to be a symphony in the sense of the European tradition, in the sense of sonata form, variations, fugal structures; I have attempted to review all these things once again.

*Sinfonia* No. 6 was first played in Cuba before an audience of three thousand, who consisted largely of soldiers of the revolutionary army, sons of workers, students from the University of Havana. I knew while I was writing it that this would be my audience. I took the greatest trouble. What was meant to emerge was this: I am looking for means with which I can glorify the proletarian revolutions of Cuba and the Third World. I bring in an NLF song and a song of freedom by Theodorakis; all the rhythmic parameters are derived from Latin American folklore. While I set about transforming the expressive means of bourgeois (European) 'new music' and my own, to turn them into their opposite, they resist and fragment. A conflict is depicted.

The use of straightforward labels (subtitles) such as oratorio, symphony, etc., for many of my works—labels that I prefer to such titles as *Pollution No. 3*, *Sonorizations*, *Tautology for conveyor-belts*, or *illuminated/not illuminated*—by no means indicates that these works are just reconstructions of the formal or thematic practices of the nineteenth or earlier centuries. One frequently finds, concealed behind bold titles and exotic packaging (and today packaging is almost everything), things whose only novelty lies in their name. In language a consensus exists that an enterprise carried out by several costumed singers, a number of instrumentalists, lighting technicians and theatre attendants bears the label 'opera'. The musician in the streets of Naples is performing a 'sonata', the whole population there is in agreement about that. When the Philharmonic, a firemen's band or the Rolling Stones come together to make music, the result is a concert, unmistakably and by no means always anachronistically.

The works and the forms of the past are, in Marx's sense, objectified nature. They are there to be appropriated by people. They are not ballast, but wealth. But that does not mean that one therefore has to be trendy and electronic. Electronics and so many other manifestations of modernity have nothing to do with the desire to do away with the establishment, apart from the fact that they are possible only because there is such a thing as an establishment.

I believe that a person should be honest enough to stand by everything that he has done. People are not ready-made products, either of socialism or of capitalism; they are, rather, people at different stages of development. A socialist is not something that one is, but *becomes*. And my musical strivings—even those that date back twelve or fifteen years, and also those that contain errors or have not succeeded—should be taken into account, for I too can be understood only in the context of my historical development, and not as phenomenon of 19 September 1970. By tomorrow this interview would look different: it could be more radical.

# Musical Life in Cuba[*]

In Cuba, as in many parts of Latin America, there is an extremely vigorous folk culture. It is Creole, in other words a combination of African and Spanish elements. In Santiago and the Oriente province this is augmented by a Haitian-French influence. In the 1920s two Cuban composers, Amadeo Roldán and Alejandro Garcia Caturla, tried to translate this music into forms of classical music, as Stravinsky, Milhaud and Chávez, among others, were doing. Both also intensified their contacts with Modernism, especially as represented in New York and Paris, and so it came about that on several occasions works by Stravinsky, Poulenc, Cage and others could be heard in Havana before they reached London, Berlin, Rome or Amsterdam. The centre of musical life was the Havana Symphony Orchestra, which was financed by the wealthy bourgeois, and could include such names as Igor Markevitch and Erich Kleiber in the list of its principal conductors. Italian conductors who worked in Cuba during the Batista dictatorship say they had never seen anywhere in the world such a sea of jewels and mink coats as in the Havana opera house.

Now the mink coats have emigrated to Miami, and the opera house has a different audience; the operas, almost without exception Italian, *Traviata*, *Tosca* and *The Barber*, serve to give pleasure to the people. After the victory of the revolution, Alicia Alonso, a great ballerina, returned from the United States and built up the national ballet company, which with its classical and modern repertoire enjoys international success. There is a separate

---

* 'Musikleben in Kuba.' From an interview with Hartmut Lück, first published in *Neue Musikzeitung*, vol 20 no 1, February/March 1971.

orchestra for opera and ballet, while the Orquesta Sinfónica Nacional is used exclusively for concerts. Many musicians emigrated after the *trionfo de la rebelión*, and there is a shortage of good string players. The missing talent is imported from friendly countries, especially Bulgaria. The next generation of young musicians has not yet been fully trained, delays being caused by the fact that all students have to spend a part of the year in clearing the land, building dikes, and working on plantations. The same applies to professionals. The orchestra, ballet and opera companies, etc., take part in the *trabajo productivo* of agriculture, on the development of which an improvement of the country's difficult economic situation depends. Three tendencies can be discerned in the work of the composers. There is an avant-garde, headed by Leo Brouwer, Juan Blanco and Carlos Fariñas. These musicians follow international developments, are interested in Cage and his disciples, and try to revolutionize elements of this music: in other words to adapt it to revolutionary goals. They enjoy great success, especially with the young audience that today dominates Havana—peasants' and workers' sons, who live in the former luxury hotels and study at the university.

This group is regarded with scepticism and mistrust by another, which tends rather to continue the nationalistic line of Roldán and Caturla. Some in these groups are members of the old communist party (which, as is well known, was hostile to Fidel's rebellion), and base their criticism on Marx, Lenin and Lukács.

Finally a third group, the youngest and as yet scarcely known, espouses the theory that all American and European influences must disappear from the art of Latin America. These young revolutionaries talk of neo-colonialism, and suspect the representatives of the western avant-garde of wanting to hinder the cultural awakening of the continent, as though they were CIA agents. This notion, which is worth consideration, brings them into collision with the work and aesthetic positions of the first group. All these debates take place in public under Fidel's motto: 'With the revolution, everything is allowed and welcomed; against the revolution, nothing.'

## Musical Life in Cuba

On my first visit to Cuba I asked: 'What kind of music was played, for instance, at the funeral demonstrations for Che?' 'Revolutionary music', came the reply. I then went into detail and discovered it was marches and songs. (There are also habaneras and pop songs about Che.) But sometimes electronic music too, generally by Blanco, is used at mass meetings; exciting, noisy, extremely cheerful music. On occasion you can hear this kind of music coming from many loudspeakers in the centre of the city; for instance as a 'sound-track' for an adapted 'psychedelic circus' (with political slogans), or for the approach to the Lenin exhibition in the Habana Libre (formerly the Hilton Hotel), for which Brouwer produced a six-channel montage of Lenin's voice. Mixed in with the noise of generators, the Beatles, and Cuban percussion, it comes from six corners of the hall, while Lenin's favourite piece, the *Appassionata*, or Mahler's 'Second', drifts down from above and mingles with the electronics.

Blanco told me how he once composed electronic music for the opening ceremony of a new village in the Sierra Maestra. The sounds thundered into the valley from the surrounding hills. A sort of natural stereophony. When it was all over, Fidel said to him: 'You did a good job, Blanco. But now I would like you to show the *campesinos* here in the Sierra what real music is. You should start with Mozart.'

Music is still not part of the primary curriculum; there is a shortage of teachers. But not everything can be done in eleven years; it is already a remarkable achievement of the revolution that there are no more illiterates. Previously they amounted to 80 per cent of the population. Several composers are interested in the important question of musical education, but there is a lack of resources, of time. . . .

Brouwer takes a class for young pop musicians, with whom he experiments with new forms. In addition he writes music for newsreels and films (he is the musical director of the state film company, ICAIC), is the author of a number of popular songs (afterwards he forgets he wrote them), and devotes the remainder of his time to composing orchestral and chamber music and giving guitar recitals. In this last capacity he travels by bus and mule to the most remote villages, where a *concierto* has never been heard, to talk about music, its history and its social significance.

Every composer (painter, writer) receives the same fixed sum of about 500 pesos (500 US dollars), pays no taxes, rent or telephone bills (like all Cubans), and is not forced to do anything in return, though he is expected to produce about one work per year. There are no royalties; all scores (paintings, books) belong to the people, and there is no extra payment for additional work such as conducting, teaching, etc. Nevertheless — or perhaps we should say, for this reason — Cuban composers work with an intensity and enthusiasm that can be explained only by the fact that they feel themselves liberated, and are happy to be able to play a part in building their revolution.

# Signs *

Composing music could be described as an attempt to set in motion essentially raw and static matter which can be represented by physical 'signs', and to wrest from it something contrary to its specific nature, something that comes into being despite it, and overcomes its rawness and muteness. The state that emerges from this victorious struggle is artificial or artistic, a work of art; from time to time an elucidatory communiqué is published to explain its genesis to the expectant public. The work itself outlives this communiqué several times over in value; the latter is forgotten, while the former retains a vibrancy, exerts influence, enlists agreement and discord—and then goes on to create fresh signs, and fresh agreement and fresh discord about these signs, often losing sight of the original object.

Alternatively, this victorious state often reaches such intensity that its effect goes beyond the intended fluctuating polyvalency, and can be interpreted and named—the expression of love, a longing for death, a hymn to the night, a message of freedom—without this meaning being revealed in any other way except through the musical signs themselves, precise, unmistakable, irreplaceable. Then this meaning spreads powerfully, in waves, and it becomes necessary to interpret it into categories. There thus arises a new conception, style, common property that no longer concerns the composer or the nature and motive of his actions. By this stage he himself is usually already gone after a life marked by obstinate rejection of his new reality.

* 'Die Zeichen.' *Texte und Zeichen* vol 1 no 2, Berlin 1955.

Once his new signs have been accepted and classified, others must soon follow. The tension has abated, the signs become academically respectable, a piece of musical history seems to be in the making; at this quasi-historical moment countless zealous writers and industrious apprentices rush into the public arena, retrace the emotions of yesterday, and proclaim them as the doctrine of tomorrow. What was once a bold leap, a signal from a lofty and distant transmitter, the reproduction of the call of a bird of death sighted only by the composer, is now transformed into a dry study, for the purpose of producing further dry studies: a computable object. The idea, artistic truth, ends up in a state of siege, a pseudo-revolution.

But excitement and tension between intervals can be produced only in a state of excitement and tension, not in a scientific manner. The mystery of these tensions lies beyond any known categories, however often such categories may be invoked to concretize this mystery; it demands that the categories be constantly questioned; it seeks no common-sense certainty; it wants something to come from these tensions, not something to be done with them. Great art is always a becoming, not a making. It speaks in a beauty, characterized by searching and uncertainty, to everything that is 'becoming'; it confuses and angers the efficient rule-bound 'makers'.

Music, and not just what is ascribed to it, is as far from being abstract as is a language, a death, a love. The mere fact that it is endlessly invented, wrested from the material, that through it something is snatched from fleeting time as it rushes by, that something is preserved, that in the concretization of time a longing is expressed and fulfilled—all this prohibits the use of the word 'abstract'.

Anyone who does not believe this must cling to the scaffolding of a narrower world made more bearable by theories. Others will set out on that more difficult path whose end cannot be foreseen: the path into a darkness filled with snares, misgivings, uncertainties and errors. One should let them go their own way, and wait for their return.

# La Cubana
## A Vaudeville *

In music-theatre, as I envisage it, music is incorporated into the drama, is performed on the stage rather than invisibly in the pit, is a concert dissolved into movement and action: demystified music.

Even concert pieces such as both of mine from last year—the Second Violin Concerto (where there is every kind of action, and a poem by Enzensberger is involved) and *Heliogabalus Imperator* (*allegoria per musica*)—are theatre music, or a kind of theatre music; at any rate a world of structures that strive to attain concreteness, to drive abstraction and inhumanity out of music. I do not know how far I have reached with my efforts, but I think further results will be discerned in my coming works too. I have just written a 'vaudeville' with Enzensberger, in which all the music is employed realistically. Music can be heard and seen in it only where it would also be heard and seen in real life. The only exceptions are the four 'chansons of the witnesses', which are performed on the apron-stage and comment on the action. All the other pieces are ingredients of the action; they are at its focus, are interwoven with it, and are triggered by and themselves trigger the action.

The theme of the vaudeville is the futility and dubiousness of art and artists, explored in the person of a Cuban music-hall queen named Amalia Vorg (known as Rachel). As previously in the case of *El Cimarrón*, Enzensberger got the material from Miguel Barnet, a

---

* 'Ein Vaudeville.' First published in *Festschrift für einen Verleger: Ludwig Strecker zum 90. Geburtstag*, ed. Carl Dahlhaus, Mainz 1973.

young writer and ethnologist living in Havana. It is based on his book *Canción de Rachel* (Havana 1969), the second part of a trilogy of documentary novels, of which the first part will be the story of a Havana family in the early years of the revolution. Barnet often spends years collecting material for his books by taping conversations; so too in the case of Rachel, whose recollections, thanks to his editing, became a document about Cuban cultural life in the first part of the century. Corruption and prostitution, which characterized the decades before the revolution, shimmer through her accounts like strings of imitation pearls, and can be found among the lumber of her egocentricity and the wretchedness of her platitudes. But whereas in Barnet's hands the subject-matter remains within the boundaries of a documentary study, and the author's critical involvement is only indirect and embodied in what he manages to uncover, when it is being reshaped into music drama it becomes far more ambivalent, and is exposed to criticism from several (especially contemporary and aesthetic) perspectives. What this means will emerge from a description of the work.

In a prologue we see Rachel as an old woman, alone and no doubt now poor, in her little apartment jammed full of souvenirs, in the company of Ofelia, her old theatrical dresser and maid. The action begins at the very moment that Fidel and his *guerilleros* are entering Havana, so the date must be 1 January 1959. The indifference and cynicism with which Rachel receives this news ('Don't get yourself all worked up, you idiot, it's only a revolution.') immediately show us Rachel as she was and is; later the witnesses say it quite explicitly, in their second chanson:

> Suicides, cloudbursts, revolts;
> we see but one person
> who does not get wet,
> who never burns her fingers,
> seemingly invulnerable and out of harm's way:
> Rachel!

Her thoughts are immediately elsewhere, with the weather, with herself and her memories ('Now, in those days. . . .'), and there follows a flash-back to the first tableau,* which is set in 1906 in the Tivoli Theatre, the scene of Rachel's first engagement. There is no development in the spoken scenes between the individual tableaux, giving the impression that they are all on the same day, as if time were standing still. Nothing seems to be happening except memory. We hear nothing about the revolution except that the theatres are closed and there is no more tea. Ofelia sits in front of the radio once, but instead of news, only crackling is heard. Even in the epilogue, when old Rachel is trying on her costumes to see which of them she would like to be buried in, nothing decisive happens, nothing changes. This scene, in which a day from Batista's dictatorship in 1934 overlaps with 1959 (a snapshot of the apartment of an old theatre diva in Havana during the revolution), fuses into something like an allegorical present, and also shows quite clearly that the authors have avoided any form of agitprop, and have stuck to the theme instead. The theme is variations on art; a theme with which the theatre can be entrusted, which concerns everyone (and politically too) who is involved with the material: stage, lighting, music, make-up. Everyone from that world can recognize himself in Rachel's mirrors or in the sets that surround her. It is, therefore, a case of *l'art pour l'art*, although not in the conventional manner desired by its proponents.

During composition I noticed something that can easily be overlooked when reading the text (and which some have indeed overlooked), namely that it is the product of an unusually vivid imagination. There is nothing casual about it. It is planned with an eye to the music, and has a telling and also somewhat calculated quality; its craftsmanship is riveted together and solid (permanently joined by springs, pins and human hair), so that composing became more and more like doing a crossword puzzle, as if all I needed to worry about was that everything fitted into the right place, like the toothed wheel of a pianola. In fact the whole piece seems to me (it

* All tableaux, unlike the prologue, intermezzi and epilogue, are set in the past and are musical scenes. Thus in the prologue, intermezzi and epilogue Rachel as an old woman should be played by an actress; young Rachel in the tableaux, on the other hand, as a singer or *soubrette* or *chansonette*.

has just been finished, so I am unbiased) cold and robust, and as heartless as could be desired. While I was composing the music in Marino in the summer of 1972, Enzensberger was building his poetry automats in Berlin; that may be a significant coincidence.

Now to the question of the active participation of orchestral players in a performance of *La Cubana*. I hope that I have not called for anything that my instrumentalist colleagues will refuse to do. (In that case, back to the pit with them!) There must be some 'ethos' or 'pathos' that makes them scurry off and shy away from experiments (that are not experiments at all), and hesitate to do things that are different from what they had thought all along. I do not want to parody the production of instrumental music, but first of all to expose it, and then activate it and bring it to a new kind of reality. There were similar things in *El Cimarrón*; the performances of those photomontages translated into music require four (exceptionally experienced) performers who sing and act, and are creatively involved in composition during the performance. Also in *Natascha Ungeheuer*, where the technique discovered in *El Cimarrón* is continued and extended to several groups of instrumentalists. Here the musicians are themselves actors. They depict ideas and situations, which their activity expresses; and their physical presence and the sound that they produce are plot, décor and message.

There are already some good examples of the new type of player that the new music drama requires, such as the cellist Hornung, the percussionist Yamash'ta, members of The Fires of London, of the London Sinfonietta, and of the Hamburg Hinz und Kunst group. I foresee more and more musicians preparing themselves to take on this new extended role of instrumentalist-actor.

In *La Cubana oder ein Leben für die Kunst* (La Cubana or A Life for the Arts) I have reduced my demands on the one hand: the technical difficulties are less challenging than in the pieces mentioned above; the work is after all intended for repertory theatres. On the other hand I have increased the degree of involvement in the stage action; ideally all the players should also be good actors.

# La Cubana: A Vaudeville

In the first tableau, which shows us the Tivoli music hall, we see the Tivoli orchestra (clarinet, saxophone, banjo, double-bass, and pianist-conductor; later a trombone is added). The players should appear incompetent, tired and harassed. There is thus already a theatrical element, but the main thing is that each should handle his music like an actor his lines: as a role that needs to be interpreted; played not 'inwards' (like chamber music) but 'outwards'. The player should watch and listen to himself. He should distance himself from himself. A direction in the piano part of the 'Duet of the perpetually rosy future' (in the first tableau) runs as follows:

To be played from memory, but without bravura (to be practised until the playing becomes automatic and 'dead'). It should not sound 'difficult', but old and hopeless. A lot of pedal. The pianist, a tired (old) woman (who will later appear as a witness, and sing mezzo-soprano), smokes a cigar while she is playing, or drinks coffee, reads a newspaper or eats a sandwich. And because of the structural simplicity of this number, the impression of an 'accompanied song' must not arise.

On the stage, Rachel and Eusebio should be as far from the piano as possible. No eye contact. 'Asynchronism' can be rehearsed if desired. The impression must be given that the singing 'harmonizes' with the piano part only by accident (and never for long).

In the 'chansons of the witnesses' waiters and stagehands play the accompanying instruments; a member of the circus band (the tuba player) joins in later. Here too there should as far as possible be no conducting, and the playing (and of course the singing) should be from memory. Folk instruments—ocarina, bamboo flute and mouth-organ—contrast with the mandoline, guitar and tuba.

Percussion instruments hardly appear in the entire vaudeville. They are excluded from all the 'Rachel' music, as well as from the witnesses' chansons, although it would have been obvious to provide the tangos, rumbas and *sones* with the percussion sound customary for these dances. But I reserve these colours and their associations for the insurrection scene (in the third tableau), and for the 'mass rhythms' (Enzensberger) at the end of the work. A whole range of unusual folk instruments is included (situated in four different places behind the stage); among them a *pandiera*, a *chocolo*, a *cabaça*, a Neapolitan *scetavaiasse*, a *Waldteufel*, and Haitian voodoo drums ('father, mother and baby').

In the second tableau there is a nine-piece band in a number called 'Music from a House'. It seems to come from a bar in a building, but cannot be seen, only heard. It mingles with Beethoven's 'Moonlight' Sonata, clumsily played (presumably by some young miss); we hear snatches from all three movements. There is also in a house opposite (or at any rate some way away) a cornet playing a tune that obviously belongs to a pasodoble, and finally the whole nocturne is extended to a waltz, which intertwines, played on a violin and an accordion by two beggars squatting by the harbour wall; the accordionist seems to be an invalid, and is drawn across the plaza on a low (ankle-high) trolley by the (blind) fiddler.

For the 'Aster Duet' between Rachel and Lucile the wind band moves off and is already out of sight, becoming softer and softer; Rachel and Lucile sing rubato (without conductor) to this music, more and more intensely. There should be an impression of fortuitousness, as in the 'Duet about the perpetually rosy future'. The same applies to the beginning of the third tableau, the circus scene. A group of *campesinos* are killing time until the performance begins. They play simple music, which should sound improvised and yet as if they were following rules that no one else knows. Their instruments are three jew's-harps, ocarina, mandoline, mouth-organ, bamboo flute (or something similar—a tin whistle of the kind that children buy at fairs would do), guitar and marimbula (African harp)—similar to those used in the witnesses' chansons, and the players should also be the same. This music-making (without conductor of course) should be something 'internal', quiet, almost apathetic, without movement, with a few spare dance-steps added later. It provides the contrast for the 'Caravan Duet', whose rhythm should differ sharply from the instrumental playing, which must be legato and rubato. Later on in this tableau there is some (conducted) circus music (two piccolos, piccolo clarinet,

clarinet, two trumpets, trombone, tuba, glockenspiel, bass drum), followed for the first time by a new sound element: Enzensberger describes a 'rhythmic cackling, howling, shouts, drumming' coming from a distance. I produced the 'rhythmic cackling, howling' and the 'shouts' with Peter Zinovieff in London on a magnificent new synthesizer. Variants of them can also be heard at the end of the work. The electronic sound is supplanted by the percussion instruments behind the stage, playing strictly in time, against which Estéban Montejo, the young *Cimarrón* (who has interrupted the circus performance with a group of rebels), together with Paco (circus acrobat) and Rachel improvise intervals (on strict rhythmical patterns) in the way already tried in *El Cimarrón*, *Versuch über Schweine* and *Natascha Ungeheuer*. Pitch is indicated only approximately, and it is therefore important for the performers to avoid singing twelve-note clichés. That is one problem; the other will be how to maintain cohesion between on-stage and off-stage. This will have to be solved in a different way in each theatre by using the house's technical capacities, but a visible conductor or co-ordinator ought to be avoided.

Now the fourth tableau (1927). Even more than the first, it is theatre within theatre (within the theatre). The players sit in a simulated pit, as if they were parodying their everyday work environment. There has to be a conductor here. In the Alhambra Theatre, as this temple of culture is known, we are plunged into the final act of a pornographic operetta about mistaken identity (the text is taken without adaptation from the original), which ends with the heroine's striptease. I have tried to construct the music so that you might imagine its composer to be an enthusiast from provincial Cuba who defies the banality and kitsch of the text, and tries 'in spite of all' to write something sublime. In the process he merely succumbs to cliché on a 'higher' level, thinking that a genius has to stand above his environment and must not allow himself to be influenced by it, and that a good composer must even be capable of setting a poster to music—I believe this requirement comes from Telemann, and was virtually met by him. He has heard Puccini and Debussy in Havana (after all we are in 1927), but is now so carried away by the events of the drama that he forgets his plan and increasingly loses sight of his aesthetic, so that his music becomes more and more swinging until he even supplies something very special in F sharp major for the striptease. This 'act' must be played in the style of a *zarzuela*—the instrumental music pedantic, without expression (with false pathos), without nudges or winks, without verve, without 'tongue in cheek', *senza leccarsi i baffi*, the singing *molto parlando*, rather like dramatic recitatives in Lehár. Every word must be understood. Only the tango at the centre, 'Magdalena's tango', is properly sung out by Rachel who is playing Magdalena, and comes on in a dinner-jacket disguised as Teodoro; she should sing with a deep voice that recalls something like Zarah Leander. The text is about the scent of perfume and cigars. The banality and futility of this 'act' is framed by a prose scene in Rachel's dressing-room.

In the fifth tableau (1934) we find only mechanical sounds, chiefly the clattering and hammering of the pianola, and right at the end the sound of an old scratched 78 record of the Alhambra orchestra playing Rachel's song 'My Illusion' (several verses of which she rendered in the fifth scene, accompanied by the pianola). Rachel leaves her theatrical life behind (in Miguel's book she does so to open a brothel); the Alhambra is closed and becomes the Shanghai Striptease; the last scene and her last song are interrupted by shoot-outs between gangsters, scenes with beggars, and a demonstration (in which Ofelia takes part). They end with the epilogue; while Rachel, an old woman, puts on a suitable dress for her burial, stagehands strike the old sets from the Alhambra, more and more junk getting piled up on stage. When she walks on to the stage in her funeral garb, a worker tosses a plump rat on to the heap of rubbish. The sound of the old record of 'My Illusion' that Rachel has put on (she wants it to be played at her funeral) becomes more and more submerged by the mass rhythm, the folk instruments played by the beggars, and a pedal point G, taken from the last note of the gramophone record and held in crescendo behind the stage on every available bass instrument, with really rhythmic shouting of 'ay!', stamping, and a variant of the electronic cackling.

*[214]*

## La Cubana: A Vaudeville

Anything solemn, all ceremony has been stripped away from the music-making, including the forbidding anonymity of the orchestra pit. The tediousness of avant-garde festival music has also been completely avoided. In his poem 'A Final Contribution to the Question of Literature?' Enzensberger first asks his 'brothers in Apollo':

| | |
|---|---|
| *Warum zitiert ihr immerfort Hegels Ästhetik und Lukács?* | Why do you constantly quote Hegel's *Aesthetics* and Lukács? |
| *warum bringt ihr euch Tag für Tag* | why do you, day after day, |
| *auf den historischen Stand?* | bring yourselves historically up to date? |
| . . . | . . . |
| *Woher diese Angst, Klassiker zu werden* | Where does this fear come from of becoming classics |
| *oder im Gegenteil?* | or of the opposite? |
| *Und warum fürchtet ihr euch davor* | And why are you afraid of being clowns? |
| *Clowns zu sein?* | of serving the people? |
| *dem Volk zu dienen?* | |

He then calls out to them:

| | |
|---|---|
| *Fürchtet euch nicht!* | Don't be afraid! |
| *Krümmt euch vor Anstrengung* | Bend your backs with effort |
| *oder schiebt eine ruhige Kugel,* | or take it easy |
| *aber habt keine Angst.* | but have no fear. |
| *Es kommt nicht auf uns an.* | We don't really count. |
| *Dafür werden wir doch bezahlt.* | That's what we are paid for. |
| *Warum gebt ihr nicht zu,* | Why don't you admit |
| *was mit euch los ist* | what's up with you |
| *und was euch gefällt* | and what you want? |
| *Ein einziges Mal,* | Just once, |
| *nur ein Vierteljahr lang,* | for just three months, |
| *zur Probe!* | try it out! |
| *Dann wollen wir weitersehen.* | Then we shall see. |
| *Niemand tut euch was.** | No one's going to bite you. |

* *Gedichte 1955–1970*, Frankfurt 1971.

## La Cubana: A Vaudeville

Through *La Cubana* we would like to set something concrete against all the efforts to identify conformist storms in cultural teacups with Marxism or with 'the revolution' (seldom and unwillingly defined more precisely); something that in its criticism also concerns the behaviour of musical avant-gardists ('Avant of what?', as Peter Maxwell Davies asks), those Rachels of the absolute and the *Weltgeist*, as found in the subsidized 'Alhambras' of today.

Not sounds, but guns could bring about social change. (Who and what will change remains open.) In the meantime we would like to deposit our bad conscience in the mortuary of Modernism, as Enzensberger puts it, in other words to free ourselves of certain *idées fixes* about culture that we might still have. As can be seen in my earlier writings from 1952–62, I have been working in this direction for two decades, though I have certainly been caught again from time to time, and gone back to doing what I've been trained to think of as my duty. Alexander Mitscherlich calls this *Trauerarbeit*, meaning what the Germans have been busy doing since the war, the magnitude of their labours substituting for remorse, for shame, and for the inability to communicate.

*La Cubana* is (nothing but) a vaudeville, and the music for it makes no contribution to the problem of workers' music; from a certain point of view it is 'élitist' *cum grano salis*. The standpoint from which I wrote the music is, however, not free from grim dialectic, which perhaps does not matter, as long as listening to and seeing the whole piece is pleasurable. But you should not rank this music with attempts to create art that can be employed in the class struggle. It makes no such claims, it is not so conceived and in any case that kind of thing would be out of place in a vaudeville.

Only the attempts described above to interweave music with action could be viewed in such a context. I would like the music to lay bare something of the history of the instrumentalists, which belongs to the history of working people. I would like the instrumentalists to interpret themselves consciously, and to extend their scope, so that they see themselves as inhabiting a realm of increased possibilities—possibilities of self-realization and self-liberation, which are assuredly a prerequisite for liberation on a larger scale.

# Opera Belongs to All *

The Germans are envied the world over for their opera houses. In the USA, in England and in France people are increasingly striving to set up new opera houses or new orchestras in the provinces. In those countries it is considered culturally progressive.

For a modern city, closing down an opera house is a decisive step towards alienation. For centuries it had been a significant part of the cultural life of a city that musicians were among its citizens. It is, indeed, due to them that an appreciation of music spread and that, on the whole, there is such a natural feeling for music in our people. All that would come to an end and cannot be replaced by touring companies, especially as they are more likely to be of a token character than a permanent local institution.

The notion that opera is 'bourgeois' and an obsolete art form is itself one of the most outdated, tedious and musty notions. There are, to be sure, outmoded styles, outdated and tedious productions, and slipshod routine that make it difficult for many theatre-lovers and young comrades to grasp the content of the works being performed. (Is that the case in Dortmund? I do not know, but cannot imagine that it is.) But this art form contains riches that are among the most beautiful inventions of the human spirit. They belong to all people; they were not written for the ruling class, but in a spirit of human brotherhood. Anyone who has seen, for example, how young workers and peasants in Havana have made symphonic music and opera their own, and how they fill the opera house, *their*

* 'Die Oper gehört allen.' A letter to a newspaper, occasioned by plans to close down the Dortmund opera house and Philharmonic Orchestra. First published in the *Deutsche Volkszeitung*, 9 May 1974.

opera house, to listen to *their* composers, Mozart, Verdi, Caturla, Beethoven, and Brouwer, will no longer be able to retain any doubts about which direction progressive cultural work must take; certainly not that of doing away with one of the fundamental factors of our culture.

It is not opera that is reactionary. What is bourgeois is an (undialectical) belief in linear progress, titillated by fashionable notions, frustrated and elitist, which calls for different forms of music and music-making as if to escape reality, to by-pass it: forms that could not exist at all, because they would have no basis (in the political and philosophical sense). Progress in art (and in artistic life) is conceivable only in connection with social progress. One must start at the foundations.

One more word on Dortmund. The Dortmund Philharmonic Orchestra is one of the finest orchestras in the Federal Republic—a so-called 'crack orchestra'. Doing away with it would mean only that the new and curious form of 'progress' in our cultural life has already progressed further than most of us had suspected or feared.

# A New Journal

*Letter to the* Frankfurter Allgemeine Zeitung*

London, 27 August 1974

Sir,

I beg the hospitality of your columns for this response to the article by your correspondent, Friedrich Hommel, 'By conviction and because it's fun', which appeared on 24 August.

Schotts, the publishers, and I are as before in complete agreement that it is necessary for the planned new music journal, which will result from an amalgamation of *Melos* and *Neue Zeitschrift für Musik*, to have a different character from its predecessors. What appears to be contentious is the addition of two members to the existing editorial board. The two in question are the music critic H. K. Jungheinrich, whose participation will contribute to sustaining and amplifying *Melos*'s reputation for contemporaneity and liveliness, and the German composer Dieter Schnebel, who will re-establish the tradition of having a composer (such as Robert Schumann and Karl Amadeus Hartmann) as one of the editors of what was the *Neue Zeitschrift*.

The negotiations have not yet been concluded, so it is odd that someone should claim to know their outcome. It could even be held that, with his article, Herr Hommel wishes to intervene in these negotiations and influence them.

What is meant to be new about our journal is that contemporary musical activity, which is in a constant state of flux, will be critically surveyed in detail. This will also make it attractive to a larger

* 14 September 1974.

readership than hitherto. A music magazine cannot afford to lag behind the general development, unless its policy is consciously to avoid contact with reality and to make its circle of readers ever smaller. More and more composers and performers are voicing the demand for a more relevant and democratic music scene. It would be foolish and unrealistic not to listen to them. A journal such as the one planned by Schotts must, explicitly and increasingly, become a forum for the free expression of opinion and open discussion.

What is intended is democratization: that is, all representative aesthetic tendencies throughout the world should have an equal right to have their say. There can be no talk of preference for any set of 'views about music and society'.

The suppositions and imputations of Herr Hommel thus have no foundation whatsoever. It is admittedly interesting—though by no means unusual—to observe that as soon as there is even rumour of new directions, people start talking about a 'break with tradition', about 'coercion' and 'ideologization'. Not exactly 'liberal' or 'democratic' behaviour.

On closer observation one notices that Herr Hommel's indignation can largely be put down to the co-option to the editorial board of H. K. Jungheinrich, who in Hommel's article is condemned by a few quotations taken out of context. Herr Jungheinrich has for several years been the music critic of the *Frankfurter Rundschau*, a newspaper that certainly cannot be suspected of plotting the overthrow of the democratic institutions of the Federal Republic.

I do not propose to go into Herr Hommel's pseudo-biographical gossip about me. But I must say something about a few points that are of more than personal significance:

1. Trying to find psychological explanations for political commitment will not do. At a time when a world-wide conflict is being waged between the forces of renewal and those of conservatism—a conflict of which, most recently, events in Chile, Portugal and Greece are symptomatic—to dismiss a person's commitment to progress as privately motivated is, at such a time, a moral effrontery that rebounds on its originator. It is, moreover, a

deliberate, planned attempt to cloud the facts, and itself constitutes commitment, but assuredly not to progress.

2.    The personal crisis referred to is of a different nature from that imagined by Herr Hommel. It is the crisis of every bourgeois intellectual who in his work is entangled in the conflicts between the old world and the new. The artist who did not notice this crisis would be insensitive, of no service to culture, and objectively abetting the perpetuation of this crisis. (Even during my alleged 'crisis of creativity' I have not altered the rhythm of my production, but if anything have intensified it. During that time numerous compositions for orchestras of varying size were produced, and often without words, despite what Herr Hommel reports.) I am a socialist, and as such neither a 'dreamy utopian' nor one of those who look upon the countries where socialism is being constructed amid much hard work as 'paradises'. A lengthy and difficult process has begun in those countries, which has as its goal a view of man that must deeply engage anyone prepared to think and comprehend.

3.    That an artist should put all his energies into making his views known is logical, and certainly not scandalous. There are various excellent examples of this in literature, and in music, albeit to a lesser extent. I must blame myself for having remained indifferent on this question for far too long, and for not having understood sooner that exerting an influence is not merely a personal right but, in the first instance, a social duty. It is taken for granted that my publishers demand this kind of involvement from their authors.

# Tristan *

One morning in early 1972, in the course of a few hours, I composed an extended piece for piano. The thematic material that was articulated—semitonal steps and sixths, chords of fourths and, in particular, diminished fifths—distantly recalls the music of Wagner's *Tristan*. Like it, my harmony seems to be moving towards an incommensurable goal, whose attainment keeps being deferred, so that a new constellation of enigmas can be posed in its place. But Wagner's music has an incandescent and exclusive quality, something totalitarian. Mine is cool, as if it were early morning, and the questioning and longing are expressed with muted voice; it comes from far away, and has, so it seems, a marmoreal sound and a depersonalized quality. Yet the most intimate and personal things, which would later be developed in my symphonic work *Tristan*, were embodied in this piano piece, which I christened *Prélude* and which was to be followed by further preludes. For the time being I left the piano piece as a sketch.

Some months later I was in London. During the day I was in Putney with Zinovieff and his computers, synthesizers and assistants. We were producing the tapes for my Second Violin Concerto; Brenton Langbein, the soloist, had recorded on individual tracks the sections that were now being transformed by synthesizer. The singer, Alan Evans, had recorded (in German and English) my setting of the Enzensberger poem that gives the concerto its structure. We filtered the voice; the sounds of vowels and consonants were analysed, unmasked, reified. But the further

---

* '*Tristan.*' (1975) *Musik und Politik* 1976.

this process went, the more it became a dismantling of the text. Finally, the words became incomprehensible; that would not do. We relaxed in the garden. At the end of the garden there were iron railings, from which one could look down on to the pudding mud-flats of the Thames.

I was freezing all the time. At night I wrote down what I heard when I was dozing or dreaming; I described it in words. A form and a name were the result: Tristan. The sounds flew around nightmarishly like the bats in Goya's etching, 'The Sleep of Reason Begets Monsters'. My pathos, my illusions, my difficulties with language. I spent three days at 26 Fitzroy Square, amid the medieval monastic furniture of Peter Maxwell Davies and in the company of his insane cat. I wrote down the score of the sounds I had dreamed about.

There were two parts, each lasting six minutes. One was for prepared piano and primitive percussion instruments; seven tracks, seven-part counterpoint. The other was for Renaissance instruments, flutes, shawms, lutes and tromba marina, and incorporated the old Florentine 'Lamento di Tristano'.

Some days later we recorded these instrumental parts track by track, and once that had been done we prepared the strings of Zinovieff's piano with clothes-pegs, strips of cardboard, drawing-pins and wire. *Vieux jeu.* Toys, whips, bells were among the instruments. We spent a whole day recording this music, Zinovieff and Geoffrey King, a composer and assistant of Davies. We threw glass marbles at the strings. They bounced around making a tittering sound, and clattered when they reached the steel frame. We bombarded bass strings with tennis-balls; that sounded like far-off explosions. It was playful, but it also had a diabolical, neurotic, evil, lunatic element. We were tense, excited, screamed at one another, were beside ourselves. To conclude, we mated an old pianola mechanism with that of the piano, and put on a piano-roll of Chopin's funeral march. Even before being processed by the synthesizer, the result on tape was of an overpowering hideousness. Now it sounded grotesque, terrifying, this violation, this battering of music. *Bruitismo.* Brutalism. Physical aggression. Clattering, groaning, howling, roaring. I have never done anything like it before, let alone heard it.

Later the first four bars of the third act of Wagner's *Tristan* were subjected to computer analysis. Late in the evening I had to go over to Putney again; the results had started to come out of the computer. Zinovieff and his lovely Victoria were sitting there and crying while, like veritable waves, the counterfeit versions flooded over us, voluptuous, soft, and mellow in their droning. Suffering and reconciliation, death and redemption in one, emerged from this hothouse; more and more new experiences of suffering, information about suffering, and new forms of suffering were accumulated on the reels. Six minutes of this material would later serve as a continuum for the epilogue of my work.

But a year would pass before then. Before I could start on the composition of the piano pieces and the orchestral music, I had to listen to the tapes again and again, until I knew them by heart, for only then could I create opposing colours and lines, and correspondences to the recorded sounds. Slowly, concrete ideas took shape. They became more vivid, thanks to a visit from John Cranko in early 1973. He had heard of my *Tristan* project, and hoped that I would adapt this music for him for a trilogy of full-length ballets. My plans and sketches were, however, already too far advanced to allow a change of course at this point, and in any case I had already promised the piece to the London Symphony Orchestra. But I said I was prepared to collaborate on his trilogy later, whereupon Cranko spent days telling me stories from old Tristan legends that he was planning to use. Many of these motifs have certainly gone into my music, for instance King Mark's love; Tristan as a beggar with his hair cropped, and recognized only by the dog; Isolde sentenced to death by burning, or given to the lepers as a whore; black Isolde; the black sail; the boathouse by the sea. John sent a draft, according to which each of the three evenings would have had a central theme: earth, fire, water. This outline did not reach me in Marino until after John's death.

The questioning and searching of the first prelude ends with a kind of answer. As in Wagner's prelude to *Tristan*, so too in mine, A

14 At rehearsal with the touring group at the first German performance of *El Cimarrón*, Berlin 1970. Left to right: William Pearson (baritone, but pretending to play the guitar), Leo Brouwer (guitar), Stomu Yamash'ta (percussion), Karlheinz Zöller (flute), and HWH

15 Scene 8 in the 1976 Covent Garden premiere of *We Come to the River*. The conductor was David Atherton, with production by the composer and sets designed by his brother Jürgen Henze. The General (Norman Welsby) is on the bench at the left

16 *Don Chisciotte* performed alfresco at Montepulciano, 1976

17 HWH applauding the 'banda' at Montepulciano, 1976

minor can be regarded as the tonal reality that never appears, that is never expressed but waits in the background. At the end of my prelude it can suddenly be heard pianissimo in the strings for thirty seconds. After about fifteen seconds it is joined by the Florentine 'Lamento', which is also in A.

To accompany the electronic sounds, orchestral music has been composed which is antiphonally related to them in every instrumental, rhythmic and dynamic detail. Hearing it later on, it sounds like an elaborate network of revelations, correspondences, answers, calls. But form is ultimately produced by development, and this is to be found in the autonomous structure of the orchestral music, which steers horizontally towards one point, gliding along on the tonality that circles ambivalently around A. Memory crops up among the long drawn out lines of the cellos, the violas and then the violins, in the organ-like notes of the full brass, and is awakened by the ecstatic sound of horns. Chopinesque piano music, garlanded with string harmonics; the colours grow darker; in deep wind passages what had been contained in the *Prélude* of the previous year is developed, darkly glittering, fluctuating, yet subordinated to the pulsing of the 'one crotchet per second' tempo (M.M. 60). By strictly fixing the tempo (on the precise observance of which the quality of a performance of the work stands or falls), a corrective has been built in which rules out chance and keeps the sound masses under control. Thus the process of creation, starting with the first sketches and ending with each new concert performance, to an increasing extent works against chaos. One could say that the entire work on this piece represents a vehement act of will against this chaos that threatens to break in from all sides.

A second monologue for piano follows the first tutti section (which is called 'Tristan's lament'). This monologue too is kept within a primarily calm tempo. There is so much time. The pianist is given the task of finding nuances between *pppp* and *ffff*. The elegiac narcissistic tone of the work is extinguished by three short orchestral variations that follow: the first is a shadowy *pointilliste* figure, the second a bobbing scherzando, the third drives forward in somewhat stormy fashion. The piano music that follows, the third prelude, takes up what has been alluded to, but now everything is in a state of unrest and agitation, as though a gust of wind had swept through the house. A three-part canon in the orchestra takes up the idea of the third prelude in three versions; the last note of this section is a C on the double-bassoon, which becomes five crescendo drum-beats on C, and for three bars we hear the opening of Brahms's First Symphony. There has been some speculation about the reasons for this unexpected visitation. I had intimated that it stands for the Enemy. What its precise meaning is should be left open; it is sufficient to know that it does not signify only the pedantic opponent of Wagner, familiar from biographies, nor merely, in the grey North Sea light of those sounds, the dreary day that Tristan dreads and hates.

Nevertheless the result of this theatrical entrance of the Enemy, of this wrenching open of a door, is that the music now no longer seems to know where to go, as if it were blinded and stumbling. For the moment it can manage no more than a few attempts to pick up the thread again, which end with a stammered reminiscence of the ostinato bass C.

All of a sudden, Tristan's madness erupts. The taped music is answered first by the piano *con pathos*, and immediately afterwards by small high-pitched percussion instruments; then wind music, dark percussion, high woodwind. Next comes a kind of composed pause bar, during which each of the string players improvises on three or four notes, by plucking strings in rapid succession, playing or tapping them with the back of the bow, or drawing it across the strings or the bridge; at the same time a woodwind sequence that had already played a role in the 'Lamento' goes past, as if on the horizon. Then a few bars of string cantilena, followed by a further fragment from the Brahms. This is pulverized; a rapt passage for solo violin is surrounded by light percussion and solo wind instruments. Powerful piano chords, clusters, piccolo trumpet. Crescendo-accelerando on the bass drum, like a cue from Kabuki theatre. This is copied ten seconds later in descent by the piano, then by the orchestra, which however ends in a ritardando, and here the montage of Chopin's funeral march begins on tape, with the orchestra playing in counterpoint: in the woodwind with a ludicrous abbreviation of the march rhythm, in the strings with percussive effects. First in the trombones and tubas, then in the horns, finally also in the trumpets with counterpoints that increase in intensity and reach a first peak in the fifth minute of playing. Violins take over the principal line, but after a few bars the brass enter again in canon, and carry this section to its acoustic and emotional climax.

The last sound dies away in two adagio bars on the strings, out of which, without a break, something new and different emerges: a sequence of burlesque dance pieces. The first, for strings only, has a waltz-like character ('Burla I'); 'Burla II' follows *alla turca*; then two *ricercari*, between which 'Burla III' (a march that shines like a prism through irregular rhythms) is inserted. These tormenting, reeling hallucinations and grotesques constitute the quest for the opening motifs, and thereby of earlier dreams and longings, which seem distorted as if in a grimace, and scarcely recognizable. Metallic beats growing louder and louder break into the second *ricercare*, until they are silenced by a scream of death, no longer simply that of Isolde or Tristan, but of the whole suffering world, which seems to burst the bounds of concert music. What can be heard on tape is an electronic elaboration of the scream of a Wagnerian heroine, broken up into many voices and colours. The utmost volume in the orchestra: weeping, howling and bird-calls, and the sound of flexatone and foghorn, all of which slowly ebb away.

On the evening of 12 September we heard of the death of Salvador Allende, and during the following days and weeks we received more and more details about the end of Chilean democracy. The first refugees arrived; we heard directly from Santiago about mass arrests, executions, the death of Neruda and the destruction of his house, burning of books, the death of Victor Jara under torture. In Rome we took to the streets with thousands of others, joined in solidarity rallies, yet were impotent and helpless. The catastrophes continued in my private life: the death of Auden at the end of the month, and Ingeborg Bachmann's horrifying death by fire. All these things made it impossible for me to write for several weeks. Not until the end of October, in Venice, did things slowly start to go better. I took little trips to Burano and Torcello, and often went to the Accademia to look at Giorgione's 'Tempesta', in whose enigmatic composition I thought I could perceive certain messages that seemed addressed to me. I lived in the house of a Japanese glass-maker, my friend Yoichi, in San Giacomo. The light was already wintry, the city without tourists; only the voices of the Venetians could be heard, in the tones of the plays of Gozzi and Goldoni; in the streets were many familiar faces who had stepped out of paintings by Carpaccio and Titian. A resigned calm settled, a Trakl-like state, and amid this I produced the piano epilogue, a sustained two-part song, introduced by microtones and shifting chords. I left sections blank, in which I would later insert reminiscences and variations of sections that had been written earlier but which in my present state I did not want to see or hear. At the end of the duet you hear over the loudspeaker a human heartbeat, and the voice of Kolinka Zinovieff who (with a slight Cockney accent) reads from the twelfth-century *Tristran* of Thomas: 'She takes him in her arms, and then, lying at full length, she kisses his face and lips and clasps him tightly to her. Then straining body to body, mouth to mouth, she at once renders up her spirit and of sorrow for her lover dies thus at his side.' Beneath this can be heard the original Wagnerian sounds from the Wesendonk *Treibhaus* song and the beginning of the third act, in extreme augmentation. Then bells chime, as though from the many towers of Venice, and are accompanied by taped electronic transformations of this old music, waxing and waning, chaconne-like, glistening like the sea on an autumn evening, when the golden and blue colours so often invoked by Trakl are resplendent, and red maple leaves float on the canals. In this light, and these sounds, this weeping and silence, everything that has accompanied this work comes together: places and people, the cemetery in Klagenfurt, the football stadium in Santiago where political 'suspects' are rounded up, the deaths and varieties of death, and the dead whose passing has impoverished mankind, while the fascists' goose-step resounds through buildings deserted by the people, and the fly-face of General Pinochet appears on the television screen, spreading such horror that clocks stop and blood congeals.

# We Come to the River *

Today I'm going to talk about new music-theatre, and in particular a work that Edward Bond and I have written. The score was finished only two months ago, and I didn't then want to think about this music for a long time. Even now the distance is very slight, but I shall try to give an account of the work all the same. Basically it began as long as ten years ago, after the completion of the opera *The Bassarids*, which conjured up the music drama of another era. After that work, where I made the tragic (pessimistically catholic) thought of Auden transparent through my music and—so it seemed to me—completely exhausted my means of expression, I could not think of music drama except as a form that would live on in a kind of archaic immobility. Yet the theatre was and is my domain; I keep having to come back to it. My music is impelled towards gesture, concreteness, visualization. It sees itself as drama, as something that inwardly belongs to life, and could not exist in tidy abstinence or in the private domestic realm.

During the ten-year gap between *The Bassarids* and *We Come to the River* my composing has thus been a continuous movement, away from the drunken hedonistic world of the bacchants and maenads, towards the contemporaries, the murderers and the victims in the new piece. It was a path full of difficulties, both artistic and moral, a time of study and practice, and such works as *El Cimarrón*, *Natascha Ungeheuer* and *La Cubana* are to be seen as preparatory stages. During this period my music became more and

* 'We Come to the River.' Lecture given at the Brunswick Chamber Music Festival, 26 November 1975. *Musik und Politik* 1976.

more clear and defined, and to an increasing extent the vehicle of messages and precise identifiable content. Its syntax is distinct, and its vocabulary, which comes from both recent history and antiquity, has consolidated and expanded itself in its lyricism and directness, I think. No change of style (whatever one means by the concept of 'style') has occurred. Style as an end in itself has never interested me; rather, new things have entered my language, and new technical experience, but primarily personal ones, which transform themselves into musical forms.

Edward Bond described his libretto as 'Actions for Music', and in fact his libretto and the actions it contains are in many respects inconceivable as a stage-play: everything that takes place—and the way in which it takes place—is aimed at music. You have to go a step further and say aimed at *my* music, namely to demand of it something that it had hitherto refused to provide. For until my meeting and debate with him I had thought that it was possible for music to adopt a passive attitude towards contemporary reality, one of the most striking phenomena of which is violence, and thereby to retreat from it into abstraction, or react merely with songs of lamentation or accusation.

It is true that in works such as *The Raft of the Medusa*, *El Cimarrón*, my *Sinfonia* No. 6 and the cycle *Voices* I had sung of heroic struggles for freedom, and had composed songs about those deprived of their legal and natural rights, songs from prisons and ghettos, dives and camps. But I did not think it necessary or possible to adopt artistic means to portray real social circumstances in such a radical manner and to expose them to the collision of art and reality, as is the case in this work. Nor would I have thought that drama and music (and the two working together) would have been capable of reproducing such a degree of reality that they themselves are completely filled with it, and exposed to rupture and damage. Nor had I regarded it as the task of the theatre to formulate anger and injury, admonition, appeal and alarm in a way that is itself frightening and alarming, itself cruel and injurious. At the beginning of my collaboration with Bond it seemed almost unthinkable that I would be able to draw music, my music, so completely into the realms of brutality, cruelty and evil as dramatic truth demanded; into realms that admittedly were known to me—known to me personally—but which I had always been able to avoid or break out and escape from, with the help of music itself and its qualities of comfort and reconciliation.

Artists enjoy the same inherited privilege as their art, namely to keep themselves at a certain distance from reality; to be able to do so, seemingly indeed to have to do so, so as to make possible a perspective and a distance which make the creative act possible. But the question arises whether this privilege has not by now degenerated into a sacrilege and whether it does not violate the social obligations of artists. Whether, perhaps, in the course of the past hundred years this distance has not increasingly led to false conceptions of art and its tasks, and to ideology, and whether present-day aesthetics is not obsolete, lagging incalculably far behind, with notions that no longer have any real object, and are just as harmful as the cruelties of the characters that Bond holds up as a mirror to the present.

Setting the libretto of *We Come to the River* was a process of learning, as composing always is learning, comprehending, understanding, insight. But to talk about this particular process of learning means, at the same time, to talk about the struggles that are being waged in the world, about the moral conflicts of individuals, no less than about the suffering and misery of millions of oppressed and exploited. The powerful, the violent, the military in this piece are people whom we come across in the street, in hotel lobbies, and in television news bulletins. It is the weak and the poor whose vulnerability and defencelessness changes into strength, and becomes a force that changes the world. The clearest example of this during the past few years has been Vietnam, where after thirty years of war a people managed to free itself from an imperialist super-power.

This took place at the time that I was engaged in work on *River*, and it seemed to me as though this victory strengthened the humiliated heroes of our piece. Reality came to their aid, gave them solidity. The music I had intended for them was no longer the voice of someone who was suffering with them, but that of a joyful identification, full of love and pride; a sound of a new certainty and determination; something simple, delicate and exact that sets itself against the absurdity of this age, against the bawling and bellowing of reaction, and rejects them, to grow towards a new age of reason and brotherhood.

Reality also provided material enough for the portrayal of the opposite side. Some months before I started composing (the first sketches are dated 14 January 1973), the fascist dictatorship in Chile had begun. Thousands of refugees were accommodated in Rome and in neighbouring villages. We heard from them at first hand about the murder squads, the concentration-camps, torture, fear, about all the repression that had been inflicted with icy, murderous coldness on people on whom the fascists were now venting their anger simply because they had taken a step towards national independence, renewal and socialism, and in a few years had shaken the forces of reaction to their foundations.

Much from these refugees' stories has gone into *River*. But the music is also filled with my own experiences. It is informed by the fear of the police that has pursued me throughout my life, in boarding-schools, barrack-yards, and detention-cells. It can identify with the young deserter, it weeps with each victim, and hates and despises the world of the fascist bourgeoisie, the murderers, the torturers and their assistants. And it generates hope, enough hope to avoid falling into pessimism, which is as harmful as every other form of frivolity.

Before I say anything more about the nature of the music and about the new forms of music drama that have grown out of it, I must give an idea of what happens in the piece.


We are in an imaginary empire. It could be a nineteenth-century one, but it could just as well be a contemporary regime. A popular rising in the provinces has just been bloodily put down by the army. The General is dictating a victory telegram to the Emperor, businesslike and professional. In the canteen, soldiers are getting drunk. A deserter is brought before the General. He is not given a chance to say anything and is summarily sentenced to death. Here too the General is not intentionally brutal, but merely efficient and without sympathy for human suffering. A victory celebration is held in honour of the General and his staff, with laurel-wreaths, victory odes, toasts to the Emperor. At the same time we see the deserter in the guardroom: telling the firing squad, waiting with him for dawn, about his childhood and about the panic that made him run away from the battlefield and try to get home. In the meantime, the General has left the festivities. When he gets back to his tent he finds a doctor waiting for him. The doctor tells him that he is suffering from a disease that will lead to blindness. There is no cure. It is the result of an old wound and must be accepted as an inevitable fate. The General can scarcely hide a growing feeling of despair but manages to control himself and force himself to return to his paperwork. At the same time the official festivities have ended and the officers have begun to amuse themselves with whores.

With the coming of dawn, the General can no longer remain at his work. He goes out on to the battlefield. For the first time in his life his eyes are opened to the suffering that he himself has caused. He sees his victims, hears the moans of the dying. He meets two women, one young and one old, who are going through the pockets of the dead for things to sell. The young woman is also looking for her husband among the dead and wounded in the mud. She is half-insane with fear and desolation. She does not know that nearby, at that very moment, her husband is being shot as a deserter.

Meanwhile the barrack square is being decorated, the new Governor arrives, the regimental banners are paraded, the victors make themselves at home. The General is distracted, as if paralysed by what he has seen that morning. His memories of the suffering human beings will not leave him alone, so he returns to the battlefield. The Governor and the officers follow the General; he is arrested when he tries to save the young woman from being shot for robbing corpses under an order given earlier by the General himself.

Soon afterwards, on the bank of the river, the group of officers with the handcuffed General come across the old woman, who has tried to save herself and her grandchild. She too dies when she throws herself into the rushing waters of the river. On the orders of the officers, the soldiers shoot at her until their magazines are empty. The General looks on helplessly. He curses the Governor. His voice has become a voice of protest. Soon his name will be written on the walls of buildings as a symbol of freedom. The General himself is silenced; the first half of the opera ends with his being led off to a lunatic asylum.

One of his former subordinates, Soldier 2, manages to get inside the asylum. He finds the General. He tells him about what is happening in the world outside: arrests, a state of emergency, torture; people are disappearing without trace. The air is thick with mistrust and fear. There is unemployment and hunger. What is going to happen? What can be done? The soldier asks the General for advice, for help, but the General turns away; it seems as though in his isolation he has lost all touch with reality. He seems to be hallucinated, it looks as though he really has become insane. The soldier leaves empty-handed. Next, the Governor visits the lunatic asylum. The Emperor has sent him to ask the General to return to duty. The General's prestige would help to stem the crisis in the empire. The outlook is bleak, things are beginning to fall apart, and not even the most brutal repression is enough to thwart the coming popular uprising. The General indignantly and contemptuously rejects the Emperor's request, and we realize that he is by no means insane. It is only that he is losing his sense of reality and the moral imperative that would lead him to act. His behaviour is hesitant, wavering ambiguity. He is no longer one of the powerful, and no longer even wishes to be one of them, but he does not know how to help the oppressed in their struggle, nor does he seek to. He continues to contemplate his own suffering. He believes that he will do least harm to himself and others by remaining immobile.

His wavering and his inability to help the rebels also mean that they will win their independence only by learning to help themselves. The General is obsolete. Even his new insights cannot lead to action. When he learns that, after visiting him, Soldier 2 shot the Governor, as a consequence of which Soldier 2 and his family were killed, he suffers a hysterical outburst of despair. Once again he feels guilty, his inactivity was also incapable of preventing bloodshed; what is worse, it is apparent that even his very inactivity and perplexity lead to bloodshed. He is someone who brings death. He now wishes truly to become insane or blind, or to die. He tries to poke out his eyes, but the orderlies overpower him, put him in a straitjacket and chain him to a block. Meanwhile the Emperor—a composed young gentleman surrounded by beautiful young girls, not unlike an Oxford-educated Indian prince—has heard about the murder of his Governor. It is suspected that the rebellious General in the madhouse is behind the assassination, since it is known that the assassin visited him there. The young ruler has told the story of an old emperor who, at the end of his life, after 999 deeds, became a hermit and, for his thousandth deed, repaired Buddha's broken staff, dying the next day. The precocious young Emperor has identified himself with this legend and has decided that his thousandth and last deed should be to render the General harmless. Two hired assassins arrive at the asylum and carry out the Emperor's orders: they blind the General. The doctor's prophecy has been fulfilled, although not in the way expected. And it becomes clear that disease and blinding are symbols and not just part of the plot of the drama.

The moment the General is blinded the scene changes in a transcendental way: the General's victims appear. It is as if their lives had never ended: the deserter comes home and embraces his wife. Soldier 2 and his family are reunited. They appear to the General as a vision; he would like to speak to them, but no one notices him. It is as if he were no longer there. And yet we have not left reality, on the contrary it is emphasized by the presence of the insane, who are frightened of the disfigured General and feel threatened by him. They push him off the block, to which he is still chained, and suffocate him beneath large white sheets; they say they are going to drown him in the river.

The oppressed have seen and heard nothing of all this, they continue singing their song to the child, which symbolizes hope, a future; and their singing, joined by more and more voices of more and more liberated people, ends with the words:

> We stand by the river
> If there is no bridge we will wade
> If the water is deep we will swim
> If it is too fast we will build boats
> We will stand on the other side
> We have learnt to march so well that we cannot drown.

To perform this work a space must be created that produces the illusion of three different stages. Each of these is allotted a small instrumental ensemble, which plays only when the action is on that stage. Stage I is in the foreground; the ensemble for it consists of 'old' instruments, including a viola d'amore, a viola da gamba, and a guitar, but also a few modern wind instruments and a piano, along with several small percussion instruments that are played by the pianist and the other instrumentalists. On the border between Stages I and II a portative organ is set up. The organist appears only twice, and plays choral fantasias on Hassler's *Herzlich tut mich verlangen* at the very beginning and near the end, when distant trumpets can also be heard from behind the stage, echoes of the martial music which has made up much of the score, and is here heard for the last time. Stage II, on which the central scenes take place, has an orchestra that consists of a string quintet, celesta, and a few brass and woodwind, as well as small percussion instruments to be played from time to time by these players. On Stage III, further in the background, there are three woodwind, deep brass, and four string instruments amplified by contact microphones.

The musicians of the three orchestras should be placed on sumptuously decorated podiums, and dressed as if for a gala performance. By contrast I envisage the sets as extremely simple and unembellished: the bare minimum to clarify the events on stage. By the side and rear walls of the stage is a great arsenal of percussion instruments: skin-headed and steel drums and, most importantly, bronze panels. A drummer, half dervish, half magician, appears at certain dramatic moments to play them. He has also some of the functions of the Greek chorus and of the fool of the Elizabethan theatre. Whenever the instrumental music is driven to silence, this drummer suddenly emerges, like an emblem of speechlessness. In the Emperor's scene he is on stage throughout and plays the *angklung* (a Balinese bamboo organ) which has been placed on the far side of the 'river' beyond Stage II. It looks rather like a clump of reeds, and thus suggests that a river is nearby; its sound is a somewhat hollow knocking and rattling, and with temple bells and antique cymbals it accompanies the Buddhist legend told by the young Emperor.

I have tried to give the three instrumental groups something of a speaking quality, something that draws them more intensively into the dramatic action than is normally the case with orchestral music in the pit. The music is not at a distance from the events on the stage; it does not comment, except on a few brief occasions, when each time there is the impression that the wordlessness of instrumental music is driving it to despair, to silence or to stepping over its boundaries, and then it looks as though it really is trying to see itself as language. This music keeps running up against the boundaries that seem to have been laid down for it in the past, and in many cases it is handled as if it were itself becoming critical, concrete, and a component of the drama. I would like to give some examples.

A casual remark by one of the whores, which can scarcely be heard, becomes two scenes later the main theme of the march played by the regimental band as its 'colours' are being paraded, and with which it noisily crosses the auditorium. At the ball in the city's banqueting rooms Orchestra III plays mazurkas and waltzes. Simultaneously, there is a duet between the doctor and the General, full of dark tragic stresses, and at the same time we hear on Stage I the monologue of the deserter condemned to death. Another simultaneous scene follows. On Stage I the parade-ground is swept, at the command of a sergeant-major (coloratura tenor, accompanied by an étude-like concertino for piccolo and piano). On Stage II the young woman thinks she has found her husband's body, while simultaneously on Stage III he is being shot as a deserter. But the music on Stage III has not changed since the previous scene; no one has told it to, and the ensemble continues to play dance music: a waltz. Thus a feeling of powerlessness is expressed at the same time as an accusation is made, and also an association with that horrifying image of the camp orchestra at Auschwitz, which by order of the commandant had to play at executions. (The surviving photograph will be remembered.) Perhaps this is one of the clearest illustrations of what I had in mind when I said that in this work music has been brought to a level of realism that I would have avoided in the past. Here violence is itself portrayed by means of an act of violence.

The sound of Orchestra III has something altogether vulgar, belching, repellent and sarcastic about it, which it loses only after the General has been blinded. The sound of Orchestra II is flexible, and can be applied to the most varied expressions, while the instruments of Orchestra I have a strained, helpless quality, but also something tender and fragile, as if in them was preserved the precious lives of children, whose voices carry the optimistic sounds of the final song.

There are a few places where all three orchestras have to play together, even though there is no simultaneous action. An example is the closing scene of the first part. The old woman jumps into the river with her grandchild; we can tell from the shouts of the soldiers that she is being swept into the undertow. Orchestra III plays an exceptionally banal hit-parade tune, until the musical material of the other orchestras begins circling the stage in the form of a canon, excited and full of passion, and is tossed around as if in a centrifuge. The music then ends in the highest registers, in harmonics, to continue from there (or rather to transcend itself) with the realistic recorded cries of water-birds—again we are on the boundaries of speechlessness.

The music of the insane in Act II plays a particular role. For the two great asylum scenes Bond has written a number of monologues, which are simultaneously spoken by the inmates, or murmured, whimpered or shouted as *Sprechgesang*. These people are the victims of violence; their monologues contain descriptions of atrocities from antiquity, from the nineteenth century and from today. We hear about lynch-justice in the USA, mass shootings by SS henchmen, Hiroshima, Nagasaki, Vietnam. Other inmates hoist imaginary sails on their imaginary boat. While doing this they sing an *a cappella* madrigal, whose mood is that of the disconsolate, hopeless situation of those who are singing it. At the end of this scene the orchestra takes up the madrigal and carries it over into the next scene, which is set in the town among the 'sane', and whose mood is of the horror of a routine, regulated existence.

On his very first appearance, at the start of the scene on the battlefield, the drummer establishes a rhythm and brings into play a further parameter for the whole piece. This rhythm will occur in ever new manifestations, constructed on the isometric principle, and always in connection with violence. Thus it also penetrates the structures of the General's outbursts in the asylum; his melismata are attached to him like the strings of a puppet. It is as though the poison of violence that is seeping into him is more and more taking control of him, like a real form of madness. The isometric combinations attain their maximum density in the shape of a four-part rhythmical canon, when the General is sitting on the block strapped in his straitjacket, before his death.

The simultaneous scenes produce a broad polyphony of language, of meanings, of musical forms of expression. There are constant cross-references between individual scenes, despite the simultaneity of independent actions. Never is anything without meaning as in the theatre of the absurd, and nothing is abstract or formalistic or random. All possibilities that were at our disposal, all knowledge and skill, indeed even virtuosity, served to create serious drama, music drama, whose every note and sentence is political, and which radically takes art at its word, and aims to take it a step further towards social truth and relevance. The three fathers beneath whose eyes this piece grew up are Monteverdi, Mozart and Mahler: the supreme realists of music.

I have already mentioned the two organ chorales, whose presence also belongs to my conception of the realistic employment of music in this work. I must go a bit further, and explain how I separated the music of war from that of the oppressed.

The music of violence has several parameters. It has signal-like calls, which are seen as typical of military music. But beyond these there are motivic nuclei, arrangements of intervals, and also twelve-note series (which slowly emerge in the course of the work; for instance for the Governor and the General not until the closing scenes, when their fate is sealed) which are intended to be characteristic of suavity, hypocrisy, indifference. During the visit to the doctor, in the third scene, material already develops that could be understood as leitmotifs in the Wagnerian sense, and it evolves in a comparable fashion, albeit less explicitly. It becomes a part of the growing crisis, and accompanies the General's destiny like his creeping sickness itself. There are short motifs that, in my sketches, bear titles like 'military honours' or 'the general becomes human' or 'blinding'. Polite society, which is associated with the thematic complex of violence, has cutting sevenths and ninths, which are, however, connected with banal sequences of melodies, and thus produce an impression of corruptness and frivolity, which keeps emerging unmistakably from the musical structures. The music that accompanies the entrance of the prostitutes is made up of the same material as that of polite society. There are often closed forms of parody, which I have provisionally termed 'character-pieces'. Besides the march with the whores' theme and the ball music, there is a coloratura aria in A flat major, with harp accompaniment, written and composed by a young lady named Rachel for the victory celebrations, and performed by her in honour of the General.

But such jests become less frequent as the tragedy progresses, and can scarcely be found in the second part of the work, which begins with the asylum scene. An exception is the aria of the Emperor (mezzo-soprano): the remarkable story of the Buddha, full of poisonous sanctimonious tonality. Unmistakably to differentiate this kind of tonalism, which we may call Parsifalesque, from the harmonic and melodic terrain of the other milieu, the world of the oppressed, was one of the most difficult problems in the entire work. I have let this material grow and enrich itself steadily throughout the entire piece, whereas the material of violence gradually becomes stiff and dies. My sketchbooks contain five melodic forms, both long and short, for the deserter, and a further five vertical chordal forms. His mother, the old woman, has her own melody, which begins with a descending minor third, just like the fish-selling market woman's aria 'Faber, mein Sohn Faber' in Paul Dessau's *Die Verurteilung des Lukullus.*

The melodies and harmonies allotted to her are, moreover, clothed in a sixteen-part chord that is spread over six octaves, which is sustained for the entire battlefield scene in ever new timbres like a pedal point or, shall we say, a raga. The young woman has an emphatically rising and falling line made up of thirds, fourths and diminished fifths, which are intended to express her state, bordering on madness, and it accompanies her scenes in constantly changing forms.

Soldier 2 and his wife have melodic material that is composed of small delicate intervals, which grows up as if incidentally in the very first scene, in the canteen, and which is developed only in the second part. The same applies to their harmonic arsenal, which can be heard for the first time in its diatonic simplicity when Soldier 2 visits the asylum and gives his account of the terrorized city. This, together with the horizontal values, determines the entire ninth scene, during which the Cabinet is meeting on Stage III (the accompanying music is made up of insipid, almost random combinations of the motifs associated with the Governor), and Soldier 2 is standing like a sentinel on Stage II, waiting to shoot the Governor, while his frightened wife on Stage I worries where he is.

At the very end the most telling motifs from the world of the oppressed reappear. They form a chain of intervals which is a metaphor for hope, a hope for love and peace that is possible only now at the end of the opera. All fear and anxiety have left the music; the end is like a new beginning in a world freed from terror and injustice.

# Don Chisciotte[*]

Translating Paisiello's Neapolitan original—one of the many *opere buffe* of its time, with its perhaps somewhat standardized and mechanical structure, sequences of recitatives, arias, ensembles— from Naples to Montepulciano, from the Settecento to the present, from the auditorium to the open air, was a sort of 'act of alienation' that Giuseppe Di Leva, the playwright, and I, undertook to attempt.

In the course of work further 'alienations' became necessary. In the original Don Chisciotte was a ridiculous butt of coarse jokes. In our version he emerges more and more as victor over his farcical environment, whereas the rural sub-aristocrats, who in the original were portrayed as somewhat frivolous and comic, but otherwise brilliant and witty characters, have degenerated into dissolute conventional types, with pimples, worn and faded elegance, stupid, deceitful, foolish. An exception is the Duchessa, not just because she is Irish. She is portrayed as a somewhat dreamy woman out of Maupassant, who has rather fewer unlikable qualities than the others and who, as a visitor from abroad, tries to find herself, and adapt herself to situations of which she would never have dreamed. Landscape painting and deer-hunting are worthy pursuits by comparison with the ignoble flirtations and comedies of mistaken identity, spawned by emotions that have become blasé to the point of foolishness. But this Duchessa, too, lacks understanding for our hero, and so she too is 'disqualified' at the end, when this entire society is congealed and petrified in its conventional gestures and

* 1978. Foreword to the score.

mannerisms, without prospects or future, while Chisciotte and Sancio set off for new adventures of the spirit and the imagination, following the tracks of the lovely dream image.

Of course Dulcinea never appears; she is present only as an idea, a phantom, an ideal, a chimera, as an abstract space outside reality—or is she? Is she perhaps closer, more tangible, more immediate than it seems? Could she with one bold thrust be brought down to earth from heaven? We have left Chisciotte his gloom, his Middle Ages, also some of the characteristics given him by Lorenzi and Paisiello. But at decisive points we have tried to make them larger than life, not least by occasionally transposing the nimble metropolitan structures of Paisiello on to the sounds of a rustic *banda*, and we have tried to create a different reality, a reality of austerity and frugal melancholy. In the sound of the *banda* there lives a quixotic spirit, where impotence, suffering and dreaming are brewed together to form a spectacular pathos, a strange kind of theatrical thunder.

In every production the *banda* should be made up of amateur wind players rather than well-schooled professionals, to prevent the intonation from becoming exact, and thereby softening the overwhelming impact of thirty to sixty out-of-tune wind instruments. Professionals would also bring into play their magisterial composure (or the illusion of it), and thereby rob the piece of its quixotic dignity. The *banda* should, if possible, be positioned some distance from the orchestra, but it must be visible on the stage or in the auditorium.

Arranging a major part of our work for a small ensemble of modern instruments was originally a response to the restrictions of Montepulciano, but finally emerged as both workable and appropriate from various points of view. This small-scale sound set against the *concerto grosso* sound of the *banda* reacts sensitively to events on stage. The sound is contemporary; it serves as a bridge, especially for the listener who has difficulties in hearing and evaluating details from the stereotyped sound of a settecento opera (or whose willingness to listen is numbed by such a sound) amid the archaicism and the cultural vacuum.

The alterations in the original score and in the text are so numerous that you can say you are dealing with a new work. Not only have recitatives and arias been added; the dramatic structures, the plot and the dialogues have been altered, and in many cases newly invented. A critical light is now cast on an art form, a society, an epoch. There is mention of poverty, the pauperization of a class, hopelessness and failure, but also of great dreams, utopia, a heroic impulse that can leave nothing unchanged and static, which appears in this comic, black, dirty 'common' piece as a positive force, as something that can be believed in and loved.

# Music for Edward Bond's *Orpheus*<sup></sup> *

At the second Montepulciano Cantiere (International Arts Work-shop) Franco Serpa, the classical scholar, gave a penetrating lecture on aspects of the Orpheus legend, showing how its ideas and images are still very much alive today and how they determine our thoughts, our feelings, and inhabit our culture as a whole. Serpa persuaded us that Greek civilization lives on in our psyche, subterranean and organic, and that not only our dreams and desires but also our decisions and actions are determined by its ideas and myths, prominent among which is the story of Orpheus.

Disquieted, from then on I collected all the information I could about the myth, whose forms often diverge in strange ways—Serpa's material and those of his references that were directly applicable to the theatre formed the major part—and sent what I had found regularly to Edward Bond in Cambridge. Serpa had said to me: 'Ci vuole un poeta' (a poet is needed) to create something out of the wealth of material, to develop a line of thought that can support the musical ideas and serve as their vehicle; a concreteness that makes sensual response possible. So I had asked Bond to help me, not least because of our friendly collaboration on *We Come to the River*.

In December 1977 I sought him out. I spent a whole afternoon walking up and down in his study, trying to answer his question *why* I wanted to write an Orpheus. By the end of my visit I still had not managed to explain it clearly, for I myself did not know; I knew only my musical reasons and desires connected with the theme in

* From a letter to Josef Rufer, January/February 1979.

question. To explain these to him, I had to refer to Monteverdi's
*Orfeo*, and to bring to mind a repeated and particularly intensive
musical experience, when I had heard this work two or three or five
years previously, and which had not only accompanied the music of
*We Come to the River*, but also helped to form all my future artistic
plans and ideas. I was able to say to him that I wanted to produce a
dramatic work, instrumental drama, where the singing voices were
replaced by gestures and dance steps, and where this muteness
made a different, instrumental eloquence necessary, a speaking
expression, which could not be interchangeable or be confused. It
had also to be narrative and declamatory, and directed without
interruption to the plot, appropriate to the meaning that it
embodied; to mirror the protoplasms of the symbols and their
effects in musical forms; and to enable them clearly to be heard, felt
and realized for the first time in this mirroring.

Bond promised to write something that would fit in with my
needs (in so far as I had managed to put them into words on that
occasion), and a few weeks later I received six or seven pages of text
which read like a visionary prose-poem. Orpheus is seen as a hero,
and as a magician and a lover; he also has something of the saint and
the preacher in him. The images, thoughts and messages of this
'Orpheus', which Bond terms a *story* so as to emphasize the
narrative nature of his work, and probably also bearing in mind the
association with the word *history*, all at once gave me something
real: a form to my music, an urgency to my ideas. The period of
questioning and searching, of preparation, was over. There now
began my involvement with Bond's interpretation. This took place
in the work process itself. In profound sympathy with his aesthetic,
all I had to do was read his signs correctly and find the appropriate
musical answer. I imagine that it will be a novel and unusual task for
choreographers and designers to find the appropriate scenic
equivalents for such a unity of poetic vision and music, and to
discover the right balance of freedom and faithfulness, which is the
first requirement for the success of a *Gesamtkunstwerk* made by
various people.

Exactly a year before Bond's text arrived I had mentioned for the first time that I would like to write an Orpheus. I can still recall it exactly: it was while I was packing my case after having conducted *Heliogabalus Imperator* in the Amsterdam Concertgebouw. A heron was sitting on a post in the misty Amstel. The previous evening at a party I had met an unusually feminine creature, reddish and mask-like, motherly like everything seductive, like Eurydice, who reigns over a wide territory that was then still unknown to me, the goddess of the dead, the dead goddess. In Berlin we say 'die tote Else', the bringer of death; the enigmatic one, with eyes turned to stone, rising up Medusa-like out of the sewer-gratings of New York, fabulous, fairy-tale-like and vulgar, equipped with the rough and touchingly coarse language of the metropolis. It seemed as though I was to be provided by the divinities of Hades and Persephone with this autumn crocus-like artifice, as if I had asked for it as 'food for the journey'. I accepted it, and carried it on my back. I have never looked back since; I made of it what I could, and learned, among other things, the prerequisites for a kind of music—once again music—which could be approached only by crossing a danger zone necessary for its discovery, and therefore unavoidable.

That this was how it would be, emerged only later, after some experiences; at that time everything was still just ideas, dreams—furnished, it is true, with horrors, misgivings, betrayal, but also with a hunger for adventure and a special kind of hellish gaiety, foolish and constantly overlapping, one thing extinguishing another from time to time. But it was deadly serious, a difficult matter. Since this 'ancestral' encounter I tend to think about my childhood and the later years of wandering and searching more often than in the past. Whenever I start work on a new piece I try to establish technical premises (and more or less fictitious autobiographical circumstances) on the basis of which it might be possible to attain that state of lightness and purity that could lead to the rediscovery of music as I had dreamed it to be when a child. Thus I am compelled again and again to invent for myself the music I most wish to hear.

By this time the three new quartets had been written (1975, 1976, 1977) and the sonata for solo violin. These works are *en route* to the

Orpheus music; and I would also describe the two sets of variations, *Il Vitalino raddoppiato* (1977) for violin and chamber orchestra, and *Aria de la folia española* (1978) for orchestra, as preparatory works, to say nothing of the guitar piece *Royal Winter Music* (1975–6), for the Orpheus music was indeed to be determined by the sound of the guitar. All Orpheus' arias begin with its tones. It is the jangling and whining of nerve-ends; it is a hundred different hues: dark, shadowy, silvery, weeping, the hollow calls of nocturnal animals; and it is the echo-sounder of history. All these things about the sound of the guitar somehow move me. I had employed it before, in the context of Greek antiquity in *Kammermusik 1958*, where the ideas of the late Hölderlin fragments 'In lieblicher Bläue' undertake to convey the German soul of the present to the land of our origins, so that I could follow along with music. Some years before that still, in *König Hirsch*, at the start of my life in Italy, the guitar was for me like a gate through which one can reach the beginnings of music, a remnant from a bygone age that still lives on, deep in the consciousness of the people. In *Royal Winter Music* the guitar is a quite contemporary instrument. The writing is full of technical innovations, the pieces that it contains are settings of Shakespeare (each deals with a character from a play) and the aim is to unfold and release the full orchestra of the guitar sound.

In the *Orpheus* music, however, its sound is like the first word; a new life is starting in its body. Its life is inward, it is the beginning of music, the vehicle for the intervals on which the work is based: F— A flat—G—E; then, like a reply, C sharp—B flat—D—E flat; and finally, like a consequence and a completion, A—F sharp—B—C. After a few introductory notes the guitar is joined by the harp— there will be many kinds of duet between the two—and then the strings gradually join in, taking up and continuing the melody. The strings are used as obbligato instruments: nine violins, four violas, four cellos, three double-basses. Further string music is provided by the harpsichord; this is conceived as an extension of the guitar and the harp, and always as a solo instrument, representing Eurydice. As the drama mounts, the whole consort of strings plays together, and the sound becomes richer, denser, more intense.

The strings accompany Orpheus and Eurydice throughout the entire work. They symbolize life, that exertion of love and of faith, directed against death, against madness. The opposing world— Apollo, the divine, law, authority, the giving father, classicism—is represented by a different series of notes: first of all by the ambiguous interval C—F sharp; then by the notes D—F— C sharp—A, which can be regarded as D minor with a leading note (if one removes the D, one finds an 'augmented' chord); and lastly by A sharp—C sharp—B, followed by the emphatic minor seventh. Further interrelations can be detected: the minor second between the fourth and the fifth note, a further *diabolus in musica* between the fifth and sixth, further minor seconds between the ninth and tenth and the twelfth and first notes. So far as the playing is concerned, the ambivalent role allotted to Apollo in this piece is built into its basic material: between the concept of divine justice, which is hard to define, and the more precise one of the diabolic; between magnificence and deprivation; incalculability, cunning and kindness; grace and extortion; unapproachability, unfathom- ability and illusion; certainty and hallucination.

The god is found guilty: beneath all the tinsel and gloss his music has an underlying quality which we can recognize as the sound of authority, the magnificence and *gloria* of Olympus. Courtly elements, Baroque music which, played on modern brass instru- ments, is here revealed as something murderously hostile, as a threat, as an expression of violence. This alternates with nimble little pastoral pieces, which are meant to recall the world of the *ballets russes*; not so much the scores, but a certain category of dance, and above all the dazzling externals, the costumes, the peacock feathers, the silks and the décors of the audience *du côté de chez Guermantes* bewitched by the orientally 'barbaric' pro- ductions; also the exclusiveness and reactionariness, and finally the transience peculiar to this refined cold world of authority. An *envoi*.

These Apollo pieces are all written for wind instruments, which are joined by a sort of continuo of percussion, bells, crotales, metallophones, and also piano and celesta: this makes the atmosphere of the Apollonian harmony glitter, giving it the dangerous oriental and archaic qualities I had in mind. One day, several years ago, after finishing the score of *We Come to the River*, I sat in the back row of the theatre at Delphi and tried to imagine how music must have sounded there; what I 'heard' is, at least partly, written down in the score of *Orpheus*. Whereas the gracious and Olympian qualities prevail at the beginning and dangers remain beneath the surface, as something you can hear rather than see, with each entry the music for Apollo becomes more violent. His last great scene is composed as a ceremonially resounding sarabande; it is like a gradually planned unmasking, a 'show of force' at the very moment when Orpheus, insane with pain at the renewed loss of Eurydice, shakes the world-order to its foundations. But Apollo's instrumentation expands and reaches down, and also denotes other gods, Hades and Persephone (whose great entrance I have depicted with a solo organ), and the world of the dead. Their musical material is also Apollo's, as if to demarcate the territory of the divine in its broader range. Whereas Apollo's sounds are primarily characterized by bright flutes, oboes and high clarinets, there are very deep registers for the inferno, including heckelphone, contrabass clarinet, tuba, and alto and bass flute. Their *espressivo*, the depiction of weeping, groaning, lamenting, which Bond's dramaturgy suggests, can be compared to that of solo instruments in Bach's settings of the Passion; even their style derives from there, the music acquiring a speaking quality as if it had been put to words. In the inferno we find for the first time instruments that are no longer clearly separated from one another: Orpheus's world, since the death of Eurydice, is so closely tied up with the underworld that for a time it appears to merge with it completely. Only in Orpheus' great aria in the kingdom of the dead—music that aims to bring hope and salvation to those who are suffering—does it once again free itself from all other instruments, and have the strings perform a broadly conceived Lied; as in all the arias, here too there are solo strings in various combinations in the foreground. This aria begins, moreover, with harp and guitar; they play one of the ritornelli from the same scene in Monteverdi's *Orfeo*; this is like an invocation, through which the melody of the strings can at last begin.

The composition of the Orpheus music could begin only after the heron had flown from his post in the misty Amstel. All the arias of Orpheus are concerned with bringing this departure about, as if as an exorcism. To be able to focus at all on an idea of Eurydice, and devise an ideal of purity and human dignity, first of all negation and hell had to be known and suffered. I think that in this score you can gauge, from the arias in particular, the struggles amid which darkness was lessened, self-deception done away with and a clear way of speaking sought, and I suspect that grief still attaches to them, and scraps of nocturnal veils.

This suspicion is also the (musical) reason—which corresponds with the requirements of the drama—why, at the very end, after Orpheus has lost his love once again and Apollo will not help him, and Orpheus has destroyed his lyre and now finds himself alone and unable to express himself, the world is without music, without salvation or hope. Something new happens yet again: Orpheus tries to play on the strings of the broken instrument. And he manages it: first one note, feeble and voiceless. Then a second, a third; a relationship forms between these three notes and new music slowly develops. Its only connection with what has gone before is that it has freed itself, launched itself from it. It is the experience of despair, madness and self-destruction on which the new tonal relationships are based, but on which however the full light of joy and happiness can now fall. What in the arias had still sounded like yearning, like dreams brushed by nightmares, is now the affirmation, the concept, the manifesto of a new idea of happiness, love and the life of all men.

The entire work is about the abolition of suffering and superstition, and it is also about the personality of the artist and, aesthetically, again about 'music as language', a theme of perennial interest to me. *Orpheus* is also, to an even greater degree, about the gestures of which music is capable.

# Benjamin Britten<sup>*</sup>

One of the first pieces of modern music that I heard as a student was *Peter Grimes*, in Mannheim in 1946. What struck me above all were the orchestral interludes, which had an organ-like beckoning and resonant quality, informed by a sense of remoteness; they seemed to me like echoes thrown back by the horizon of the sea. Hearing the work again on subsequent occasions confirmed this impression. This element of landscape, of making a landscape visible in its colours and contours, seems to crop up in many of his works, and the landscape is always that of England. Three works immediately come to mind: the *Serenade* for tenor, horn and strings; *Les Illuminations*; and the *Nocturne* for tenor and chamber orchestra. In all three you can sense the vicinity of the sea; you can hear the facets of grey, silver-grey, ash-grey, white and mother-of-pearl of which the low-lying sky is composed, and amid which all the things of the world that appear in this music—men, animals, plants and flowers—have taken on a matt, withdrawn and quiet quality. When I describe it in this way, however, all I am providing is a description of the terrain, and I have so far been speaking only of colours, atmospheres, of the scent of the Suffolk meadows and of the wind whispering or howling across them. Not of the syntax.

I never had a conversation with Ben about music. Only on one occasion did I hear him talk about it, in the late 1950s in the little hall in Aldeburgh. He was standing next to me during the rehearsal of a piece by a contemporary whom he did not admire, and was confiding his displeasure to the dachshund under his arm; after a while he left. We shared a kind of wordless friendship; there were always others around whenever we saw one another, and so neither he nor I spoke about music or related subjects. But I did dedicate my *Kammermusik 1958* to him, as a true act of homage and an expression of gratitude for the inspiration that his works had given me. Ten years later he dedicated his setting of Brecht's *Children's Crusade* to me. During the period after the 1968 Hamburg *Medusa* scandal, when my political views had suddenly been thrust into the limelight in a hostile and almost intolerable fashion, thanks to a massive media campaign, and performances of my works in the Federal Republic were rapidly decreasing and the theatres were rejecting my pieces, I saw him one night in London at the house of mutual friends. He put forward Aldeburgh as a place where my new works could be performed, and I took up this offer soon enough—which is how it came about that *El Cimarrón*, which had been written in Cuba, received its first performance on 22 June 1970 *chez* Britten at the Snape Maltings.

Several years previously he had been present at the German premiere of my *Novae de Infinitio Laudes* in Cologne (1962). On the morning after the concert he came to my hotel and left for me a long letter about my piece; it was a letter full of sympathy and warmhearted comradeship. This gesture had something of the politeness and good manners that were once perhaps taken for granted between artists, but have now completely been lost in the wake of that ludicrous so-called competitiveness—a better word would be marketing—which makes the producers of works of art into individuals who have to corner sectors of the market for themselves.

I should have written Ben a letter at least as long, after hearing his *War Requiem* for the first time—but I didn't get round to it. This work had a shattering impact on me; it found me exhausted and perplexed after the 1966 premiere of *The Bassarids* in Salzburg. The *War Requiem* seemed to me to be a work whose urgency had banished all stylization, and had drawn its expression from an intense capacity for suffering. Moreover the connection with the great requiems of the past seemed natural and unproblematic; it seemed to result from a necessary affinity with Bach, Berlioz and Verdi, to whom Ben had built a bridge that, even after the completion of the *War Requiem*, could still be used by him and us, his younger colleagues. It was as if the demands of the subject had mobilized new forces in him, which is why it is like a battle fought with armour and heavy artillery: it is not just a work with a mass appeal unrivalled in our time, composed in profound seriousness and with an enormous investment of effort, but at the same time a compendium of significant answers to the questions of construction, syntax and semantics. This work represents the other side of Ben's music: a world in which the lyrical is denied, and whose contours have been elaborated in a hard and indeed temperate and unornamented manner. This is no doubt the product of maturity. It has been fully realized for the first time in the *War Requiem*, as great drama, but it can also be found in the earlier works, if not as a predominant factor. And if in the early works he still employed parody and stylization, such characteristics increasingly gave way to a more chiselled manner, which no longer admitted anything but austerity, dismissing every superfluous effect, every trace of ornament.

I have no difficulty in outlining Britten's historical background. I see as his first ancestor William Blake. I come to this of course by way of Ben's setting of 'O rose, thou art sick' in the *Serenade*. (The first time I heard this piece it scared me to death. I have tried again and again to set this poem myself, without success.) There is Elizabethan music; there is magical poetry that has been married to it. In its delicate fragility it is this music that reaches back to the early works I've mentioned, and it reappears in the late works, transformed, rethought, in a new shape. Because there is a strong national sense of history in his thought and action, there is Britten the pacifist with socialist tendencies, and Britten the young composer who worked with the literary avant-garde, primarily with W. H. Auden, and came to elaborate his own aesthetic, not without their influence. More background is provided by a number of English composers of the late nineteenth century. You can detect an emphatically non-Continental musical thinking; no trace of the

Vienna School, not even of its traditionalistic side; on the other hand there is perhaps an English variant of the *Neue Sachlichkeit* of 1930–5, and French elements (already conveyed in English models) in so far as these are worth mentioning outside of the world of Debussy. For there is not a trace of Debussy to be seen, and Ravel too is by-passed: the one, I suppose, on account of his overstraining of the concept of style, the other because of his artificiality and his lack of passion; both must have struck Britten as unusable.

For the rest, he in fact was born with his own style, and had merely to develop it in a consistent manner, with eyes open to what was going on in the world, with a sense of reality that subsequently also determined his practice. He is one of the best examples of pragmatic musical thinking, which is why you can find pieces for children and beginners that are easy to sing and to play—indeed his oeuvre contains a remarkable amount of music for young people. But there is also technically and intellectually demanding chamber music; the development of the Lied; and the operas—virtuoso and dramatically sophisticated works full of popular appeal—almost all written for the touring English Opera Group and its practical and financial constraints.

There was also Britten the conductor, and the unusually gifted pianist. (Whenever did he find the time to practise?) Ben was a practical man, a modern musician, an inspirer and initiator. To return once more to his oeuvre, I feel that the relationship between his native lyricism and his dramatic manner, something that he worked and struggled for, is a source of conflict inherent in almost all of his works. The one allays the other; the one corrects the other; the result is a tense, shaping interaction that also ensures constant development, and prevents stagnation and repetition.

It was painful to see how illness overcame him and made his work more difficult, and *Death in Venice* seems to me already to bear traces of the weakness that would soon overpower him. The 'in memoriam Benjamin Britten' at the head of my Fifth Quartet is meant to convey my empathy with this remarkable man; my grief at his death, which came thirty years too soon; my respect for his work, for his struggle; my joy at his victories, and my admiration for his mastery.

# Paul Dessau*

I got to know Paul in the winter of 1948. The writer, Grete Weil, who later wrote the libretto for my first opera, *Boulevard Solitude*, brought us together in Berlin. I often visited him in his study in the Deutsches Theater; I was permitted to inspect the still unfinished score of *Lukullus*, and I did so gratefully, with a great deal of curiosity and a strong desire to make up for lost time. In this room, filled with mountains of books, piles of music, photographs of productions and an old piano, there was also a little corner for me; it was there that I worked on the fair copy of my Third Symphony. Sometimes Paul took me with him to the neighbouring Theater am Schiffbauerdamm, so that I could watch Brecht rehearsing his adaptation of Lenz's *Der Hofmeister*, and later also attend the premiere, full of vigour and presented with many fresh ideas that still prove fruitful today. I was even once introduced to Brecht, in the 'Möve', and I can still vividly recall his handshake, his friendly grin, his lively eyes, his clothes and his cigar.

During that time Dessau was working closely and continuously with Brecht, whose spirit was, as it were, present at our discussions; and I had the opportunity of seeing Brecht at work during the closing stages of the rehearsals for his production. These encounters had a special impact on me, and the production style of *Der Hofmeister* was of direct and lasting influence on my own work for and in the theatre. It was Dessau who introduced me to Brecht's theory of art, for at that time nothing had yet been published.

I remember how excited I was that such a busy and famous man as Dessau could give so much of his time to a young unknown

* March 1979: Dessau died three months later, on 28 June.

musician like me. No one has ever spoken to me of Mozart with more understanding and more love than Paul, and in everything that he said his aesthetic was revealed, which I liked a great deal, and which made me reflect for the first time on the role of the artist in society. For him the task of the composer consisted and consists in a constant dialectical rapport with everyday life, in inter-relationships, and in an altogether feverishly combative existence. I was perhaps too young then, and still too caught up in the Cold War climate of the West, fully to understand everything that Paul said about political things. For this very reason he tried to open my eyes and enlarge my view of the world, and I did in fact learn, and attained a better understanding of certain things; Paul made them concrete and tangible. I grasped how he was deeply concerned to see and shape music as a living component of the world; as speech and reply; as an instrument of the class struggle, in which process he strived also to incorporate inherited means of expression that had been brought to the latest stage of their technical development. I learned from him how a composer can develop possibilities of realizing this concern, how tradition can intervene and help to mediate expression, how history can remain living and con-temporary, even in the context of the latest achievements. I can think of no one else today who has so much grace in his thought and writing, so much humour—real, knowing humour—so much wit, and yet is never ironic or hurtful. The brio that dominates a score like *Puntila*, determining the sound of the whole, and can be detected in the smallest nuances of the instrumentation, is firmly in the tradition of comic opera from Mozart to Rossini to *Falstaff*; a frenetic, unremitting realism—what a delight, what intelligence, what fine workmanship! This score is a summation of the whole of Dessau; it can also be found in his filigree chamber music, his songs, both tender and hard, and his austere polyphonic symphonic music. I believe that many of these works are not yet sufficiently known internationally, and that their potential has not yet been realized; but this will come, for this is music that belongs to the future, and whose humanistic seriousness and historical decisive-ness will urgently be required.

## Paul Dessau

Dessau didn't influence my music; at any rate, not technically. We talked mainly about the classics, and not very much about contemporary music. We did sometimes show one another our latest pieces—and were astonished by the patience with which we read the scores, down to the most minute detail.

My friendship with Paul endured, and even when I went far away from Berlin and started to live in southern Italy, from 1953, our exchange of letters and ideas never ceased. We met as often as we could, in Berlin and Italy. Paul and his wife, Ruth Berghaus, were there when the Hamburg 1968 premiere of *The Raft of the Medusa* was broken up, and we saw one another often during the time of the West Berlin Vietnam congress. I attended many of his premieres and concerts, just as he took an interest in my work in a spirit of critical friendship and friendly criticism. I am therefore indebted to him for many valuable pieces of advice, and without a doubt many of his suggestions have gone into my work and made it richer and more solid. This was not just during the last ten years— during which we also came much closer to one another in political matters—but much earlier, indeed right from the start. My friendship for him was always mingled with a certain admiration, as if for an elder brother of whom I could be proud, because of his sincerity, his courage, his energy, and his refusal to compromise. Paul expects everyone to be as strong and intelligent and talented as he is, and he is quite right to do so: this is a programme. I myself am no longer going to achieve it, but I know that one day the whole world will be inhabited by *uomini sociali*, and they will be as pure and healthy and inventive, and as full of love and brotherhood, as my marvellous old friend Paul.

# The Montepulciano Cantieri, 1976–80 *

Montepulciano (Lat. Mons Politianus), in the province of Siena, on the saddle between the Orcia and the Chiana valleys, is a small ancient town with a population of 15,000 modest and hard-working people. They live in neat small houses among fortifications, renaissance buildings, enormous churches, monasteries, a bishop's palace, a law court (which recently was given a larger building for its needs, the renaissance Palazzo Magnanet that many people had hoped would become the residence of a music and arts school), a town hall (the city is administered by the communists in coalition with a socialist minority), a jail, various rather good primary, secondary and grammar schools, a communal *scuola di musica*, a small seventeenth-century theatre built into the rock of yet another fortress, some banks, more offices, one small hotel, *carabinieri* barracks (in a Medici fortress), all this surrounded by an Etruscan wall built when the town was founded.

It lies in the middle of what is called a *zona depressa*, an economically underprivileged area. Agriculture, mainly the production of olive oil and wine, is the major and almost exclusive source of income. The population is falling, the young people want to leave for a big city. The winters are long and cold, with a lot of snow. There is no entertainment, except television and cards, there isn't even a regular cinema. The town is set in a magnificent austere landscape that somehow reminds one of the Scottish Highlands.

In the autumn of 1975, the town council and the regional government in Florence, after a first abortive attempt to stage a

* 1981, written by the author in English.

music festival in Montepulciano, wrote to me for advice. So I went to Montepulciano (which is about 120 miles north of Rome), looked around, talked to the local councillors, collected opinions, and left again, taking the problem away. It seemed to me that a regular music festival of some quality would be much too expensive, and would not altogether meet the cultural needs of the people. Bearing in mind all I had heard, I felt it was necessary to think of something which would put an end to the artistic starvation in Montepulciano. No child had music lessons in school, the *scuola di musica* was empty (there were only two untuned old pianos), the theatre was always closed, once a week a mediocre film was shown in the cinema (owned and run by the church). The one and only 'artistic' activity was organized by a priest called Don Marcello. He wrote, composed, and staged the annual *Bruscello*, spurious folklore plays based on old sagas and *stornelli* (metrical verse), and performed by local amateur actors. He accompanied their liturgical singing on an electric organ which had produced the same faulty harmonics ever since 1939.

I thought that, perhaps, first of all one ought to try to excite the citizens' curiosity about the arts, which might eventually lead to some kind of appetite for them. The *poliziani*, intelligent and orderly people who had been deprived of the enjoyment of good music and theatre for so long, and whose ancestors had been too crushed by poverty and the class struggle to be able to enjoy those arts which they thought to be the privilege of the wealthy, were now educating their children to be part of a new and progressive *italianità*, and I felt they were ready for the arts, whether they knew it or not. I thought that efforts should be made to ensure that in the not too distant future this town should have its own cultural life, with everybody, young and old, developing a passion for, or at least an interest in, one of the many forms of artistic expression that exist in European culture.

I thought it might be possible in Montepulciano to prove that music is not abstract and useless, not a mere pastime, and that it could do even more than improve the moral climate, as Stravinsky had hoped. I believed that it could raise the economic and social standards of the community, and, last but not least, that it would help to make the town a pleasanter place for its inhabitants and visitors.

During the weeks following the preliminary meeting with the city council, I talked to various young friends and told them of the plan that was gradually emerging. The first musician I talked to was, I remember, Homero Francesch, the Uruguayan pianist. I asked him what sort of fee he would expect for joining us, and he said he would do so for nothing, and so would many other players he knew. I sought suggestions, opinions, offers, and from then on I went to Montepulciano regularly, with musicians and theatre people, to look at the premises, to discuss art and theatre with the inhabitants (among whom many loyal and kind friends emerged), to hold informal meetings and to give small concerts (at one of these I performed and analysed the first movement of Mozart's Symphony No. 29 with a decrepit provincial chamber orchestra). Eventually a scheme emerged. We worked on the lines that the summer performances we were planning should involve as many local people of all ages and classes as possible. We hoped that this might help to break the barriers between artists and the public, and that it might inspire the local people to try out their own ways of reacting to music. We hoped to do a lot of popular music, too, and to play such *musique savante* that would somehow meet their expectations. Everything we planned was meant to be a bridge between the past and the present as between city people and country people, and between artists and other working people and craftsmen. The workers, the children, and the young were our principal objects of attention.

In October 1975, a group of composers spent a week in Montepulciano, working on a German collective opera called *Der Ofen* (The Furnace), a protest against air pollution in big cities. All the composers who were in this team later wrote other pieces for Montepulciano and worked there, playing, teaching, contributing new ideas, and bringing in new names all the time. I think they all fell in love with the place, the people, and the 'Festival' which we now called the 'Cantiere', meaning a workshop where young artists could invent and experiment with new forms of communication. We were all seeking new audiences who might initially be sceptical, mistrustful, or indifferent, but whom we hoped we could win over, changing them and bringing them the joy of discovering and understanding another dimension in themselves. My composer-colleagues in this venture were Peter Maxwell Davies, Thomas Jahn, Henning Brauel, Fabio Vacchi, Geoffrey King, Niels Fréderic Hoffmann, Richard Blackford, and Wilhelm Zobl.

I myself had the idea of arranging the score of Paisiello's comic opera, *Don Chisciotte* for performance by the local band. The idea was that this would be the major event of the planned Cantiere, and be given in the open in the huge square, the Piazza Grande. In the October days of 1975 I had the rare opportunity of hearing the band rehearse, and it was instantly clear that they would never be able to learn such music in eight months, let alone play their wind and brass instruments (on which they never practice) throughout an entire opera. What could I do? I didn't want to lose the band, the most musically committed body we had in Montepulciano. So, with the help of Henning Brauel, I orchestrated the arias and ensembles for a small group of professionals. This turned out to be a mistake: the delicate sound of the ensembles was swept away by the strong wind that blew across the square. I reserved to the band, whose sound not even a hurricane would drown, the *sinfonia* and frequent short interventions whenever Don Quixote had one of his pathetic adventures. So for the following year's band-event Henning Brauel wrote incidental music for the play *Orfeo* by Agnolo Ambrogini, called 'Il Poliziano', Montepulciano's great son, Lorenzo di Medici's court poet and political adviser. We had hoped that some of the band, although amateurs, might be able to play Brauel's polyphonies, which he was convinced were readily playable. I had persuaded Franco Lizzio, a retired conductor of the Milanese tramworker's band, to come to Abbadia S. Salvatore, a neighbouring town which boasted the best band in the district, but after two weeks of rehearsal he gave up. The difficulty lay in the long notes that Brauel had written; everything was in slow tempi. He'd thought that would make it easier, but the speed showed up the faulty intonation of the amateur musicians in a most unfortunate fashion. The music was eventually performed by the wind and double-basses of the Cantiere symphony orchestra (that was extra work for them). But we used bands again, even in that year, and 1979 brought an apotheosis of band music when amateur bands, and one made up of Cantiere professionals, were placed on the four sides of the square and just played selected pieces from their Italian opera repertoire. To go with this music Jörg Schmalz, a young German choreographer, using volunteer dancers from the West Berlin Opera House created a romantic ballet in two acts, *I Muti di Portici* (dancers are indeed usually all mute . . .), based on the story of the dumb girl and Masaniello, the seventeenth-century Neapolitan terrorist. This production was an enormously popular success, not least because it ended with fireworks representing the eruption of Vesuvius. So we at length found a way to spur the band of Montepulciano on to excel itself, and it will surely continue to do so, providing ever better music for the community.

We hoped to win the children's interest with *Il Palazzo zoologico*, an opera specially written for them and the first Cantiere by Thomas Jahn. The libretto was written by London children to whom Edward Bond had introduced us. They gave the composer three wonderful one-act plays that were somehow linked. The libretto was translated by Montepulciano children, other children designed the costumes and the sets, while the opera itself was performed with professional singers and musicians. This was a truly delightful show: the first contacts had been successfully made, and would create more links with the children's world. They would begin to express themselves through art, and in a few years they would take over the whole place.

We knew, from our discussions in the town hall, in the streets, cafés, and private homes, that almost everybody would expect an Italian opera to be put on. I didn't quite know how to go about it — for instance, how to find the singers? — and I asked Sandro Sequi, the producer, for advice. He and Riccardo Chailly (whom Sandro brought us and who stayed with us for three years) staged a wonderful *Turco in Italia* in the first year. We assembled a cast of young volunteer singers from various countries, a similar orchestra (based on a small Zurich string ensemble led by Brenton Langbein), and a male chorus (we had forgotten about this until the last moment, and the budget hadn't allowed for it anyway) composed of coaches, conductor, friends and myself. We sang from a box while the action was executed on stage by a Milanese mime group that had unexpectedly turned up. The production (in original nineteenth-century sets) was brilliant, and made a favourable impression on the *poliziani*. One of the production assistants was Carlo Pasquini, a local talent who one year later staged *The Soldier's Tale* with his friends acting and dancing, and young English musicians playing the music. This was produced as a street theatre piece, and it was toured around the villages and small towns around Montepulciano. More *poliziani* were involved in the final *spettacolo* in the first year, *Tradimenti*, a happening invented by Memé Perlini, a Roman avant-garde producer of promise, and his designer Antonello Aglioti. It took place in the Edmondo d'Amicis school, on all three floors, in corridors, classrooms, even in the lavatories, and was a kind of exhibition of the horrors of provincial life, with its bigotry, frustrations, its hopelessness, its weird and absurd petit-bourgeois habits. There were horrible, funny and revolting things to be seen, sadism, sodomy, blasphemy, suicide, all this repeated constantly, but all these things were suffused with a kind of sad beauty ( = art). The audience walked around in the school, from room to room, and was, needless to say, absolutely shocked by what it saw, just as Perlini had intended it to be. This was to make things more difficult for us.

Our work had been watched with considerable mistrust by those in the community who had not voted for the coalition local-government, and some people had been hoping all along that the devil (who was surely hiding in Paisiello's, Rossini's, and P. M. Davies's scores, in the libretti, in make-up and costumes, in the behaviour of the foreigners, and in the whole noise that music makes), would eventually make a mistake and show his red cloven hoof. And so he had done, not only in Perlini's horror show but also in the main square, some days before, when an Italian folk group called Canzoniere Internazionale had sung some irreverent songs, in a programme called *Siam venuti a cantar Maggio* (We've come to sing the ancient May songs) and where, in the same programme, a group of citizens had performed the ancient play *Sega la vecchia* (Saw the old woman in two—the personification of winter), a kind of popular Tuscan 'Rite of Spring', reciting and singing the certainly neither very tender nor pious prose of centuries ago. An outcry was organized, posters appeared on the Etruscan walls saying 'La Comunita d'Impegno Cattolico PROTESTA' etc. . . . The antagonism, which exists all over the country, between a reactionary and clerically dominated bourgeois Italy, and a new class of progressive and therefore rather anti-clerical forces, came out into the open and was dramatized in the events at Montepulciano.

More disagreeable things followed. A sit-in was staged, by the Milan mimes and Mr Perlini, in front of the curtain in the theatre, on the last evening of the 'Festival'. The mime group refused to go on stage in the second and last performance of *Turco* unless the mayor paid them their travel expenses, which he had refused to do for some trivial bureaucratic reason and because Aglioti, the designer, had bought fresh pizza for 200,000 lire without permission from the administration, telling the baker the Cantiere would pay, and had rather foolishly paved a classroom with it in the *Tradimenti* show. A vociferous argument now took place in the theatre, during which Perlini called the mayor a *buffone* and an eminent Rome music critic, Dr Fedele D'Amico, stood up and suggested that the travel money for the mimes be collected among the audience, on condition that the mayor sacked himself on the spot. There were more insults and shouting. I had no idea how to break that deadlock, until the leader came to me saying that the orchestra wouldn't play unless the mimes were given their money. So that was that, I explained the situation to the audience, and everyone went home. All the efforts we had made to bring about a local *compromesso storico* seemed in vain. (Later, believe it or not, this Montepulciano scandal was discussed in the Italian parliament.) The opposition now had a lot of proof that the leftist administration was full of destructive and bolshevistic tendencies.

The morning after the scandal the mayor asked me would I consider continuing my work with the Cantiere, in spite of everything that had happened. I told him I didn't like scandals, I didn't think that the outrage he had provoked had been unavoidable, even if he'd wanted to uphold a principle and show his citizens how uncompromisingly correct the new communal administration was. I told him I felt correctness and bureaucracy were not exactly the same thing. I said I would try to continue, but on condition that he would from now on help to prevent this sort of thing, and refrain from acting without consulting me. Anyway, I must admit he had also been helpful in various difficult moments, and somehow, in spite of all the contradictions and shortcomings, the first attempt at a Cantiere Internationale d'Arte had been made and had found quite a number of supporters among the townspeople. And a new style had been found.

Many of those who had worked there in the first year felt like coming back, and did. My friends Helen Grob (international correspondence and organization, rehearsal and performance schedules, accommodation and public relations) and Fausto Moroni (Italian correspondence, administration, finance, organization of transport and of the highly acclaimed *mensa*) agreed to continue their work, too, and did so for five years. In this time they gradually involved young *poliziani* in the administration and taught them how to cope with all these complicated and sometimes chaotic problems, and I think they managed to set up all the basic organizational structures necessary for future Cantieri. They invented a style of administration equal to the particular demands.

Peter Maxwell Davies had given a composition class in the first year, and his Psalm 124 and *Missa super l'homme armé* fantasy were the musical base on which Perlini had built up his *Tradimenti*. His pupils had contributed small pieces to the Perlini show as well, and had written others for a guitar music competition in the main square (with a jury of citizens), the pieces being played by young Italian guitarists who had taken a course with Julian Bream. Unfortunately Max could not return because he founded the St Magnus Festival in Orkney, which takes place at exactly the same time of year as the Cantiere. However, he sent us a new string quartet for our 1980 cycle of music for young players. Jenny Abel the violinist, Peter Locke the pianist, Garth Knox the Scottish viola player, and many more have returned almost every year. Jan Latham-Koenig, who began in Montepulciano as a pianist, conducted Paul Dessau's children's opera *Orfeo e il sindaco* and Milhaud's *Les Malheurs d'Orphée* in the second Cantiere, and continued to play and to conduct for us year after year. In 1978, he conducted a ballet choreographed by William Forsythe to *Aria de la folia española*, and in 1980 he appeared as a dancer in *Pavane pour une infante défunte* with choreography by Ron Thornhill. He helped to prepare the locally cast production of *Pollicino* that he conducted in 1980, the first clear sign of a new musical life in Montepulciano, and joined the group of young Italian and non-Italian artists who ran the 1981 event. Here he conducted the premiere of Ferrero's children's opera *La Figlia del mago*, with professionals on the stage, but *poliziani* in the pit. Hinz und Kunst, the Hamburg instrumental group that had played the music in *Palazzo zoologico* in 1976 and given a concert with new music, in 1978 brought us a street theatre play, written by themselves, called *Il Mongomo a Lapislazzuli*. Lorenzo Ferrero, who had helped with the electronics in an avant-garde *son et lumière* show in the first year, had *La figlia del mago* premiered in the sixth Cantiere, after having in 1977 contributed a brass trio called *Plutone* to a cycle of new and old instrumental pieces about characters and situations in the Orpheus myth. Thomas Jahn, who had composed the children's opera in the first Cantiere, wrote the music for William Forsythe's exciting full-length ballet *Peccato che sia una sgualdrina* ('Tis pity she's a whore). In the fifth Cantiere this was performed in the main square, danced and marvellously acted by volunteers from the Stuttgart company, and with an English chamber choir, and local fans. The ballet was scored for a percussion group and the *banda* (this time supported by the band of Chianciano).

The involvement of the townspeople increased with the years. By the second Cantiere, there was a full-length show in the Piazza Grande, entirely written by a group of Montepulciano intellectuals, and performed by bands, actors, and a choir of Maggiaioli singers from Castiglion d'Orcia who sing an impressive ancient homophonous chant that reminds people of the sorrows and hardships of the feudal past, but which is not much taken to heart by the young who don't think those times and tunes worth remembering. This play was called *Villan d'un Contadino* (The Villainous Peasant). It told of the grim past, and the struggles for freedom and better living conditions by the former generations in these austere valleys. Two years later, in 1979, Antonio Fatini, a local boy of thirteen, had his satirical play *Una storia della fine del mondo* performed in a circus tent, acted by boys and girls from the town and from nearby Todi, and some of the amateur players. The music, performed by the Grimethorpe Colliery Band, consisted of a suite of cheerful marches, tangos, foxtrots and waltzes, written in the thirties by Eugenio Garosi, the (late) mayor of S. Quirico d'Orcia, a neighbouring town. The Yorkshire miners made an enormous impact on the southern Tuscan *banda* scene that year, giving various concerts and visiting Abbadia S. Salvatore, a mercury mining town whose pits were closed down about ten years ago. Everybody there is in *cassa integrazione* (on the dole), but the British were received with pomp and ceremony, and gave a magnificent concert in the piazza there. Visits by English musicians became more and more frequent with the years, and since the third Cantiere the orchestra has been entirely British. In 1980, the London Young Musicians Symphony Orchestra came and performed the incredible feat of rehearsing and giving two performances of Rossini's *Cenerentola*, two of a ballet programme, and five symphony concerts—all this in four weeks and before packed houses. In 1977, the Cambridge University Chamber Choir came, and returned the next year, not only singing and acting in *Masnadieri*, in *La vida breve*, in an *a cappella* opera *De todo encanto amór*, written for them by Jochem Slothouwer, the Dutch composer, and singing mass in the churches on Sundays (which pleased the clergy), but also giving many concerts with and without instruments. They also improved the reputation of the Cantiere by their courtesy and civilized behaviour.

# The Montepulciano Cantieri, 1976–80

In the fourth and fifth years, a choral group composed of young professional London singers, led by Howard Arman, worked on pieces as diverse as *The Threepenny Opera*, *Perséphone*, *Peccato che sia una sgualdrina*, and *Cenerentola*, as well as in cantatas, masses, and many *a cappella* concerts. But the numbers of Italian and foreign artists and students has also risen over the years. Every young artist who joins a Cantiere will find that Montepulciano is a place where he can learn a lot, study repertoire, and explore his potential as a soloist. It is an ideal place for postgraduate musicians preparing themselves for their first jobs, and it is a workshop in this sense as well as in the sense of improving the cultural life of Montepulciano. Hard work is the principle, the Cantiere is not a holiday; it is, at its best, a holiday working place for the artists who choose to go there. Everybody who does is supposed to know what is expected of him there, and why he has chosen to go. This has not always been clear, even though we have always held regular discussions with the artists, and occasional ones also between artists and the people who live there. Everybody who goes to Montepulciano must know he is expected to conduct himself as a civilized contemporary artist. Friendships have developed, especially among the young. People inspire each other, barriers are broken down, bridges have been built.

All this was very pleasant to see. And yet, a considerable number of the inhabitants, the reactionary part, the opposition, elderly *democristiani* (although not all of them), continued to jeopardize our work, denouncing it as communist propaganda, trying to denigrate the participants, and refusing any kind of co-operation, although they were grateful for the commercial benefits brought by the Cantiere. An anonymous author (one supposes it was Don Marcello) attacked us every week in the only paper published in Montepulciano, *L'Araldo Poliziano*. But almost from the beginning, Antonio Fatini, (the author of *Una storia della fine del mondo*, the play we produced in 1979 in which the mayor, the bishop, the *maresciallo dei Carabinieri* and some other people are acidly satirized—only the clergy protested) and his friends produced a photocopied monthly paper called *Montepulciano Notizie* in whose pages a less dark and less sinister voice could be heard, fresh and irreverent, and an eloquent advocate for the aims of the Cantiere.

After the third year, in 1978, I thought that something drastic should be done in order to accelerate the didactic process. There was not enough participation from the young people yet. We needed someone to live in Montepulciano all the time, to be able to teach music to anybody who wanted to learn, and to activate the cultural life of the community, especially in the dreary winter days. One of the most faithful Cantiere workers who had been in at the start, having hitch-hiked to Montepulciano from Lewes in Sussex, was Gastón Fournier Facio, a musician and sociologist, whom I had met in 1975 in London. In Montepulciano he had started as a stage-hand, then advanced to production assistant, then became the organizer of fringe events. He also made himself responsible for most of the programme notes, which he wrote in plain prose that could be understood by everybody. In 1978 he took his M.A. at Sussex University, and should have returned to his native Costa Rica. But I managed to persuade him to stay and convinced the Board (which consists of local craftsmen, peasants, workers, wine people) and the City Council to hire Gastón, who was by then very popular in Montepulciano, as an *animatore culturale*. After the usual bureaucratic difficulties and infuriating delays, they did. If they hadn't, I would have given up trying to direct the Cantiere. I think no one has ever regretted engaging Gastón.

Gastón established himself in Montepulciano in January 1979. He had learned to play the recorder because his plan was to teach this instrument to the children in order to give them a basic knowledge of music. Schott, the music publishers, donated a set of Orff *Schulwerk* instruments, so that the children would also be able to learn by playing percussion instruments. After six months, Gastón had trained up a group of thirteen children and youngsters, called *Concentus Politianus*, to the point where they performed on the Cantiere fringe. A few weeks later, the group asked me to write something for them. I agreed to write the opera *Pollicino* for them to perform in August 1980, thus giving the Concentus players a goal, and creating the problem of finding twenty-one children and four adults who could sing and act the piece. I wrote it between October and March, after which Latham-Koenig, Gastón and I immediately auditioned hundreds of primary school children, and found what we were looking for. Peter Locke was hired by the city council to spend the following months in Montepulciano in order to teach the children we had chosen how to use their voices and how to sing—and he got stunning results. He also coached the adults, four members of Don Marcello's *Bruscello* who had thought they could sing, but in fact had a very hard time indeed learning the notes, the rhythms, and the intonation. The children, on the other hand, had no musical problems at all because nobody told them that the music was difficult. Gastón patiently rehearsed his Concentus (now numbering forty-one players) for months and months, and then Jan arrived and pulled all the strands together. Lilly Decker, a young producer from Cologne, taught the singers how to act, and Peter Nagel, the German neo-realist painter, organized the children in the making of the lovely sets and costumes they had created for themselves. On 2 August 1980 *Pollicino* was premiered, an Italian opera, made in Montepulciano, involving seventy-seven children, before a packed audience of Montepulciano families. From now on, there would be no stopping these children any more.

I have now confidently handed over the direction of the Cantieri to others, though I shall continue to watch their future development with the greatest interest, and to provide whatever help and advice I can. By 1981, at the time of writing, the number of Concentus members has risen to over sixty. The city council has engaged another Costarican, Marisol Carballo, to teach singing in all the schools, and to found a choir. This choir appeared in the 1981 main square show *Il Re Nudo* which was acted and sung almost exclusively by Bruscello members and other *poliziani*. Don Marcello has died. But the Bruscello he founded will go on. New plays will be written for the group, they will be trained, rehearsed, and they will sing properly. One day, who knows, why not, they might like to play the classics, Macchiavelli, Shakespeare, Aristophanes. The band will eventually play in tune, thanks to training in the Concentus, and will be able to draw on a larger and more adventurous repertoire. Already a few youngsters from the Concentus have decided to study an instrument; one has chosen the violin, all the others woodwind. Unfortunately, they still have to leave their town to study. I hope one day that won't be necessary. We are only at the beginning, but there are signs that Montepulciano is changing. Some young people have founded a book publishing house, others are taking to re-establishing crafts that have been forgotten or seemed useless, like paper-making, bookbinding, art photography, designing and painting. There are at least three active poets and playwrights, and parents are now eager for their children to be involved in the Cantiere and the Concentus. They have realized these are better pastimes than television or drugs, and they have probably also noticed that the children who make music are happier than those who don't. There are now about a hundred of them in the choir. I have reason to hope that one day Montepulciano will be a place where music is at home, and the other arts will be at home there, too, and nobody will feel like going away any more.

# A Letter to Young Artists<sup>*</sup>

When in 1963 signs of anti-Semitism were once again writ large on church and synagogue walls, and anonymous vandals had begun to desecrate gravestones, four friends and myself quickly conceived and wrote a collective composition which we called *Aufstand: A Jewish Chronicle*. Our idea was to compose a protest and a warning against the acute danger of sliding back into the dark and dreadful world of Nazi-fascism.

The five composers were Paul Dessau and Rudolf Wagner-Régeny from the Democratic Republic, and Boris Blacher, Karl Amadeus Hartmann and myself from the Federal Republic. Our scores were written quickly, but we had to wait until 14 January 1966 before the work got its first performance at a public concert conducted by Christoph von Dohnányi with the radio orchestra in Cologne. A recording of the performance was later broadcast by all the West German radio stations. The first performance in the Democratic Republic took place the day after the one in Cologne and was conducted by Herbert Kegel in Leipzig. Since then *A Jewish Chronicle* has also been performed in Yugoslavia, in Switzerland, and in the United States. The work has also now been recorded.

The composers who contributed to the work knew well enough that their protest could not of itself prevent the rise of neo-fascism. But it would have been impossible for us to have kept silent and done nothing. We remembered how too often in the past artists had kept their own counsel, and how disastrous their silence had often

* 1981, written in English.

been in the Third Reich. We all believed that any kind of warning would be preferable to the kind of non-political evasiveness that indicates only indifference and insensitivity. The five of us had all, each in his own way, been brought face to face with his own life in having experienced the gruesome events of the Nazi era. We all had personal experiences to bring to the work, the bitterness of emigration and emargination, the horrors of the war, and of the problems that come from belonging to any kind of minority. Our protest was against *racism*, probably the most nauseating aspect of fascism. Even if our collective composition only had a modest and limited impact, it at least helped to get other people going. It is no longer unusual to find artists of the younger generation concerning themselves with present-day phenomena and reflecting social reality in their work. And it is obvious that there is now no one whom one could really call a fascist artist any more. How could any human being, gifted with intelligence and creative imagination, accept and even identify with the stupidity, brutality and misanthropy of neo-fascism?

If, however, any proof were needed that the alarm sounded by *A Jewish Chronicle* was scarcely heeded by anyone, it would be sufficient to observe what is actually going on these days in capitalist countries, and not only in the Federal Republic. The swastikas on walls all over the place are only the backdrop to a horror show whose acts include sado-masochistic sexual behaviour, paramilitary activities, terrorism, and even the 'uniform' styles of certain fashion designers. Art has shown itself by no means immune to these developments, often reflecting or reacting to neo-fascist influence, consciously or unconsciously, in an altogether sinister way. Since the horror show is enacted mostly by members of the younger generation, one concludes that it is a reaction to the officially brutalized environments in a world that no longer appears to have any room for hope, perspective, or free choice. For many young people it seems to have become too difficult to go on believing in progress, to work hard on the positive side of life where the primitive and barbaric instincts of racism would disappear through the acceptance of an enlightened humanism, and where fraternity would win through and peace be possible at last. Their goal seems to have receded far away into the distance. Those who are responsible for this are those who hold the reins of power, among whom there are too many intolerant, racist and disdainful people.

I believe that rarely in history have art and artists had a more important task to fulfill than the one we are confronted with today.

Art has to go right among the people. Art has to mobilize its inherent combative spirit and go into the attack. The fight must begin in the primary schools and continue in the streets, in the universities, in the media, and in the ancient temples of the muses. No occasion should seem too unimportant to young artists for them to miss the chance to assert an anti-fascist stance. I would like to call upon all young artists to see themselves as torch-bearers of humanism, actively confronting injustice and every fundamental error of which our century has been guilty. Fight the inarticulate and comfortable philistine complacency that troubles the world everywhere, from the tables of the provincial bistro up to the minister's office. Find out from where this complacency stems and where it inevitably leads! Help establish and maintain the rights of minorities and combat prejudice against them! Regard yourself as part of an avant-garde opening the door to a more profoundly democratic way of thinking. Every verse you write, every painting you paint, every lesson you give, every bar of music you write or play, can be a move against those who want to reverse the wheel of history, to use the power of the police and of blackmail to drag you back into their own sullenness. Don't lose heart. Don't let yourselves be persuaded to take part in any dubious scheme. Analyse and be conscious of the motives behind your own actions, identify your work with your lives, and remember that your efforts represent the work and lives, the fears and the hopes, of millions of people. You are asked to defend them, and to accompany them on their way to the future. Your job is to touch the sensibility of the masses—you have to try to get through to them by whatever means you can. Your work is not for the celebration of the bankers, prime ministers and presidents of today. There is a new task for your work, one that has never existed before and has never been more urgent. Art must now take the side of the repressed, the humiliated, the offended. Art is to take the part of the weak and the poor, and to gain vigour and impulse from its need to be a voice for the oppressed.

I ask you to arm yourselves with scepticism, patience and irony, to trust your resourcefulness and imagination—these will be your surest guides to the way in which your art will play its vital role in the shaping of a new and better society.

# Index

Compiled by Pauline Del Mar

*Henze's works are indexed by title*

# Index

# Index

# Index

# Index

# Index

# Index

# Index